Trinidad and Tobago

TERRIFIC and TRANQUIL

Golden Jubilee Edition

*Commemorating the 50th Anniversary
of Independence, 1962 to 2012*

Edited by Arif Ali

Rainbow Nation

"If we are able today to speak proudly of a Rainbow Nation, united in its diversity of culture, religion, race, language and ethnicity, it is in part because the world set us a moral example which we dared to follow. This achievement is bound to last because it is founded on the realisation that reconciliation and nation-building mean, among other things, that we should set out to know the truth about the terrible past and ensure it does not recur."

Nelson Mandela
Rajiv Gandhi Lecture, New Delhi, India, 25th January 1995

Published in the United Kingdom
by Hansib Publications Limited
P.O. Box 226
Hertford, Hertfordshire, SG14 3WY

www.hansibpublications.com

ISBN 978-1-906190-37-8 (Hardback)
ISBN 978-1-906190-46-0 (Paperback)

This revised Third Edition published in 2013

First Edition published by Hansib Publications in 2000
Second Edition published by Hansib Publications in 2007
Third Edition published by Hansib Publications in 2012

A catalogue record for this book is available
from the British Library

Design and production by Hansib Publications Ltd
Printed and bound in the United Kingdom

The Ministry of Tertiary Education and Skills Training

Senator the Honourable Fazal Karim
Minister of Tertiary Education and Skills Training

To:
Daniele
with my Highest
regards for a
great future
collaboration

from Fazal

1st February 2014.

Higher education and training play a pivotal role in the development of a rich, diverse, highly capable and adaptable human resource pool. This in turn facilitates the development of a more diversified and knowledge intensive economy. As Minister of Tertiary Education and Skills Training (TEST), I am therefore charged with the responsibility of empowering our future leaders with the necessary skills and training required in this dynamic, technologically advanced and fast paced globalized environment.

At the Ministry of Tertiary Education and Skills Training, in accordance with fulfilling our mandate, we have initiated a multi-pronged approach which includes a suite of strategies, programmes and projects in alignment with our objective. Foremost amongst these strategies has been the expansion of the Government Assisted Tuition Expenses (GATE) programme to include Vocational Training, in the interest of providing greater access to free, quality education to our citizens and ensure that we have a sustainable supply of trained professionals to respond to the needs of this nation's industry.

The Ministry has also facilitated the ease of access to tertiary education by expanding the facilities available to students, through the start of construction of the University of the West Indies (UWI) South Campus in Penal/Debe, the UWI Open Campus in Chaguanas and the College of Science, Technology and Applied Arts of Trinidad and Tobago (COSTAATT) Main Campus in Chaguanas, and the expansion of training provided by COSTAATT in Sangre Grande. With a focus also on Technical and Vocational Education and Training (TVET), several new TVET Training centres have been opened, including the MIC/YTEPP Tobago Technology Centre and new Youth Training and Employment Partnership Programme (YTEPP) training facilities in Tobago, Point Lisas and Waterloo.

To guide further initiatives within various sectors, the Ministry has developed a National Policy on Tertiary Education, and has established a number of new and accredited qualification schemes such as the Caribbean Vocational Qualification (CVQ). With responsibility also for government's health care training; apprenticeship centres; and teacher training, under the ambit of the Ministry of Tertiary Education and Skills Training, a Nursing and Allied Healthcare Training and Education Facility in El Dorado will soon be established, which will assist us in increasing our population of qualified healthcare professionals.

To narrow the gap between the demand and supply of labour, with particular regard to our nation's youth, we have expanded access to the On The Job Training (OJT) programme, and have been instrumental in the establishment of Workforce Assessment Centres that has proven to be a critical measure to ensure workers have an opportunity to have their skills assessed and certified.

Contents

Acknowledgements

"But there has to be a point in time when the consensus of opinion regards a change as having taken place. In the case of Trinidad and Tobago, that point was October of this year: you made it. You are now a developed country."

Arthur Snell, British High Commissioner, Trinidad and Tobago Newsday, 31 October 2011

A very big thanks to all of the following, some of whom may not even be aware of how helpful they were during the past year while we were working on this book. Your time, advice, ideas, articles, photographs and your hospitality at all times are much appreciated.

Thank you to Prime Minister Kamla Persad-Bissessar's administration, whose cooperation at all levels encouraged and supported the 50th Anniversary book, which is a joint Government / Private Sector project. Often referred to as the "Gold Book", we hope that the reader will find the contents of Trinidad and Tobago: Terrific and Tranquil of interest.

Thanks to **Hansib Publications** staff and associates in the United Kingdom and Trinidad and Tobago, namely, **Managing Editors Kash Ali** and **Ansel Wong**, Richard Painter, Shareef Ali, Alan Cross, Ella Barnes, Dorothy Wong, Justin Joseph, Peter Kanhai, Anji Benjamin, Kendrick Sooknarine, Relindor Kanhai, Neesha Thompson, Michael Belcon, Vino Patel, Ian Marsh, Josephine Learmond-Criqui, Moti Persaud, Cordelia Andrews, Dwayne Andrews and Wayne Gregory.

Thanks to George Stanley Beard, Cornell Buckradee, Winston (Gipsy) Peters, Tim Gopeesingh, Fazal Karim, Jennifer Jones, Vel Lewis, Surujrattan Rambachan, Vasant Bharath, Ganga Singh, Wade Mark, Stephen Cadiz, Rupert Griffith, Devant Maharaj, Chandresh Sharma, Lindsay Gillette, Bhoendradatt Tewarie, Anil Roberts, Fuad Khan, Rajiv Shandilya, Emmanuel George, Roy Boyke, Joshey Mahabir, Cherrylene Lewis, Brinsley Samaroo, Kelvin Ramnauth, Shirley Bahadur, Kristy Joseph and Collin Partap.

Thanks to Carlene Cross, Radha Permanand, Neisha Ghany, Ravi & Rishi Rampersad, Vanessa R Williams, Karima Ali-Dookwah, Ramesh Chadeesingh, Natalie Dookie, Lazena Abdool-Gay, Bernadette Bacchus, Matthew Sammy, Fabian Carew, Christopher Alexander, Amer Haidar, Josanne Leonard, Francis Williams-Smith, Jill Robertson, British Airways, Sonal Vyas, Debbie Surjusingh, Prof. Andrew Ramroop, Merle Latchman, Rakesh Patel, Hugh Henderson, Andy Ali, Susan Malco, Shafina Hallal, Ann Braithwaite, Lawrence Ruiz, Eric Feniet, Ian Gould, James B. Solomon, Naparima Girls High School, Jenifer Gittens, Charlie's Black Pudding, Shivana Laughlin, Gizelle Morris, Janet Furlonge, Denise Dorant, Caribbean Airlines Limited, Giselle Noella – London, Yolande Agard-Simmons, Bridgid Sutherland, Leroy Clarke, Christopher Laird, Neil Latchman, Victoria Lenzoi Lee, Terence Walker, Sasha Mohammed, Janice Learmond-Criqui, Keith Diaz, Prof. Patricia Mohammed, Joe & Lennie Dalsingh, Vicky Jones, Tyrone Gopee, Napier Pillai, Leslie Palmer, Tony Martin, Maureen & Deryck Murray, Moneera Mohammed, Beresford Hunte, Naithalin Juman, Tisha Marajh, Nayantara Gayah-Hassan, Stacy Bond, Shurla Henry-Gibson, Gillian Friday, Terrance Juraman, Don Sylvester, Avenash Ramsoobhat, Lynette Guevara, Jeewan Ramcharitar, Pamela Lee-Persad, Shem Baldeosingh, Ashwin Creed, Sunita Pahuja, Mitra Mahabir, Paul Carrington, Fazad Mohammed, Carolyn Ali, Routie Badal, Ken Emrith, Kelvin Mahabir, Teelack Singh, Geoff Patton, Debra Coryat-Patton, Rishi Permanand, Trevor Dean, Lisa Agard, Arthur Snell, Mario Sabga Aboud, Narend Sooknarine, Everard Snaggs, Roberto Peon, Omar Khan, Rawle Winston Titus, Winston Williams, Edwina Leacock and Richard Young.

Thanks to the writers/contributors (in alaphabetical order)
Yolande Agard-Simmons, Patti-Anne Ali, Dr Michael C. Belcon, Michael Coryat, Nicholas Dean, James Fuller, Hamid Ghany, Farah Gopaul-Fuller, Gideon Hanoomansingh, Glenroy Joseph, Alana Jute, Giselle Laronde-West, Josephine Learmond-Criqui, Simon Lee, Cherrylene Lewis, Ministry of Arts & Multiculturalism, Prof. Patricia Mohammed, Sasha Mohammed, Mandilee Newton, Surujrattan Rambachan, Jewan Ramcharitar, Leela Ramdeen, Ronald Ramkissoon, Joan Rampersad, Dr Kris Rampersad, Amon Saba Saakana, Dr Brinsley Samaroo, Prof. Clement K. Sankat, Sonja Sinaswee, Narend Sooknarine, Donald Stollmeyer, Dr Bhoendradatt Tewarie, Tourism Development Company, Rawle Winston Titus, Trinidad and Tobago Electricity Commission, Sheldon Yearwood and Angus P. Young.

Thanks to the photographers (in alphabetical order)
Ian Abraham, Shirley Bahadur, Ian Brierley, Stephen Broadbridge, Oswin Browne, Elizabeth Desiree Chung, Calvin French, Marcus Gonzales, Government Information Services Ltd, Gary Jordan, Keystone/Hulton Archive/Getty Images, Josanne Leonard, Robert Lerich/Dreamstime.com, Andy Lyons/Getty Images, Ryan P. Mannette, Ministry of Agriculture, Ministry of Arts & Multiculturalism, Noel P. Norton, Salim October, Pniesen/Dreamstime.com, Wendell Stephen Jay Reyes, Tom Shaw/Getty Images, Alex Smailes, James B. Solomon, Narend Sooknarine, T&TEC and Tourism Development Company.

I would also like to mention the wonderful cuisine – from the humble 'doubles' to the 'aloo pie' – that Arlene and Henry Loy have produced at the original First and Last Bar at No. 3 Manzanilla since 1947, and all the local and international foods served in the hotels, restaurants and other establishments; not forgetting the 'bake and shark' and the ubiquitous 'roti and curry' and 'oil-down'.

Thanks to the scores of Trinidad and Tobago nationals, from all walks of life, whose paths we crossed while working on this momentous book that marks the 50th Anniversary of Independence.

And finally, to Pamela Mary for caring so much.

Arif Ali, June 2012

Supporters

Hansib Publications is grateful to the following Ministries, businesses and organisations for their support:

Accreditation Council of Trinidad and Tobago
Agricultural Development Bank
Angostura Limited
ArcelorMittal
Atlantic LNG Company of Trinidad and Tobago
Book Specialist
Books and Office Supplies (Tobago)
BP Trinidad and Tobago
Caribbean Discovery Tours Limited
Caribbean Industrial Research Institute, UWI
Cariflex (1994) Limited
Chaguaramas Development Authority
Charrans Bookstore
Environmental Management Authority
eTeck and invesTT
Guardian Shared Services Limited
Hyatt Regency Trinidad
Ishmael M Khan & Sons Limited
Jet Printing
Justin Works
Kanhai Real Estate
Keith Khan's Books Etc Limited
Lexicon Trinidad Limited
Maurice Sedwell (Savile Row) Limited
Metropolitan Book Supplies Limited
Michael Belcon
Ministry of Arts and Multiculturalism
Ministry of Education
Ministry of Energy and Energy Affairs
Ministry of Finance
Ministry of Food Production, Land and Marine Affairs
Ministry of Foreign Affairs
Ministry of Health
Ministry of Housing
Ministry of National Security
Ministry of Planning and The Economy
Ministry of Public Administration
Ministry of Public Utilities
Ministry of Science, Technology and Tertiary Education
Ministry of Sports and Youth Affairs
Ministry of Trade, Industry and Investment
Ministry of Transport
Mohammed's Bookstore Associated Limited
Mootilal Ramhit & Sons Contracting Limited
National Carnival Commission of Trinidad and Tobago
National Gas Company
National Infrastructure Development Company Limited
National Library and Information System Authority
National Lotteries Control Board
Neal and Massy Foundation
Nigel R Khan
Office of the Attorney General
Office of the Prime Minister
Office of the Speaker
Pizza Boys Group of Companies
Point Lisas Industrial Port Development Corporation Limited
Richmond Motors (BMW)
RIK Services Limited
Sagicor Life Inc
School of Business and Computer Science Limited
Scotiabank Trinidad and Tobago Limited
Sun Tings
Telecommunications Services of Trinidad and Tobago
The Cascadia Hotel and Conference Centre
The Petroleum Company of Trinidad and Tobago Limited
The Port Authority of Trinidad and Tobago
The Trinidad and Tobago Civilian Conservation Corps
The Trinidad and Tobago Housing Development Corporation
Tourism Development Company Limited
Travel-Plus Services Limited
Trinidad and Tobago Bureau of Standards
Trinidad and Tobago Coalition of Services Industries
Trinidad and Tobago Defence Force
Trinidad and Tobago Electricity Commission
Trinidad and Tobago Film Company
Trinidad and Tobago Fire Service
Trinidad and Tobago Free Zones Company Limited
Trinidad and Tobago Insurance Limited
Trinidad and Tobago Mortgage and Finance Limited
Trinidad and Tobago Prison Service
Trinity Insurance Brokers Limited
University of the West Indies (Bookshop)
University of the West Indies (Principal's Office)
Urban Development Corporation of Trinidad and Tobago Limited
Venture Credit Union Co-Operative Society Limited
Water and Sewage Authority of Trinidad and Tobago
Worldwide Bankers RE Limited

Rio Sobo. *Photo courtesy Tourism Development Company*

Foreword

In his Independence Day address on 31 August 1962, the first Prime Minister of Trinidad and Tobago, Dr Eric Williams, counselled,

"...whatever the challenge that faces you, from whatever quarter, place first the national interest and the national cause. The strength of the Nation depends on the strength of its citizens."

Fifty years on, the current and first female Prime Minister of Trinidad and Tobago, Mrs Kamla Persad-Bissessar, has committed her premiership to build a society,

"which cherishes life, honours diversity, generates prosperity, encourages innovation and acts with compassion to its most vulnerable citizens."

Both Prime Ministers are at the extreme ends of the 50 year journey of Trinidad and Tobago as an independent twin-island nation, with each playing seminal roles in directing the development of the country,

a country whose diversity is widely acknowledged – diversity in its history, population, flora and fauna, arts, culture, music, lifestyles, religion, cuisine, investment opportunities, infrastructure and environment.

Now led by Mrs Kamla Persad-Bissessar, the first female Prime Minister of Indian heritage in the Western Hemisphere, Trinidad and Tobago is poised to initiate a social and economic transformation to ensure the nation's survival, growth, competitiveness and sustainability. This twin-island nation is a truly dynamic duo offering two distinct markets – Trinidad, "the place for business"; and Tobago, a holiday paradise that is "clean, green and serene".

The country has published its medium term policy framework to create prosperity for all. The government is putting in place a programme of actions to navigate the major challenges of the new global economic and political landscapes. It is extending attractive opportunities to stimulate internal and external trade and ▶

PHOTO: STEPHEN BROADBRIDGE

Beach football. *Photo: Stephen Broadbridge*

Port of Spain. *Photo: Stephen Broadbridge*

investment so that Trinidad and Tobago will become the regional hub for the Caribbean and Latin America and be a global player in and a haven for trade and investment.

The country's creativity is an integral part of this transformation process and the cultural industries are being developed to international standards to showcase the talents of its artists and practitioners through the inflows of visitors and tourists and through exports.

In the immediate future, the country will continue to boost tourism and

tourism investment with several areas targeted for investment and growth, including niche areas such as sport, leisure, health, business & conference, festival, film, culture, eco and boutique hotels. The goal is to create a quality destination of first choice with world class customer service.

Partnerships are being encouraged to create transformational initiatives to boost productivity and increase competitiveness, to confront obstacles to the successful industrial and cultural development of the nation and to create more wealth, and in so doing, adding to the country's energy based economy.

Fifty years of Independence, and 35 years as a Republic, have marked the country's rapid evolution from British colony to sovereign state. As a sovereign state, though small, Trinidad and Tobago have gifted the world with numerous individuals of outstanding merit, including Dai Ailan ("mother of Chinese dance"), Rudranath Capildeo (physicist), Heather Headley (singer), Brian Lara (cricketer), Sam Mendes (film director), Peter Minshall (designer), VS Naipaul (writer) and Edmundo Ros (band leader) and is the birth place of the only musical instrument to be invented in the 20th century – the steel pan.

This twin-island Republic is the gateway to golden opportunities and experiences for both the investor and visitor.

Port of Spain. *Photo: James B. Solomon*

Paramin Mountain village. *Photo: Stephen Broadbridge*

Laventille. *Photo: Salim October*

PHOTO: STEPHEN BROADBRIDGE

PHOTO: STEPHEN BROADBRIDGE

Smokey & Bunty bar in St James. *Photo: Ian Brierley*

PHOTO: STEPHEN BROADBRIDGE

PHOTO: ELIZABETH DESIREE CHUNG

Temple in the Sea. *Photo: Wendell Stephen Jay Reyes*

Bamboo canopy'. Photo: *James B. Solomon*

Rincon Waterfall. *Photo: Stephen Broadbridge*

Maracas Bay. *Photo: Wendell Stephen Jay Reyes*

Beach at Maracas Bay. *Photo: Gary Jordan*

Gasparee Caves are located on Gaspar Grande, an island seven miles off the coast of Trinidad. *Photo: Stephen Broadbridge*

PHOTO: MARCUS GONZALES

PHOTO: IAN BRIERLEY

PHOTO: STEPHEN BROADBRIDGE

PHOTO: IAN BRIERLEY

Maracas Falls. *Photo: Ian Brierley*

PHOTO: IAN BRIERLEY

PHOTO: SALIM OCTOBER

PHOTO: SALIM OCTOBER

PHOTO: IAN BRIERLEY

PHOTO: IAN BRIERLEY

The NAPA building against the backdrop of Port of Spain.
Photo: Ian Brierley

Independence Day parade. *Photo: Wendell Stephen Jay Reyes*

PHOTO: STEPHEN BROADBRIDGE

Fort George overlooking Port of Spain.
Photo: Ian Brierley

Goat Island (in the foreground) and Little Tobago are located approximately 2.4km off the north-eastern coast of Tobago. Also known as Bird of Paradise Island, Little Tobago is an important breeding site for sea birds such as the red-billed tropicbird. The building seen on Goat Island is the former home of 'James Bond' creator, Ian Fleming. *Photo: Oswin Browne*

FACTS & FIGURES

Full Name
Republic of Trinidad and Tobago
Known as: "Land of the Hummingbird"

Capital
Port of Spain in Trinidad is the national capital.
Scarborough is the capital of Tobago

Trinidad and Tobago gained independence from Britain on 31 August 1962 and became a Republic on 1 August 1976

Location
Southernmost Caribbean islands of the Lesser Antilles archipelago and situated off the north-eastern coastline of mainland South America, 12 km (7 miles) off Venezuela.

Area
Trinidad: 4,828 sq km (1,864 sq miles)
Tobago: 300 sq km (116 sq miles)
Total: 5,128 sq km (1,980 sq miles)

Population: 1,325,000 (2011 est.)

Nationality: Trinidadian / Tobagonian

Languages: English (official language), Hindi, French, Spanish, Chinese

Religions
Roman Catholic 26%, Hindu 22.5%, Anglican 7.8%, Baptist 7.2%, Pentecostal 6.8%, other Christian 5.8%, Muslim 5.8%, Seventh Day Adventist 4%, other 10.8%, unspecified 1.4%, none 1.9% (2000 census)

Ethnic groups
East Indian 40.3%, African 39.6%, mixed 18.4%, Chinese 1.1%, European 0.6%

Literacy: 98.6%

Geography
Trinidad has three mountain ranges. The highest, the Northern Range, is an extension of the Andes mountain chain and runs along the northern coast. The Central Range runs diagonally across the country while the Southern Range runs along the southern coast. The highest point, El Cerro del Aripo, is 940 metres (3,084 ft) above sea level. About 40 per cent of all land is undeveloped forest and woodlands.
Tobago lies 30 km (19 miles) northeast of Trinidad. The highest peak, Main Ridge, is about 576 metres (1,890 ft) high.

Climate
Tropical. Daytime temperatures average 31ºC (87ºF) and are moderated by the northeast trade winds, while nights are a cool 21ºC (69ºF). The islands have two seasons: dry, from January to ▶

TRINIDAD

VENEZUELA

The Dragon's Mouth
Huevos
Boca de Navios
Boca de Huevos
Boca Grande
Chacachacare
Monos
Boca
Patos

CAR

GULF OF

LEGEND

—— Main Roads
—— Other Roads
〰 Highways
Rivers & Streams
Bathing Beaches
Airport
Leatherback Nesting Site
Gas Stations
① Scotland Bay
② Gasparee Caves
③ Chaguaramas Golf course & Edith Falls
④ Chaguaramas Bay
⑤ Paramin
⑥ St. Andrew's Golf course
⑦ El Tucuche
⑧ Maracas Water Fall
⑨ Fort Abercromby
⑩ Mt. St. Benedict Church & Monastery
⑪ Caura Valley
⑫ Trincity Mall
⑬ Asa Wright Nature Centre
⑭ Paria Waterfall
⑮ Heights of Guanapo
⑯ Aripo Caves
⑰ Caroni Bird Sanctuary
⑱ Divali Nagar Site
⑲ Chaguanas Potteries
⑳ Waterloo Temple
㉑ Ajoupa Pottery
㉒ La Vega Garden Centre
㉓ Pointe-a-Pierre Wild Fowl Trust
㉔ Devil's Woodyard
㉕ Oropouche Lagoon

N
W E
S

Guapo
Point
Fortin
Point Fortin
Point Rouge
Irois Bay
Cap-de-Ville
Granville Bay
Cedros Point
Irois
Cedros Bay
Granville
SOUTHERN MAIN
CHATHAM RD
Buenos Ayres
Los Gallos Point
Bonasse
Chatham
Columbus Bay
Fullarton
Erin Bay
Corral Point
Isolte Bay
Isolte Point
Eri
Icacos
The Serpent's Mouth

CARIBBEAN SEA

BEAN SEA

St. George

Saut D'Eau I.
La Vache Pt.
Morne Pt.
Maracas Bay
Batata Bay
La Vache Bay
Diego Martin R.
Blue Basin
Maracas Bay Vlg.
Maraval Coco Rd.
Carenage
Petit Valley
St. Peter's Bay
Five Islands
St. James
Laventille
Barataria
PORT OF SPAIN
El Soccorro
Santa Cruz
Maracas
Maraval
St. Ann's
Cascade
San Juan
Curepe
St. Joseph
Tunapuna
Tacarigua
Dinsley
Arouca
D'Abadie
Curepe

Las Cuevas Bay
Chupara Point
Fillette
Chupara Bay
Blanchisseuse Bay
Blanchisseuse
Las Cuevas
Paria Bay
Madamas Bay
Brasso Seco
El Cerro del Aripo
Hollis Reservoir
Cumaca

Grand Matelot Point
Matelot Bay
Matelot
Grande Riviere Bay
Grande Riviere
San Souci Bay
San Souci
Salybia Bay
Toco
Galera Pt.
Forest Pt.
Redhead
Cumana Bay

ST. DAVID

Guayamara Pt.
Rampanalgas
Balandra Bay
Salybia
Saline Bay
Matura

ST. ANDREW

Valencia
Oropuche
Upper Fishing Pond
Lower Fishing Pond
Sangre Grande
Cumuto
Caigual
Cheeyou
Upper Manzanilla
Manzanilla Pt.
Manzanilla Bay
Lower Manzanilla

Lopinot
Guanapo
Carapo
San Rafael
Caroni Arena Dam
Cunaripa
Howson
Coryal
Carmichael
Mount Harris
Mamon
Four Roads
Talparo
Piarco International Airport
St. Helena
Caroni
Cunupia
Longdenville

ARIMA

CARONI

Bird Sanctuary
Caroni Swamp
Cacandee Settlement
Jerningham Junction
Barrancones Pt.
Barrancones Bay
Waterloo
Carapichaima
Chaguanas
Chase Village
Todd's Road
Mundo Nuevo
Mamoral
Flanagin Town
Brasso
Tabaquite
Caparo
Freeport
Preysal
Gran Couva
Couva
California
Cangrejos Pt.
Cangrejos Bay
Lisas Bay
Point Lisas
Claxton Bay
St. Margaret
Pointe-A-Pierre
Marabella
Vistabella

NARIVA
Biche
Charuma
Cuche
Navet
Navet Dam
Nariva Swamp
Brickfield
Mayo
Tortuga
Gasparillo
Williamsville
Busy Corner
New Grant
Tableland
Poole
Rio Claro
Ecclesville
Mayaro
Guatuaro Pt.
Point Radix

ATLANTIC OCEAN

SAN FERNANDO
Mon Repos
Canaan
Ste. Madeleine
Princes Town
St. Julien
Lengua
Sixth Company
Third Company
Indian Walk
Preau
Cipero Ste. Croix
Barrackpore
Penal
Debe
Avocat
Fyzabad
Thick
Pluck
Siparia
Los Bajos
Palo Seco
Sadhoowa
Morne Diablo
Basse Terre
Moruga
La Lune
Moruga Pt.

VICTORIA
MAYARO
Guayaguayare
Rustville
Guayaguayare Bay
Galeota Pt.
Grand Cayo Pt.

Palo Seco Bay
Quinam Bay
Roja Pt.
Negra Pt.
Curao Pt.
Canari Bay

COLUMBUS CHANNEL

| 0 | 5 | 10 Miles |
| 0 | 2 | 5 Kilometres |

27

May, and wet, from June to December. There is a short dry period around mid-September – Petit Carême. Trinidad and Tobago are just outside the usual path of hurricanes and other tropical storms.

Time Zone
One hour ahead of Eastern Standard Time (EST) Four hours behind Greenwich Mean Time (GMT), year round.

Government
Trinidad and Tobago is a parliamentary democracy. The Head of State is the President who is elected by an Electoral College of members of the Senate and House of Representatives for a five-year term. Executive power is vested in the Prime Minister and Government following elections every five years. The local government body in Tobago is the Tobago House of Assembly.

The country's first female head of government, Mrs Kamla Persad-Bissessar, was elected on 24 May 2010. She leads a coalition government – The People's Partnership.

Legal System
The legal system is based on common law and statutes. The judicial system comprises Magistrates' Courts and the Supreme Court which is made up of the High Court and the Court of Appeal. The Industrial Court deals with labour matters. The Judicial and Legal Service Commission appoint judges to the Supreme Court. The Attorney General is responsible for the administration of the legal and judicial system. Final appeal from Trinidad and Tobago courts is to the Privy Council in England but the People's Partnership government has announced its intention to make the Caribbean Court of Justice its final appeal court.

Population and Workforce
Trinidad and Tobago's estimated population is 1.3 million of which 55,000 are in Tobago, 300,000 in Port of Spain and 150,000 in San Fernando. The average life expectancy is 70.3 years, with 72 per cent of the population between 15 and 64 years.

Immigration, Work Permits & Visas
Visitors to Trinidad and Tobago must possess valid passports and return or ongoing tickets. Visitors from most Commonwealth countries do not require visas for entry, except Australia, New Zealand, India, Nigeria, Papua New Guinea, Sri Lanka, Tanzania, Cameroon, Fiji Islands, Mozambique, Tonga, Uganda and South Africa. Visitors from other countries are allowed to enter Trinidad and Tobago for periods of up to three months without a visa.

Work permits are required for business stays in excess of 30 days. Work permit forms can be obtained from the Ministry of National Security,

Temple Court, 31-33 Abercromby Street, Port of Spain (Tel: 623 2441/5, www.nationalsecurity.gov.tt).

Airports
Piarco International Airport is located about 45 minutes from the capital city, Port of Spain. It is a vital hub for international air traffic in the Caribbean. There are non-stop daily scheduled flights to and from major international cities.

ANR Robinson International Airport is located 7 miles (10km) from Scarborough.

Non-stop Flying Times to Trinidad and Tobago:
Barbados 35 mins; Caracas 55 mins; Frankfurt 9 hrs 40 mins; Houston 5 hrs 30 mins; London 8 hrs 20 mins; Miami 3 hrs 30 mins; New York 4 hrs 50 mins; Puerto Rico 90 mins; Toronto 5 hrs 50 mins; Zurich 9 hrs 10 mins.

Major Airlines
American Airlines (868) 821 6000
Air Canada (868) 669 4065
British Airways (800) 247 9297
Caribbean Airlines (868) 625 7200
Continental Airlines (868) 624 2764
Delta Airlines (868) 624 8952
LIAT (868) 627 6274
Virgin Atlantic (868) 631 7470

Seaports
The main seaports are located in Port of Spain and Point Lisas. The Port of Port of Spain handles dry and general cargo, break bulk, containers and passenger traffic. The Point Lisas Industrial Port Development Corporation Ltd (PLIPDECO), mainly a bulk port for industrial commerce, also handles container and general cargo traffic.

There are two fast ferries (T&T Express and T&T Spirit) and one conventional ferry (Warrior Spirit) travelling daily between Trinidad and Tobago.

The CARICOM Jetty, at the Port of Port of Spain, operates the Passenger Inter-Island Ferry and receives, stores and delivers CARICOM cargo and multi-purpose containers for trade within the Caribbean region.

A water taxi ferry service connects Port of Spain and San Fernando.

Agriculture products
Cocoa, rice, citrus fruit, coffee, vegetables, poultry

Industries
Petroleum and petroleum products, liquefied natural gas (LNG), methanol, ammonia, urea, steel products, beverages, food processing, cement, cotton textiles

Export commodities
Petroleum and petroleum products, liquefied natural gas (LNG), methanol, ammonia, urea, steel products, beverages, cereal and cereal products, sugar, cocoa, coffee, citrus fruit, vegetables, flowers

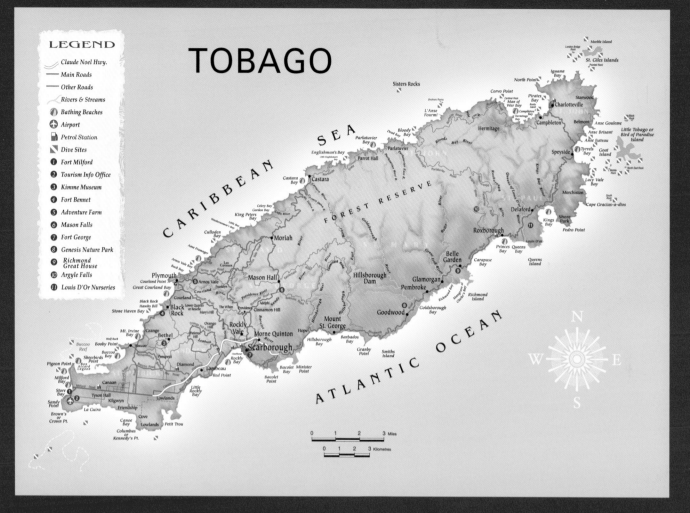

TOBAGO

Export partners
United States 44.2%; Spain 6.1%; Jamaica 5.1% (2010)

Import commodities
Mineral fuels, lubricants, machinery, transportation equipment, manufactured goods, food, chemicals, live animals

Import partners
United States 27.8%; Russia 11.5%; Brazil 7.8%; Colombia 6.9%; Gabon 4.3%; China 4.2%; Canada 4.2% (2010)

Natural resources
Petroleum, natural gas, asphalt (the Pitch Lake on the south-western coast is the world's largest natural reservoir of asphalt), eco-tourism

Membership of international organisations include:
Caribbean Community and Common Market (CARICOM) since 1 August 1973, Caribbean Development Bank (CDB), Group of 24 (G-24), Association of Caribbean States (ACS), Food and Agricultural Organisation (FAO), Group of 77 (G-77), Group of African Caribbean and Pacific (ACP) countries, Inter-American Development Bank (IDB), International Monetary Fund (IMF), International Labour Organisation (ILO), Interpol, IOC, ISO, International Telecommunications Union (ITU), Organisation of American States (OAS), UNCTAD, UNESCO, UNIDO, United Nations, WHO, World Intellectual Property Organisation (WIPO), World Trade Organisation (WTO)

Money and Exchange Rate
The currency of Trinidad and Tobago is the dollar (TT $ = 100 cents). Notes are in denominations of TT $100, $50, $20, $10, $5 and $1. Coins are in denominations of 25, 10, 5 and 1 cent.
The Trinidad and Tobago Dollar is tied to the US Dollar and floating at US $1 = TT $6.40.
The exchange rate for other major currencies is approximately:
£1.00 to TT $10.68
Euro 1 to TT $8.63
Some items are subject to 15% value added tax (VAT).

International dialling code: 868

Police	999
Ambulance	811
Fire	990

Internet country code: .tt

NATIONAL ANTHEM

Forged from the love of liberty
in the fires of hope and prayer
with boundless faith in our destiny
We solemnly declare

Side by side we stand
Islands of the blue Caribbean Sea
This our native land
we pledge our lives to thee

Here every creed and race
find an equal place
And may God bless our nation

Here every creed and race
find an equal place
And may God bless our nation.

Written by Patrick S. Castagne

NATIONAL PLEDGE

I solemnly pledge to dedicate my life
To the service of my God
And to my country.

I will honour my parents,
My teachers, my leaders and my elders,
And those in authority.

I will be clean and honest in all my thoughts,
My words and my deeds.

I will strive, in everything I do
To work together with my fellowmen
Of every creed and race
For the greater happiness of all
And the honour and glory
Of my country.

Written by Marjorie Padmore

COAT OF ARMS

The Coat of Arms was designed by the late George Bailey and was first used following independence in 1962.

They show at the top a coconut palm in fruit and a ship's wheel representing the nation's colonial past. The national birds of the country – the Scarlet Ibis (found in Trinidad) and the Cocrico (found only in Tobago) – hold up the shield on which two Hummingbirds, another national bird, are depicted. Also on the shield are three Spanish galleons, the principal motifs of Trinidad and Tobago's British colonial seals. They all stand on three hills which represent the Trinity.

The national watchwords, "Together We Aspire, Together We Achieve" form the base on which the insignia stands.

NATIONAL HOLIDAYS & CELEBRATIONS

New Year's Day
1 January

Carnival
Variable (February/March)
Though not a public holiday, most offices are closed on the two Carnival days; always the Monday and Tuesday before Ash Wednesday

Spiritual Baptist (Shouter) Liberation Day
30 March

Good Friday
Variable (March/April)

Easter Sunday
Variable (March/April)

Easter Monday
Variable (March/April)

Indian Arrival Day
30 May
Commemorating the arrival of indentured labourers from India

Corpus Christi
10 June

Labour Day
19 June
Marking the labour uprising of June 1937

Emancipation Day
1 August
Commemorating the emancipation of enslaved Africans on 1 August 1883

Independence Day
31 August
Trinidad and Tobago gained independence from Britain on 31 August 1962

Republic Day
24 September
Trinidad and Tobago became a republic on 1 August 1976

Diwali
Variable (October/November)
Celebrating the Hindu festival of lights

Eid ul-Fitr
Variable (October/November)
Marking the end of the Muslim fasting month of Ramadan

Christmas Day
25 December

Boxing Day
26 December

Clockwise from top left – Scarlett ibis, national bird of Trinidad. *Photo: Tourism Development Company*; Cocrico, national bird of Tobago: *Photo: Stephen Broadbridge*; Chaconia, national flower. *Photo: Stephen Broadbridge*; National flag; Coat of Arms. *Photo: Ian Brierley*

NATIONAL FLAG

The national flag of Trinidad and Tobago was first used in 1962 when the nation gained its independence. Designed by the late George Bailey, it is made up of a black stripe bordered in white on a red background, each colour representing an element in the character of its land and people.
RED represents the vitality of the land, the warmth and energy of the sun and the courage and friendliness of its people. **WHITE** represents the sea which surrounds the land, the cradle of its heritage, the purity of its aspirations and the equality of its people under the sun. **BLACK** represents the dedication of the people joined together by one strong bond. It is the colour of strength, of unity, of purpose and of the wealth of the land. The colours were chosen to represent the elements Earth, Fire and Water and to encompass the nation's past, present and future and to inspire it as one united, vital, free and dedicated people.

NATIONAL MOTTO

"Together We Aspire, Together We Achieve"

NATIONAL FLOWER

The national flower of Trinidad and Tobago is the chaconia (*warszewiczia coccinea*). Also known as the 'Pride of Trinidad and Tobago' or 'Wild Poinsettia', the chaconia was named in honour of the last Spanish Governor of Trinidad, Don Jose Maria Chacon (1784-1797). This indigenous, wild, forest flower has long sprays of magnificent vermilion that are said to bloom around the anniversary of Trinidad and Tobago's Independence (31 August).

NATIONAL BIRDS

Scarlet Ibis (Trinidad)
Cocrico (Tobago)

INDEPENDENCE DAY, 31 AUGUST 1962, RED HOUSE
Mary, Princess Royal (1897-1965), fourth from left, and Governor Sir Solomon Hochoy (1905-1983), fifth from left, among the officials attending the flag-raising ceremony at the Red House to mark the independence of Trinidad and Tobago from Great Britain. The nation's first Prime Minister, Dr Eric Williams, is pictured second from left. *Photo: Keystone/Hulton Archive/Getty Images*

The road to Independence

There were many patriots in Trinidad and Tobago who dedicated their lives to ending the stifling colonial relationship with Britain.

Captain Arthur Andrew Cipriani (1875 – 1945), of Corsican descent, was such a patriot who was elected leader of the Workingmen's Association which he converted into the Trinidad Labour Party in 1932. He was a member of the Port of Spain City Council from 1921 to 1941, serving as Mayor on several occasions.

Two other trade unionist/politicians were prominent at the time – Tubal Uriah Butler (1897 – 1977) and Adrian Cola Rienzi (1905 – 1972).

These leaders were at the forefront of the strikes in the oil and sugar belts from 1935 to 1937. These confrontations led to the birth of the trade union movement and the creation of the Oilfield Workers Trade Union (OWTU) and the All Trinidad Sugar Estates and Factory Workers Trade Union both founded in 1937.

Rienzi was elected continuously to the San Fernando Borough Council from 1937 to 1942 serving as Mayor from 1939 to 1942 and elected to the legislature from 1938 to 1944, having been elevated to serve on the Governor's Executive Council during 1943 to 1944.

Butler served in the Parliament from 1950 to 1961.

In Tobago, James Biggart, first elected in 1925, never failed to highlight Tobago's potential as a prime tourist resort and the urgency of better communications between the two islands. An agriculturalist, he was a constant advocate of Tobago's cocoa and animal production.

Biggart was succeeded by Alfonso Philbert James (1901 – 1962) better known as "Fargo". A contractor and trade unionist, he represented Tobago in the legislative Council from 1946 to 1961.

There were many women who took part in the pre-independence struggles. During the battles of the 1930s, the names of Elma Francois and Daisy Crick stand out. Both women were actively engaged in organising the workers, both were arrested but they left their indelible mark on the agitation for better conditions.

Audrey Layne Jeffers (1896 – 1968) also stands out prominently. In 1936, she was elected to the Port of Spain City Council and from 1946 to 1956 she performed creditably in the national legislature.

In the 1950s and 1960s other stalwarts continued the struggle. Albert Gomes (1911 – 1978) was certainly one of these.

Equally important from the 1950s to the early 1970s was Bhadase Sagan Maraj (1920 – 1971). Rising through the trade union movement, Maraj was instrumental in providing leadership to the Hindu community as he brought the many groups into the Sanatan Dharma Maha Sabha in 1952. He was elected to the legislature from 1950 to 1961 and again in 1968.

In 1960, Maraj handed over political leadership of the Democratic Labour Party (DLP) to Dr Rudranath Capildeo (1920 – 1970), a lecturer in mathematics and physics at London University. Dr Capildeo was elected leader as a match for Dr Eric Williams, his erstwhile teacher at Queens Royal College in Port of Spain. The DLP fared badly under Capildeo's leadership and in 1967 he was disbarred from the Parliament because of continuous absence.

Dr Capildeo's brother Simbhoonath Capildeo (1914 – 1990) was a better politician. He was, alongside Bhadase Maraj, a co-founder of the Sanatan Dharma Maha Sabha and he was a prime mover in the construction of Hindu schools during the 1950s. He was an elected member of the legislature from 1956 to 1961. ■

U nder British rule, Trinidad and Tobago was a classic Crown Colony – a ruling elite, appointed by the Governor of the territory, operated the Legislature.

In 1925, following years of agitation, constitution reform made it possible for some members of the Legislative Council to be elected for the first time. The majority of citizens did not enjoy the right to vote as adult suffrage only came to Trinidad and Tobago in 1945 with the first largely elected legislature becoming a reality in 1946.

The world wide depression of the 1930s did have an impact on Trinidad and Tobago. Thus the 1930s was a period of restlessness and agitation for workers rights, improvement of socio-economic conditions and for greater and more effective participation in the political process.

Economically, sugar was in decline; there were severe droughts and disease was spreading across cocoa fields, resulting in a dramatic increase in rural unemployment. There was a recessionary impact on oilfield workers as well. Workers in general became more radical. The end result was Labour Riots between 1934 and 1937 which spread across the West Indies.

The causes of the riots were investigated by the British through two Commissions. The second of these, the Moyne Commission, recommended housing construction, agricultural diversification, more representative government and preparation of a middle class to support eventual self government. The result was universal adult suffrage for all citizens over the age of 21 in 1945.

Individuals and political groupings backed by unions and workers did emerge out of the 1930s radicalisation. But party politics was loose, electors tended to chose popular individuals and so the Legislative Council which emerged under adult suffrage was not as effective as it might have been, even though the shift had been made from appointed to elected members.

The more radical elements of labour, led by Tubal Butler, won seats in the Legislature but were not influential in government. After the 1950 elections no member supportive of Butler's leadership was chosen to sit on the Executive Council. Other leaders, sympathetic to labour, but more conservative, such as Albert Gomes, began to emerge.

World War II (1939-1945) would have also made a significant impact on Trinidad and Tobago. The development of Chaguaramas and Wallerfield as American bases created jobs and opportunities for thousands of workers at higher wages and under better conditions. By the end of World War II citizens of Trinidad and Tobago now had higher expectations for a better standard of living and quality of life. It is in this climate that the country was becoming ripe for coherent political leadership and it is in this context that Dr Eric Williams, and the political party that he founded, emerged in 1955.

The first serious political party in Trinidad and Tobago was the People's National Movement (PNM) founded in 1955 by Dr Eric Eustace Williams. It was established, in intention, as a broad-based nationalist party and in 1956 won a narrow victory at the polls. The British strengthened the PNM's hold on the Legislative Council by making appointments sympathetic to the party to allow it to govern with a clear majority. With British support, Cabinet government replaced the Executive Council in 1959 and Dr Eric Williams became Trinidad and Tobago's first Premier.

With the emergence of Williams and consolidation of the PNM, traditional labour leadership which had contributed to the emergence of a nationalist spirit, was effectively eclipsed and had to recede. And because the PNM, though espousing a nationalist ideology, rallied its base support with what seemed like ethnic nationalist fervour, the stage was being established for ethnic rivalry in the politics of Trinidad and Tobago.

Labour leadership of the 1930s, 40s and 50s had been able to build cross ethnic alliances. The People's National Movement even while pursuing the objectives of, first Federation of the West Indies and then, Independence for Trinidad and Tobago, found it difficult to do so. Attempts at building an opposition party in the period after 1956 also had its ethnic dimension and the political party system which began to emerge from that time was largely rooted in ethnic alliances in a country in which the two major ethnic groups were African and Indian. ∎

Dr Bhoendradatt Tewarie, Senator and Minister of Planning and the Economy

MILESTONES IN THE FIFTY YEARS SINCE GAINING INDEPENDENCE

During the fifty years of independence, there have been several milestones and events that helped to shape Trinidad and Tobago. Chief among these are:

1962   Trinidad and Tobago achieves Independence from colonial rule and joins the Commonwealth

1962   Trinidad and Tobago Defence Force (Regiment, Coast Guard, Air Guard and Regiment Reserves) under Brigadier Joffre Serrette is established

1962   Calypsonian Kade Simon, "Yul Bryner", wins the first ever Independence Calypso competition from among a stalwart field of bards

1964   Edwin Roberts wins the country's first Olympic medal in athletics – Bronze in the 200 metres at the 1964 Olympic Games in Tokyo, Japan

1966   Broadcast of Freddie Kissoon's 'Zingay' (23 May), the first local play to be televised on TTT

1969   Harold, Kwailan & son Pierre (five years old) circumnavigate the globe in a 40ft ketch called Humming Bird II, between 1969 to 1973

1970   "Black Power" – a wave of public protests and riots for greater political autonomy, involving – Raffique Shah, Rex Lasalles, Makandal Daaga (Geddes Granger) and Winston Leonard to name a few

1974   Trinidad and Tobago Air Services is formed by the government

1976   Trinidad and Tobago becomes the first Presidential Republic within the British Commonwealth

1976   Hasely Crawford triumphs in the 100m sprint at the Montreal Olympic Games in the winning time of 10:05 seconds

1977   Trinidad and Tobago's Janelle "Penny" Commissiong wins Miss Universe title

1978   Bert Manhin wins the country's first ever medal in shooting at the Commonwealth Games

1980   Tobago gains semi-autonomy and the Tobago House of Assembly is created

1980   BWIA becomes BWIA International Airways after a merger with Trinidad and Tobago Air Services and becomes the national airline

1981   Dr Eric Eustace Williams, the nation's 1st Prime Minister, dies (29 March) and is succeeded by George Chambers

1981   Trinidad and Tobago gets a major Iron and Steel manufacturing/fabricating entity

1981   The Trinidad & Tobago Stock Exchange formally opens – 26 October

1981   Jacob Delworth Elder, the "cultural guru of the nation", receives the Hummingbird Medal for his cultural research and the development of Trinidad and Tobago

1984   Trinidad and Tobago participates for the first time in the Paralympics Games and Rachael Marshall wins three medals (Gold in Javelin and Shot Put; bronze for freestyle)

1986   A new political Party – led by Mr Arthur N.R. Robinson – defeats the Peoples National Movement (PNM); the first time that the PNM would lose an election and ANR Robinson becomes the nation's third PM

1986   A son of the soil, Anthony Pantin is ordained the 10th Archbishop of Port of Spain

1986   Ms Giselle Laronde wins the Miss World title

1987   Noor Mohammed Hassanali appointed as President – The first of East Indian heritage and Muslim faith

1988   Karen Dieffenthaller becomes the nation's first swimming Olympian and sets a national record for the 200m freestyle at the games in Seoul

1989   Mrs Glenda Morean-Phillip becomes the first female to hold the position of President of the Law Association of Trinidad and Tobago

1990   Amoco Renegades Steelband performs with Jean-Michel Jarre in Paris at the concert celebrating Bastille Day, 14 July. Live audience, circa 2 million

1990   An attempted coup (27 July) by the black extremist Muslim group, the Jamaat al Muslimeen, led by Yasin Abu Bakr, that lasted five days

1991   PNM wins the election and Patrick Manning is chosen as Prime Minister

1993   Adrian Camps-Campins – The first national to have his designs used by UNICEF as a postcard

1993   Le Roy Clarke. First artist to be conferred the title of "Master Artist" by the National Museum & Arts Gallery of Trinidad and Tobago

1993   Trinidad and Tobago is signatory to Ramsar Convention on Wetlands. Designated three sites of international importance – Buccoo Reef, Bon Accord Lagoon complex & Caroni/Nariva Swamps

1994   Brian Lara records the highest English County Cricket score (501 not out) playing for Warwickshire against Durham

1995   For the 1st time, two Parties joined to form a coalition government – the United National Congress (UNC) and the National Alliance for Reconstruction (NAR) – and Basdeo Panday becomes Prime Minister

1995   The Securities and Exchange Commission is established

1995   Shouter Baptist Public Holiday is declared, celebrated annually on March 31

1997   ANR Robinson appointed as President – The first citizen from Tobago to hold this post

1998   Ms Wendy Fitzwilliam wins the Miss Universe title for Trinidad and Tobago

2001   The 1st time elections resulted in a tie. Both the PNM and the UNC secured 18 seats in the General Elections of the year

2001   Sir Vidiadha Surujprasad Naipaul TC awarded the Nobel Laureate Prize for Literature

2001   Revised Treaty of Chagaramas creating the Caricom Single Market & Economy (CSME)

2002   Peter Minshall presented with Emmy Award, Academy of Television Arts and Sciences 54th Annual US Primetime Emmy Awards, "Outstanding Costumes for A Variety or Music Program" for his Opening Ceremony of the 2002 Olympic Winter Games

Dr Joseph Lennox Pawan is named a 'Hero in Health' by the Pan American Health Organisation for his research on bat rabies – a classic in epidemiological studies

Agreement to establish the Caribbean Court of Justice (CCJ) comes into force

Brian Lara records the highest Test cricket score (400 not out) for the West Indies against England

Inauguration of the CCJ in its New HQ in Port of Spain

Trinidad and Tobago – Soca Warriors – qualifies for the FIFA World Cup in Germany

Sheldon Bissessar sets IHRA World Record in the IHRA Top Dragster category three times from 2007 to 2011

Natural gas discovered in the north west of Tobago

Richard Thompson, Ace Trinidadian Track Athlete. Silver at the 2008 Beijing Olympics, Silver at the World Athletics Championships in Berlin in 2009, Silver as a member of the Trinidad and Tobago 100M Relay team in Beijing Olympics and Silver with the Trinidad and Tobago 100M Relay squad in Berlin in 2009

King Carlos I & Queen Sofia of Spain visit Trinidad and Tobago (16 February 2009). First state visit of a Spanish King to Trinidad and Tobago

Fifth Summit of the Americas in Port of Spain attended by US President Barack Obama

Trinidad and Tobago wins the first prize in the category of 'sweetness' and 'fruity' in the prestigious 'Salut du Chocolat' in Paris, France

Angela Persad is elected the first female President of the Trinidad Chamber of Commerce and served for two consecutive terms

2010	Trinidad and Tobago wins the first prize in the category of 'fruity' and 'floral' in the prestigious 'Salut du Chocolat' in Paris, France
2010	Kamla Persad-Bissessar, Trinidad and Tobago's first female Prime Minister defeats the incumbent Peoples National Movement (PNM), by a resounding 29 seats to 12
2010	The Hon Kamla Persad-Bissessar becomes the Commonwealth Chairperson in Office, and in so doing, becomes the first female to hold this position
2011	Trinidad and Tobago wins the first prize in the category of 'spicy' in the prestigious 'Salut du Chocolat' in Paris, France
2011	The Horticultural Society of Trinidad and Tobago wins one of the nine Gold Medals at the Chelsea flower Show in London
2011	The Tobago Medal of Honour, the island's highest honour, is given to its first recipients – ANR Robinson, James Biggar and APT 'Fargo' James
2011	The Ken Gordon "School in Journalism and Communication Arts" attached to COSTAAT is established
2011	The members of the European Union Council on Tourism and Trade in Bucharest, Romania, voted Trinidad and Tobago as the best tourist destination and the best cultural destination in the world for 2012
2012	Naparima Girls High School celebrates its centenary
2012	Trinidad and Tobago Police Service established 215 years ago (30 May 1797)
2012	Trinidad and Tobago celebrates its 50th Anniversary of Independence

Additional material by Michael Coryat

Y YEARS OF CHANGE

e advent of republicanism was the highlight f a suite of changes that took place during the ifty years of independence for Trinidad and go. The apparent intention was to shift from n identity in respect of the symbols of the State ds a more indigenous reality without disturbing stem of government and, thereby, the political ty of the country.

o this end, in 1969, Trinidad and Tobago uced its own system of National Awards that ed the Trinity Cross, the Chaconia Medal, the ning Bird Medal and the Public Service Medal rit.

om the 1970s onwards, there were public es for the Trinity Cross to be renamed as it had stian-influenced background that challenged its lusiveness in a multi-religious society such as ad and Tobago. After successful litigation in the s and the report of a National Awards Committee, inity Cross was replaced in 2008 by the Order

In 2011, the Medal for the Development of Women was added as a new national award category.

The political challenges faced by the State over the last fifty years have included five changes of government (1986, 1991, 1995, 2001 and 2010) and two major social uprisings which threatened to overthrow civilian government (1970 and 1990) and both of which were unsuccessful.

In 1970 there was an army mutiny and widespread civil unrest, while in 1990 there was a failed coup d'etat by the Jamaat-al-Muslimeen.

In 1986 the PNM were defeated for the first time in a general election. This event opened the door to a period of political change that would make Trinidad and Tobago a functioning democracy that could enjoy peaceful civilian changes of government while having simultaneously rejected outright the previous violent options that were presented in 1970 and 1990.

Hamid Ghany, Senior Lecturer in Government at the University of the West Indies

The first intake of pupils at St Francois Girls' College, which was established in the same year that Trinidad and Tobago achieved its independence, 1962. Fifty years later, in 2012, the college's steel orchestra was crowned National Junior Panorama champions for the second time (see p.56). *Photo courtesy St Francois Girls' College/Noel P. Norton*

A brief history of Trinidad and Tobago

"Here every creed and race, find an equal place."

Geological evidence indicates that, before human settlement, Trinidad was part of South America and then separated following a shift in the tectonic plate. The national bird, the Scarlet Ibis, symbolically illustrates this ecological and geological connection with South America as it is native to both the continent and Trinidad.

Recorded history of the country begins in 1498 but the human history can be traced to thousands of years before. The oldest human fossils found – Banwari Woman – would place human habitation to at least 7000 BC. Between this time and the arrival of the first European, the descendants of Banwari Woman interacted with other islands and settlements in South America, relying on fishing and agriculture for survival.

The first peoples called Trinidad 'Kairi' or 'Iere', which means "the land of the hummingbird" but it was a European who named Trinidad. During his third voyage to the New World in 1498, Italian explorer Christopher Columbus spotted the Trinity Hills with its three distinct peaks on Trinidad's south-eastern side and christened the island "La Ysla de la Trinidad" or "Island of the Trinity". Tobago, he called "Bella Forma", which means beautifully formed land.

However, Tobago's present name is believed to be a corruption of "tobacco" which was grown by the Amerindians at the time.

The systems and institutions of the first peoples of these islands soon gave way to the dominance of the European incursions. The Spanish established Trinidad's first capital at San Jose de Oruna in 1592, but neglected their new possession in favour of the riches of South America. Meanwhile the Dutch, French and English fought for control of Tobago.

At the end of the 18th century Spain welcomed Roman Catholic settlers to develop Trinidad. The subsequent influx of French planters and their slaves transformed Trinidad into a sugar colony, which the English promptly seized in 1797.

Britain established the foundation of most of the country's institutions; in law, politics and education. The British slave trade introduced new populations of enslaved Africans to work the sugar, cocoa and coffee plantations. They were the largest group of settlers in the country.

The abolition of slavery in 1838 resulted in the influx of indentured workers from China, Madeira and mainly India until 1917, alongside Syrian/ Lebanese immigrants in later years. Some 150,000 East Indians, who brought Hindu and Moslem traditions with them, have permeated every aspect of daily life from cuisine to religious festivals.

Today, all these groups have established the roots of modern Trinidad and Tobago. The country has had its share of socio-political upheavals but never at the expense of the society's trademark harmonious democracy.

The twin-island Republic of Trinidad and Tobago stands out globally as a place where people of all ethnicities, religions and cultures live in harmony, tolerance and unity. The country remains as a beacon of harmony and unity for the world, demonstrating how a diverse history can lead to a positive culture and a place where, to quote the words of its national anthem, "every creed and race, find an equal place". ■

Sasha Mohammed

The people who came

The twin islands of Trinidad and Tobago are arguably the most cosmopolitan in the world; they truly represent the world on two islands. The early foundations were laid by the Amerindian ancestors who welcomed the Spaniards but were soon enslaved by them. Today the nation has a small but vibrant group of descendants of first peoples who went by many names: Tainos, Chagnauese, Nepoios, Chaima, Yao, Warau, Lokono and Araucas. Spanish settlement from the 16th century added French planters and their slaves from Grenada and St Domingue and British conquest in 1797 brought a new element to the mix. These European conquerors brought their slaves and bought others from travelling slave traders. When slavery was abolished in 1838 and Africans abandoned the plantations there were new infusions of Portuguese, Chinese and Indian who were deemed necessary to maintain the plantation system. The joining of the two colonies of Trinidad and Tobago in 1889 added a substantial number of African labourers to the already heterogeneous population.

Added to this ethnic pot-pourri were the many religions which accompanied these settlers. The major religion was Roman Catholicism which continues to flourish and is today the largest religious group. As the British tightened their control in the 19th century they made every effort to make Anglicanism the dominant faith and when the Asians arrived they brought in new elements such as Confucianism, Hinduism and Islam. Christian missionaries were encouraged to convert the non-Christians and so there were Moravians, Baptists, Methodists and Presbyterians. The Presbyterians, mainly from Canada, targeted the Indian population. In the 20th century there have been significant revivals of African derived religions such as Shango, Orisha and Shouter Baptists.

The religious diversity matches the ethnic variety.

Each one of these diverse groups has left their imprint on the society. The Amerindians have bequeathed a rich heritage of plants such as cassava, arrowroot, cotton, topi-tambu, beans, squash, maize, sweet potato, pineapples and avocadoes. From them we have learnt the use of annatto (roucou) as a colouring agent and the comfort of the hamaca (hammock). These were the people who provided the first labour force for the establishment of villages and plantations. The Africans who replaced the disappearing first peoples continued the process of development European-style. This saw sugar as the dominant crop up to the end of the 20th century. Like the Amerindians, the Africans brought valuable plants to the islands: yams, moko, plantain, peas, medical herbs and foods like pay-me and chillibibi. Islam was first brought to the Caribbean by slaves from West Africa.

The demand for new labourers saw the emergence of Portuguese, Chinese, demobilised soldiers from the British West India Regiment, African Americans who had fought for the British in the Anglo/American War of 1812-1815 and finally Indian indentured labourers from 1845 to 1917. The discovery and commercial exploitation of petroleum oil from the First World War (1914-1918) attracted thousands of immigrants from the smaller islands, particularly from the 1930's.

The fact that the nation has been able to manage this diversity and to use it to propel itself into the 21st century, is a tribute to the mature leadership which these many talents has been able to generate. Challenges have arisen over the years but these have been managed and stability has been maintained. As the nation celebrates its 50th anniversary of Independence there is much to be proud about. ■

A celebration of Creole traditional dress and dance.
Photo: Elizabeth Desiree Chung

The cultural landscape

Trinidad and Tobago's culture is a cornucopia of sometimes unexpected delights, reflecting an extraordinary diversity compressed in a small place. These two islands can boast of an ethnic mix unrivalled by even the mega metropoles: Amerindians, Africans, Asians, Europeans, Arabs and any and every possible combination derived from these.

Language is the first indicator of this heady brew. Place names like Naparima and Chacachacare recall the original Amerindian inhabitants; Sangre Grande, Palo Seco and Rio Claro, the first (Spanish) European settlers; the French Creoles, who arrived in the late eighteenth century, gave us Blanchisseuse, Champs Fleur and Sans Souci, while the English grafted Plymouth, Scarborough and Fort St George onto existing settlements. It's pure Trini inventiveness that has put places like Hard Bargain, Never Dirty or even Monkey Town on the map. The Trinidad English Creole spoken by all from labourer to diplomat, retains elements of Spanish, French and Bhojpuri.

A quick sampling of cuisine provides a delectable entrée to Trinidad and Tobago's culture. Depending exactly where in the twin-island republic you're dining, the menu can cater to the most catholic of tastes. National dishes include African-creole pelau (rice, peas and meat) and East Indian roti (a thin flour wrap filled with meat and vegetables). An East Indian breakfast might be tomato choka accompanied by sada roti; African-creoles will offer buljol (spiced saltfish, onions and tomatoes) or smoked herring.

Tobago lunch is the iconic curried crab and dumpling, while no river excursion is complete without Indian-style open-fire cooked curried duck. Beach fast food is strictly bake and shark, while the 24/7 snack is Doubles (a 'bara' sandwich of

▶

Sunday school. *Photo: Stephen Broadbridge*

Celebration during Diwali. *Photo: Stephen Broadbridge*

Clockwise from top – Emancipation Day celebrations. *Photo: James B. Solomon*; Tassa drummers. *Photo: Shirley Bahadur*; Heritage Festival in Tobago. *Photo: Oswin Browne*; Carnival. *Photo: Salim October*; Tamboo bamboo band. *Photo: Wendell Stephen Jay Reyes*

steaming hot chick peas, garnished with spicy condiments).

No Sunday lunch table is complete without macaroni pie, stewed chicken and red beans or potato salad and Christmas requires its own distinctive menu, from the boiled ham, to the pastelle, black cake and sorrel drink.

Food for the soul is provided by an equally eclectic mix of world and indigenous religions. There are Roman Catholics, Hindus, Anglicans, Muslims, Presbyterians, Seventh Day Adventists, Jehovah's Witnesses, Methodists, and Moravians. Along with many Pentecostal

sects there are devotees of the indigenous Shouter or Spiritual Baptist and Yoruban Orisha faiths; Bobo Shantis, Rastafarians and Kali worshippers.

A number of religious festivals are now celebrated by the entire national community. Besides Christmas, with its distinctive Spanish-derived parang music, these include the Hindu Spring festival Phagwa, the major Hindu festival, Diwali, November's Festival of Lights and the Muslim Eid ul-Fitr, marking the end of Ramadan. A unique confluence of Hinduism and Christianity is celebrated after Easter at La Divina Pastora festival in ▶

The 85ft Hanuman statue in the grounds of the Dattatreya Mandir in Carapachaima. *Photo: James B. Solomon*

Cathedral of the Immaculate Conception in Port of Spain. *Photo: Ian Brierley*

Dattatreya Mandir. *Photo: Wendell Stephen Jay Reyes*

Santa Rosa church in Arima. *Photo: Ryan P. Mannette*

Temple in the Sea at Waterloo in Chaguanas. *Photo: Ian Brierley*

Phagwa celebrations. *Photo: Stephen Broadbridge*

Siparia, where the Black Virgin is worshipped by Catholics and Hindus alike. Hosay, which was originally a sacred Shi'ite Muslim observance, commemorating the martyrdom of the prophet Mohammed's grandsons Hassan and Husein, is now celebrated at the end of Muharram by all elements to the mesmeric beat of tassa drums.

Among a plethora of secular festivals, the mother of them all is Carnival. From its origins as an exclusive entertainment for French planters, with balls and masked parties, after full Emancipation in 1838, it developed into a wild celebration of liberty by the ex-slaves. Carnival evolved into a focal point for Creole creativity: in song, dance, costuming, political and social commentary. Stickfighting, calypso, steel pan; traditional masquerade

characters like the Midnight Robber, Jab Jab, Pierrot Grenade, the mud bands of J'ouvert as well as the gorgeously costumed mas bands-all owe their existence to Trinidad's Carnival, which has spawned similar festivals worldwide, including Europe biggest street event, London's Notting Hill Carnival.

Other festivals like Trinidad's Best Village and Tobago Heritage help preserve and highlight folk forms and customs, like the Moriah Old Time Wedding, storytelling and Tobago's unique tambrin music which accompanies the reel and jig ancestral dances. ∎

Simon Lee, London-born journalist has travelled and written about the region extensively

The national character

Ask any Trinbagonian inside of Trinidad and Tobago about what they think of their country. They are likely to give you a list of deficiencies and under-achievements which contribute to its under-development.

Ask these same individuals this very same question, *outside* of the islands, and you are likely to hear, in glowing terms, about its charms, uniqueness, achievements, development and potential in industry and commerce, education, culture, health, infrastructure, tourism, communication and many other areas.

Each view, though seemingly diametrically opposed and contradictory of each other, may be easily supported with fact, figures, statistics and evidence.

Fifty years since Independence, the attitudes of Trinbagonians to their country and the accommodating, multicultural character of its people remain its most defining elements.

Whilst it continues to baffle development planners who, in considering only conventional and oft-borrowed-from-abroad developmental markers, point to the highly critical environment and laid-back attitude as a drawback, reflecting an absence of self-appreciation and patriotism and officials continue to scratch their heads over how it may be addressed, the ability of Trinbagonians to laugh at themselves has particular charm, especially in putting business or leisure visitors at ease.

These unique elements define the democratic character of the place which accommodates contentions and conflicts as a way of life and allows the judiciary and media, independence of thought – necessary components for progress.

This melting pot is as much part of the *Trini limestyle* and the Carnival mentality which, though often expressed as negatives, is at the core of what drives the engine of growth of these two small islands. This provides the vibrant, effervescent, innovative, creative and spontaneous edge that is replicated in all of national life and in the numerous festivals including Carnival, Diwali, Hosay, Eid ul-Fitr, Emancipation and the Chinese Boat Festival.

It exemplifies a multicultural spirit and accommodation of diversity that is second to none in the world. The blend of world cultures, festivals, practices and habits from Africa, Europe, Asia, the Middle East and elsewhere sustains an environment of social stability and cohesion in the face of differences that lends an ease to doing business in the country.

These essential elements which are considered crucial to creating a conducive environment for progress and development exist almost as part of the natural landscape, assets and resources of Trinidad and Tobago.

Fifty years on, Trinidad and Tobago has enhanced its natural endowments of petroleum and mineral resources, tropical forests and a climate of sun, sea and sand with two bonus ingredients: ease of doing business and diligence about the business of leisure.

Dr Kris Rampersad specialises in the comparative analysis of Caribbean development issues in culture, education, literature, gender and media in global contexts

Local fashion designers Karen and Kathy Norman draw heavily on traditional art and fashion fused with the unique Carnival costumes produced by designers such as Peter Minshall.
Photo: Josanne Leonard

Creativity in Trinidad and Tobago

Trinidad and Tobago's cultural potpourri has generated a society bristling with creative passion and vigour. And, with a long and proud history of linguistic and musical expression, these islands continue to push boundaries with musical fusions, innovative designers, globally-acclaimed writers, artists and dancers and now a burgeoning film industry.

MUSIC

Trinbagonians natural affinity with rhythm and a strong tradition of singing and music meant, music of all genres, whether of 3/3 or 4/4 timing, was and is still embraced by the whole nation.

Trinidad and Tobago is famously the birthplace of calypso – which spawned piquant social commentators like Lord Kitchener and the Mighty Sparrow – and steel pan – the only acoustic musical instrument invented in the 20th century. Yet there is plenty more including a classical music tradition, indigenous art forms and their vaunted exponents such as the infectiously-energetic beats of calypso's child, soca, (Machel Montano, David Rudder), Latin American-inspired Christmas music, parang (Lara Brothers) and its Tobago equivalent – tambrin, led by shallow goatskin drum and haunting fiddle.

The influences, fusions and reinterpretations that resulted included the often ribald lyrics of soca-parang (Scrunter) and East Indian-derived chutney-soca (Rikki Jai); added to which innovators like Zanda, Liam Teague, Boogsie Sharpe, Andre Tanker, Clive Alexander and Mungal Patasar are celebrated in the fusing of calypso, pan, jazz and Indian music leading to today's innovative exponents, such as Etienne Charles.

A recent innovation, the 1980s, Rapso is a crossover genre whose chanted lyrics derived from African oral traditions, developed by Launcelot Layne and Brother Resistance and seen to great effect in the songs of 3 Canal and charismatic wordsmith Ataklan.

The strong lineage of classical music saw many Trinbagonians, musicians, conductors and singers studying at internationally renowned institutions and conservatories – Royal College of Music, Royal Academy of Music, Guildhall School of Music and Drama, the Royal Military School of Music (UK) and The Julliard School (US). When they were not studying, they were competing in music festivals. Two Trinbagonians are known to have competed in The Kathleen Ferrier Awards ("the UK's most prestigious singing awards"), winning their respective categories – Sandra Browne Hart (1971) and Tahirah Osborne (2010 – Young Singers).

Three key choirs have also helped to shape Trinidad and Tobago's classical music landscape – the Marionettes Choral (1963 – Jocelyn Pierre & June Williams Thorne, the first choir said to blend voices with the steel pan), The Love Movement (1972 – Bernadette Scott) and The Lydians (1979 – Joyce Spence). Two of the people who helped influence this aspect of the Trinidad and Tobago culture, amongst others, are Geraldine Connor and Pat Bishop. During this time, the former Trinidad Opera Company was also an influence and training ground for Trinbagonians.

Parang musicians, the Lara Brothers. *Photo: Marcus Gonzales*

The steel pan was invented in Trinidad and Tobago and is the only crafted acoustic musical instrument to be developed in the twentieth century.
Photo: Stephen Broadbridge

Master Savile Row tailor, Professor Andrew Ramroop

PHOTO: JAMES B. SOLOMON

Chutney soca artist, Rikki Jai

Most recently, The Classical Music Development Foundation of Trinidad & Tobago (2005 – June Nathaniel, a graduate of the Royal College of Music in Piano & Singing, Annette Dopwell and Christiane McGahan) was formed to promote classical music.

Other Trinbagonians who have gone on to achieve international recognition include: Heather Headley, Jeanine de Bique, Jill Gomez, Natalia Dopelwell, Simone Sauphanor (sopranos), Anne Fridal and Lorna Myers (mezzo sopranos), Neil Latchman and Ronald Samm (tenors), Brian Green and Roberto Salvatori (baritones) and Barry Martin (bass).

On the instrument side, some notable names excelling in the international arena include Faye Clinton (cellist), Enrique Ali (pianist), Liam Teague and Mia Gormandy (panist).

Trinbagonians can also be found holding the conductor's baton and two such persons are Kwame Ryan and Richard Tang Yuk.

In addition to Tahirah Osborne, Trinbagonians currently striving for international recognition include Christian Joel, Natalia Dopwell, Rahel Moore, Renée Solomon and Rory Wallace.

FASHION & DESIGN

The annual festival of expression which is Carnival was described as 'living art that we make fresh every year' by Emmy Award-winning designer Peter Minshall. Minshall's towering dance mobiles have brought a unique flavour to Olympic Games and World Cup football opening ceremonies and restored a high-art approach to costume design. His Carnival baton has been taken up by Brian MacFarlane, whose costumes remain the season's most eagerly-anticipated.

In mainstream fashion, Meiling, Claudia Pegus, Peter Elias and Heather Jones have forged international reputations whilst the sartorial excellence of Savile Row Tailor, Andrew Ramroop, is seen to great effect on the world's top dressers.

PAINTING & SCULPTURE

In painting and sculpture, the arrestingly vibrant murals which adorn the Queens Park Oval's perimeter walls are visual testament to the country's continued pool of artistic talent. The line has stretched back through modern-day exponents such as Ken Crichlow, Carlisle Harris, Peter Sheppard, LeRoy Clarke, Ralph and Vera Baney, Jackie Hinkson, Shastri Maharaj, Christopher Cozier and through Isaiah James Boodhoo, Carlisle Chang, Noel Vaucrosson and Boscoe Holder right back with the 18th century European-trained landscape artist Jean Michel Cazabon and 19th century Expressionist painter Theodora Walter. German-born Tobagonian-based sculptor Luis Kimme's life-sized, and life-like, wooden sculptures vividly depict subjects in traditional Trinbagonian costume and are highly-prized works.

The richness of the country's artistic traditions, pre-independence, included the works of Sybil Atteck and M P Alladin who absorbed foreign styles while developing their own. Since Independence, sculptor Pat Chu Foon together with several others created rich indigenous iconography, while a younger generation, building on this platform, experiments with installation, conceptual and performance art. *By Simon Lee, James Fuller and Josephine Learmond-Criqui*

THE STEEL PAN

The steel drum ("steelpan" or "pan" to aficionados) is Trinidad's major contribution to the world of instrumental music; the only crafted acoustic musical instrument to be developed in its entirety in the twentieth century.

The first pans were created in the late 1940s as a result of a long standing ban on African drumming that existed since slavery, prompting young men, primarily of African descent, to resort to other ways of creating musical rhythms.

Tobago tambrin band. *Photo: Oswin Browne*

Around Carnival time, as the music spilled into the streets, alternative ways were found to create rhythms. This included the "Tamboo Bamboo" which consisted of bamboo sticks of various lengths struck together or on the ground to create African rhythmic patterns.

To create a more musical sound and to cope with the fragility of the bamboo, metal objects were added to these "tamboo bamboo" bands including dustbins, tin cans, biscuit drums, etc that maintained the rhythms of the 'lavways' (the chanting and singing of popular songs at Carnival and Stick Fights by 'chantuelles') and the riffs of the frontline bugle players.

The US Naval base in Port of Spain and the oil refinery at Pointe-a Pierre were both sources for discarded oil drums and the next steps in the evolution of these discarded 'pans' into a crafted musical instrument – Pan – was almost inevitable.

The banning of bamboo after 1937 and the ban on Carnival that was imposed during World War Two allowed the bands time to experiment and enterprising young men like Neville Jules, Winston "Spree" Simon, Andrew 'Pan' De Labastide and Ellie Mannette were ready to introduce a functional steel pan based on the 55 gallon oil drum to the public when the carnival ban was over.

These pans were capable of playing simple melodies and from that humble beginning the full steelband was born, capable of introducing the world to a new musical experience at the 1951 Festival of Britain.

Since it origins, there have been many innovations to the original steel drum. Pans in a modern steelband, what Neville Jules called 'the family of pans', cover the entire range of a conventional orchestra from the lowest bass to the alto and soprano range.

Today, the steel pan is enjoyed and played by amateur and professional musicians of all genres, including the classics, jazz and of course calypso. *By Glenroy Joseph*

NEAL & MASSY TRINIDAD ALL STARS STEEL ORCHESTRA

The steelband movement in Trinidad and Tobago has a rich and colourful history. There are many bands whose individual narratives are central to this collective history; none more so than the Neal & Massy Trinidad All Stars Steel Orchestra. Developed between the First and Second World Wars, All Stars, as it is affectionately known, was born of an innate and explosive creativity.

The band's roots go deep and its turbulent early beginnings and explosive creativity is the hallmark of steelband music today.

"Hell Yard Boys" was the name they gave themselves back in 1935; Hell Yard being a poor area on the banks of the East Dry River in Port

Born Leroy Calliste in 1941 in San Fernando, Black Stalin won the Calypso Monarch title five times between 1979 and 1995 and was also crowned Calypso King of the World in 1999. In 2008, he was conferred with an honorary doctorate by the University of the West Indies for his dedication and contribution to calypso music and culture in Trinidad and Tobago.
Photo: Stephen Broadbridge

St Francois Girls' College Steel Orchestra celebrate winning the National Junior Panorama competition in February 2012. Their victory had the additional poignancy of being achieved in the same year that their school marked fifty years since its establishment. *Photo: Shirley Bahadur*

of Spain. The movement away from "tamboo-bamboo" to pan had only just begun. But this original name changed several times – to "Second Fiddle", then to "Cross of Lorraine" and finally "All Stars", chosen because of the perceived superior ability of the players. Soon after the war, "Trinidad" was added.

In 1982 the contributions of Trinidad All Stars to the steelband movement were recognised by the Government of Trinidad & Tobago with the presentation of a national award – the Humming Bird Medal (Gold). Four years later, the band was again honoured with an award from the Port of Spain City Council.

One of the many achievements of the band was its pioneering of classical music on the road, played to the rhythm of calypso. This highlighted the capacity of the steelpan to go beyond the previously self-imposed musical bounds of calypso or boleros.

Trinidad All Stars was the first band to play the pan with two sticks. For the first time, both the melody and the harmony could be heard played together. The band made the first "Quatro Pans" later called the *Grundig* and the guitar pans. A former captain of Trinidad All Stars, Neville Jules, also had the privilege of making the first bass pan.

The band's accomplished musicians have maintained a standard of excellence through their innovative mastery of the instruments. They have secured first place victories in the biennial Music Festival on six occasions, have won the National Panorama Competition eight times, the Bomb Competition on countless occasions and successfully held nine Classical Jewels concerts.

The band has toured and performed extensively throughout the world. *Source: Neal & Massy Trinidad All Stars Steel Orchestra*

LITERATURE

While Carnival dominates popular culture, Trinidad and Tobago's creativity is well represented in other forms. Trinidad's literary tradition established by the 1930s Beacon Group, in which CLR James figured prominently, has produced two Nobel Laureates: the island-born novelist Sir Vidia Naipaul (2001) and St Lucian-born poet Derek Walcott (1992), who founded the Trinidad Theatre Workshop during his sojourn, from the 1950s through to the late 1970s.

Sam Selvon launched the vernacular Creole voice on the world literature scene with his *Lonely Londoners*, while VS Naipaul's younger brother Shiva wrote several novels before his premature death. Other notable writers include Neil Bissoondath, Earl Lovelace, Michael Anthony, Elizabeth Nunez, Canada-based Harold 'Sonny' Ladoo and Ismith Khan.

In his work, Earl Lovelace chronicles the struggle for cultural validation and the complexities of a developing nation. His 1996 novel Salt won the Commonwealth Writers Prize. Other Commonwealth Prize Winners include Wayne Brown, Robert Antoni and Lawrence Scott. Baker, painter, sculptor and writer; the indefatigable Willie Chen and the tortured Tobagonian poet Eric Roach also emerged in the early independent years.

Among the many gifted women writers are novelists: Merle Hodge, Elizabeth Nunez, Dionne Brand, Shani Mootoo, Barbara Lalla and poets: Jennifer Rahim and the 1989 winner of Cuba's prestigious Casa de las Americas prize, Nouberse Phillips.

The new generation of writers is led by Kevin Baldeosingh, Raymond Ramcharitar and performance poet Muhammed Muwakil.

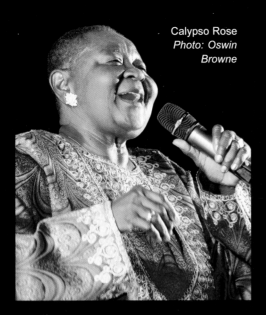

Calypso Rose
Photo: Oswin Browne

THEATRE ARTS

Both African and Indian heritages have produced vibrant dance forms. If the 'wine' and 'chip' of Carnival are best known along with limbo, there are African styles like the kalenda or stickfight dance, bongo (traditionally danced at wakes), congo, juba and coromanti and Creole forms such as the Belair and the Tobago reel and jig. Beryl McBurnie, founder of the Little Carib Theatre, revitalised dance with her regional research in the 1950s and 60s. Classical Indian dance as kathak and kuchipudi flourish alongside folk forms and the dances of Hosay and the Ramleela re-enactment of the Hindu epic the Ramayana.

The vibrancy of modern, jazz and contemporary dance styles was pioneered by several Dance Schools and Companies. Chief among these were The Caribbean School of Dance, Joyce Kirton's, Les Enfants, celebrating their 50th anniversary in 2012, Molly Ahee, Carol La Chapelle and Eugene Joseph.

Founded in 1957, Caribbean School of Dance has produced a number of students who went on to study with the world-renowned Julliard or Alvin Ailey and developed professional careers in the international arena. These include: Roger Shim – Royal Winnipeg Ballet (Canada) and later the Geneva Ballet (Switzerland); Rachel Ganteaume – Joffrey Ballet (New York); Paul Dennis – The Limón Dance Company (New York); Celisse Johnson – Brooklyn Dance Company (New York); Natalie Rogers-Cropper – The Garth Fagan Dance Company (New York); Peter London – The Martha Graham Company (New York); Solange Sandy – The Alvin Ailey Dance Company (New York), Nadine Mose – Ballet Hispanico and Elisa Monte Dance Company (New York), Ronald Taylor – Dance Theater of Harlem (New York), Terry Springer – Coreoarte (Venezuela). ■

By Simon Lee, James Fuller, Josephine Learmond-Criqui

EXEMPLARS AND ICONS

During the 50 years of independence every citizen made personal sacrifices and contributions that supported and facilitated the development of the country. Many have been recognised for this by the bestowing of the country's highest awards; others by their peers, professional bodies and families and yet more by international acclaim. In recognition of the 50 years of independence, we have narrowed our choice to 50 individuals who were born in Trinidad and Tobago, remained there for the greater part of 1962 – 2012 and are exemplars and icons:

M.P. Alladin
George Bailey
Wayne Berkeley
Pat Bishop
Sheldon Bissessar
Victor Bruce
Tubal Uriah Butler
Rudranath Capildeo
Carlisle Chang
Ellis Clarke
Hasely Crawford
Jacob Delworth Elder
Roger Gibbon
Kenneth Gordon
Geoffrey Holder
Ray Holman
Harold & Kwailan La Borde
Christopher Laird
Colin Laird
Brian Lara
Giselle Laronde-West
Rose McArtha Lewis
Earl Lovelace
Kama Maharaj
Satnarayan Maharaj
Rhonda Maingot
Rachel Marshall
Dom Basil Mathews
Pat Mathura
Beryl McBurnie
Machel Montano
Glenda Morean-Phillip
Deryck Murray
Anthony Pantin
Mungal Patasar
Sundar Popo
Narsaloo Ramayah
Mannie Ramjohn
Hazel Ward Redman
Aldwyn Roberts
Earl Rodney
David Rudder
Jit Samaroo
Len "Boogsie" Sharpe
Daisy Voisin
James Lee Wah
George Weekes
Justa Werges
Anthony Williams
Dwight Yorke

Celebrating Diwali, the Hindu Festival of Lights
Photo: Stephen Broadbridge

Festivals and celebrations

INDEPENDENCE DAY

Independence Day, 31st August, is celebrated with military-style parades with the uniformed services – Police, Fire and Prison bands – marching through the streets to the accompaniment of live music. The evening is marked by the presentation of National Awards for outstanding achievements in a ceremony held at the President's House.

EMANCIPATION DAY

The 1st of August is Emancipation Day, a national holiday, to commemorate the abolition of slavery.

The celebration usually includes a procession through the streets of Port of Spain to the Queen's Park Savannah and the Emancipation Village – a showcase of music, arts and cuisine reflecting the country's African heritage.

DIWALI

Diwali is a Festival of Lights that is marked by the lighting of deeyas which are made from clay and filled with oil or ghee. Devotees also clean their homes and surroundings, wear new clothing and give charity to the needy.

The observance of Diwali is to get devotees committed to the spiritual path and ultimately attain illumination by becoming one with God. As Hindus light the lamps in their houses, devotees are reminded to light the lamps of wisdom, goodness and God-consciousness in themselves. It is through this, that they can attain the "Light of Lights" – God.

REPUBLIC DAY

Trinidad and Tobago became a Republic on the 1st August 1976. The event is celebrated as a public holiday on September 24th because this is the date when the first Parliament met under the new Republican Constitution.

SPIRITUAL (SHOUTER) BAPTIST LIBERATION DAY

Spiritual Shouter Baptist is a unique religion specific to Trinidad comprising elements of both Protestant Christianity and African dogma and rituals. It is a dynamic and vibrant religion representing both the spontaneity and rhythms of Africa and the restrained, traditional tenets of Christianity. 30th March marks the repeal of the Shouter Prohibition Ordinance which banned the activities and observances of the religion.

INDIAN ARRIVAL DAY

Indian Arrival Day is celebrated as a public holiday in Trinidad and Tobago on the thirtieth day in May and commemorates the beginning of indentured servitude when the first labourers from India were brought over in May 1845 on the ship Fatel Razack to work on the sugar cane plantations.

Celebrating Trinidad and Tobago's African heritage. *Photo: Salim October*

Independence Day parade. *Photo: Shirley Bahadur*

Each year, Indian Arrival Day is commemorated and celebrated in several ways; notably by the staging of a re-enactment of the arrival of the Fatel Razack and celebrations in music and dance.

JAZZ EXPERIENCE

The Tobago Jazz Experience is a celebration of jazz and indigenous music of the Caribbean. Scheduled for April each year, the visitor will not only experience the music but able to savour and participate in the cultural and historical practices that define Tobago as an ideal destination.

PARANG

The term 'Parang' is derived from the Spanish word 'parranda' which means a spree or a fête. In Trinidad, parang is the songs that are sung during the Christmas season.

Traditionally, musicians called parranderos entertain members of the community by visiting house to house. However, these visits take place in fewer areas in Trinidad with the songs being given prominence through air play on radio and television. The official parang season runs from October to January 6th (The Day of the Kings or Dia de los Reyes).

LABOUR DAY

Labour Day (19th June) is the anniversary of the historic labour riots of 1937, the culmination of intense activism by workers resulting in strikes and riots on the sugar plantations and in the oil fields.

FOOD FESTIVALS

Trinbagonians love their food and competitions and food festivals provide an ideal opportunity to practice both. There are several food festivals, some with competitive elements, all over the islands and throughout the year but the most celebrated ones are Taste T&T, The Tobago Culinary Festival and the Blue Food Festival.

Taste T&T is the Tourism Development Company's annual culinary festival and is undoubtedly the gastronomic highlight of the year. Both the focus and the programme for each year are unique and is usually held in the latter part of the year.

The Tobago Culinary Festival is in May at the Pigeon Point Heritage Park and the Blue Food Festival is in October at Bloody Bay, Tobago.

BEST VILLAGE

Counties (administrative districts) compete each year for the Prime Minister's Best Village Trophy.

The competition's finale is in October or November when winners of various categories – storytelling, cuisine, dance, music, theatre, etc – are announced. A highlight is the crowning of the Best Village Queen – La Reine Rivé.

AMERINDIAN HERITAGE DAY

Descendants of the first peoples of Trinidad and Tobago celebrate their ancestry and heritage with a smoke ceremony and street procession in Arima on the 14th of October.

SANTA ROSA FESTIVAL AND CARIB QUEENS

Each year on the Sunday nearest 23 August, Trinidad and Tobago's Santa Rosa Carib Community (SRCC) celebrate their biggest festival in Arima: the Santa Rosa Festival in honour of their patron saint, Santa Rosa de Lima – patron saint of the New World, whose feast day is 23 August. This is a joint celebration with the Catholic Church. As well as a Church service, a Carib shaman performs a smoke ceremony dedicated to Carib ancestors. In 2011 ▶

3 Canal performing at the Tobago Jazz Experience. *Photo: Oswin Browne*

Ole Time Wedding celebration in Moriah, Tobago (left). *Photo: Oswin Browne*; Amerindian Heritage Day. *Photo: Salim October*

the SRCC celebrated 225 years of the feast of Santa Rosa.

Hundreds join the celebrations from across the country. A statue of the Saint is decorated and carried through the streets of Arima in a procession by members of the SRCC, led by the Carib Queen, other Roman Catholics and well-wishers. The procession returns to the Church and at the end of the service, participants share breakfast and socialise.

Indigenous Amerindians – Caribs and Arawaks – have lived in Trinidad and Tobago for over 6,000 years before Columbus came to these shores. When the Spanish colonised Trinidad and Tobago in 1592, there were about 40,000 Caribs in Trinidad and Tobago. Today, according to the SRCC's Website, about 12,000 people in Northeast Trinidad are of Amerindian descent.

Many places in Trinidad still maintain their Amerindian names, for example: Arima, Aripo, Arouca, Caroni, Carapichaima, Caura, Chacachacare, Chaguanas, Couva, Cunaripo, Guaico, Guayaguayare, Mayaro, Mucurapo, Naparima, Oropouche, Paria, Tacarigua, Tamana, and Tunapuna.

The SRCC has a Titular Queen, Jennifer Cassar, and a President, Ricardo Bharath Hernandez. Cassar was elected by the Community's Council of Elders in 2011 following the death of the previous Queen, Valentina Medina. Other former Queens include: Justa Werges, Edith Martinez, Maria Werges, Ma Gopaul and Dolores Medrano.

'Santa Rosa Festival and Carib Queens' feature by Leela Ramdeen, Attorney-at-Law, Education Consultant and Chair of the Catholic Commission for Social Justice

HERITAGE FESTIVAL

The largest and most renowned of all Tobago's Festivals, 'Heritage' is a multi-event showcase of Tobago's dance, music, religion, rituals and cuisine. The Festival is staged at several villages with each village having its own signature event. The most celebrated of this is the village of Moriah's Ole Time Wedding.

PHAGWA OR HOLI

Phagwa or Holi is celebrated in the months of Phalgun and Chaitra in the Hindu calendar that corresponds to March or April. It is a festival of fun that celebrates springtime and renewal and one of the main features of the day is the Festival of Colours when people are squirted with brightly-dyed water called 'abeer'. This is Pichakaree, an art form in which humanity is the canvas.

A special type of folk song called Chowtal is sung during the course of the festival and the music is usually played with only two instruments – the dholak (a hand drum) and the majeera (cymbals or percussion instrument). 'Chutney', a localised English, Hindi style of music is replacing the traditional chowtal.

MUSLIM FESTIVALS

In Trinidad and Tobago, several Muslim Festivals are celebrated: Eid ul-Fitr, Eid ul-Adha and Hosay.

Eid ul Fitr is a solemn festival when Muslims give thanks for the blessings they have received from Allah, celebrate the victory of the forces of good over evil, forgive their neighbours for ill feelings and spread peace. It is also a time for

Tassa Drummers. *Photo: Marcus Gonzales*

giving thanks for completing another period of fasting for the holy month of Ramadan.

Eid ul Adha is a festival of sacrifice or 'Greater Eid', commemorating the willingness of Abraham to sacrifice his son Ishmael as an act of obedience to god, before god intervened to provide him with a ram to sacrifice instead.

Hosay is a Shi'ite Muslim procession commemorating the martyrdom of two Muslim Princes that is, in Trinidad, a colourful processions with flags, spinning moons and elaborate replicas of temples called 'Tadjahs' accompanied by tassa drumming and chanting. The procession ends at the water's edge and the tadjahs and the moons are thrown into the water as offerings.

Prime Minister, Kamla Persad-Bissessar participating in the Hindu celebration of Pagwa. *Photo: Gary Jordan/TDC*

UNDERWATER CARNIVAL

In July at Pigeon Point. Tobago will be taking Carnival beneath the sea with the Tobago Underwater Dive Festival. Themed Underwater Carnival, the event is designed to showcase the destination's rich and diverse eco-system and the explosion of marine life that can be found off the island's shores. Hosted by the Tobago House of Assembly Tourism Division (THA) and the Association of Tobago Dive Operators (ATDO), the week-long event will provide both experienced and amateur divers opportunities to fine-tune their skills while exploring the enchanting world beneath its aquamarine and cobalt blue waters.

THE BOCAS LIT FEST

The NGC Bocas Lit Fest is a major literary event in Trinidad and Tobago that provides a forum for bringing writers together with Caribbean readers. The four-day Festival, held annually during the last weekend of April, includes readings, writing workshops, panel discussions, debates, performance poetry, film screenings and the announcement of the winner of the annual OCM Bocas Prize for Caribbean Literature which carries US$10,000 for the best book of either fiction, non-fiction or poetry. ■

Cherrylene Lewis currently works at the Government Information Services Limited as a Presenter/Reporter

hristmas is a special season but for most Trinbagonians one stands above all others.

Each Boxing Day the yuletide season is dismissed, executed by the Carnival guillotine, as parang is dropped and the airwaves are opened to wall-to-wall soca. Releases of songs which will vie for the Road March title heighten the anticipatory air, as does the calendar of must-attend fetes.

That anticipation is unleashed at Carnival's curtain-raiser J'Ouvert. Literally translating as 'The day opens', J'Ouvert starts in the witching hours of Carnival Monday and continues through till dawn. These early exchanges are characterised by masqueraders plastering one another liberally with multi-coloured muds to a joyous backbeat of soca. It's peculiarly moving and watching the dawn rise over Port of Spain's skyline, as shadowy silhouettes dance on top of walls, is something everyone should experience once in life.

But it's Carnival Tuesday, judging day, when everyone fully dons their finery; as is apparent by the cars crammed with masqueraders heading into town, all tasselled armbands, mirrored plastic sequins and shining faces, the resplendent ostrich feathers of the girls' headdresses bent against roofs.

An eight-hour workout awaits, for which many have got in shape and for which just as many haven't. Throughout the day, bemused stragglers charge about all over, amidst frantic phone calls and texts, trying to relocate their section. 'Where de band? Where de band?'

The shower trucks, spraying revellers in cooling water mists, are in constant use as the searing Caribbean sun takes its toll. The vibrations of the heavy base and energetic soca tempos shake the roadside buildings and the street beneath your feet. There is a euphoric unity of spirit; it's two days of not caring, getting on bad, of uninhibited bank managers and insurance clerks partying like naughty teenagers, and of random people appearing in your photographs in compromising positions. It's pure joy. Truly the 'Greatest Show on Earth'.

James Fuller

CARNIVAL TIME

Jump in de streets, and wave yuh hand,
Sweet island beats, in dis carnival band,
Drinking sweet rum, and dancing,
Hot,hot sun, yet still prancing.

Everything stop for mas to play,
Everything start back on Ash Wednesday!
Aright now is time for fun,
In this sweet Trinidad sun!

Listen to the steel pan,
Dance, chile, woman or man!
The music will take you away,
On Carnival Monday or Tuesday!

Monday morning is mud and j'ouvert,
And is de grandstand on de nex' day
Carnival nice fuh so!
Wit sweet,sweet soca and kaiso!

So whether yuh pay the devil a shilling,
Whether yuh on de corner chilling,
Whether yuh jus bussin a lime,
In Trinidad nuttin better than carnival time!

Rishi Permanand

Modern interpretation of the Midnight Robber
Photo: Ryan P. Mannette

THE MIDNIGHT ROBBER: A TRINBAGO SLAVE RELIC OF DEFIANCE

The Midnight Robber made his first carnival appearance in the early 1900s, but may have already been in existence during and after slavery. The most important point to observe is his use of the boast, the invincibility of self and having the power not only to inflict the gravest cruelty to humanity but also to have powers over the cosmic elements: the sun, moon, stars, planets, earth, rivers, rain, storms, lightning, and so on. The sources that constitute the repertoire of the Midnight Robber appear to be directly influenced by the world of slavery recreated so startlingly by the late Arnim Mitto Sampson in his essay on the origins of kaiso published in the Caribbean Quarterly (1954).

These figures were larger than life and engaged in the use of the word as weapon to inspire, kill, maim or inflict mortal damage on a living person. These motifs or themes are structurally resonant in African traditional poetry of the boast genre, although in Europe there is a semblance of this in the court jester who could heap insults even on the King on a special day of celebration. But this does not fit the Midnight Robber genre and the late Brian Honoré, himself a formidable wordsmith, recognised Africa as the source of the Midnight Robber's speech.

Although the Robber appears to be immoral with his extolled vile deeds, his victim has relentlessly been the "mock man" – the hypocrite, the purveyor of untruth. Thus the Midnight Robber adopts the language of boastfulness in order to express his fearlessness and powers. Every

Robber from the beginnings of the phenomenon to the present day has as his victim the mock man who can be identified as a slave owner and the modern day overlord and exploiter.

The speeches of 94-year old Essaw Millington, the oldest practising Robber, Andrew "Puggy" Joseph, Andrew Bedeau and Brian Honoré, all reflected the profound sophistication of the ritual of language and performance and impacted deeply on the consciousness of Trinbago and the world through the resources they pulled from ancestors in perpetuating an aspect of our memorial history.

John Stollmeyer is one of the most poetic eclectic and profound exponents of the ancestral models we have inherited in modern times. Though the word constitutes the seismic centre of the Robber's purpose and meaning, his original dress, created from flour bags with impressive symbols and motifs, with a cutlass or dagger in his hand, reminiscent of Shango/Ogun, a massive and decorated broad-brimmed hat reminiscent of the Wild West cowboy, his dramatic, frightening appearance, is in fact the facade which empowers and energises his speech, giving it meaning and context.

A bold and extroverted character, the Midnight Robber's original themes have been extended over the years by many practitioners who now embrace ecology, politics, natural disasters and industrialisation issues. The Midnight Robber lives on...

Amon Saba Saakana is the author of 'The Colonial Legacy in Caribbean Literature' and the film, 'Ida's Daughter: The World of Fintou Pearl Springer'

J'ouvert!

Photos by Stephen Broadbridge

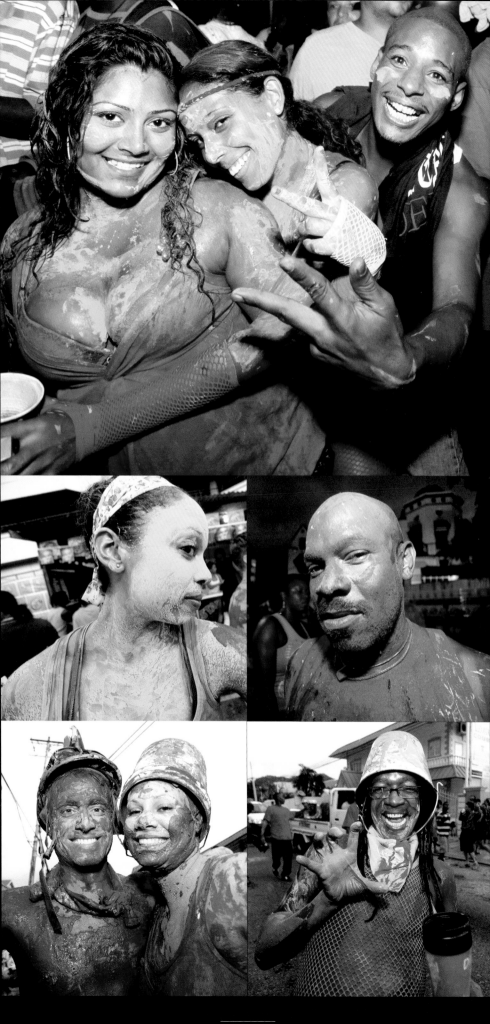

Kiddies Carnival!

Photos by Stephen Broadbridge

A typical beach lime Photo: Stephen Broadbridge

Living and lifestyles

C onsidering the volume of blessings which have been showered upon this tiny twin-island Republic, it is hard to imagine a Divine Being not being a patriot or patron of Trinidad and Tobago.

The proof is in the numerous times the country has watched natural disasters such as hurricanes and earthquakes knock at its door, only to turn round at the last moment for an alternate destination.

But there is no better attestation to divine kinship with and favour for our country than the masterpiece that is our people.

ETHNIC DIVERSITY UNMATCHED
There is no other place on earth that can surpass Trinidad and Tobago's racial composition. Every creed and race does indeed find an equal place in our land, playing together as children, walking alongside one another on our bustling streets and gyrating against one another at parties.

The country's ethnic and racial diversity stems from its rich history of conquerors and settlers, but has grown thanks to the immigrants who have come here to work in our various industries, particularly oil and gas, and others who came to find a safe, wholesome place to raise their families.

Trinidad and Tobago is also the land of the *dougla*, the word used to describe the burgeoning mixed race population. The word was first used to describe Indian-African racial hybrids, but today, dougla is used to refer to any person of mixed race. In Trinidad and Tobago, douglas are highly favoured for their unique blend of physical characteristics, marrying the classic and exotic features of beauty. The rise of the "dougla race" can be seen as the perfect representation of the ethnic harmony that generally exists in the country.

LINGO
In 2011, respected international news network CNN globe-trotted in search of the world's sexiest accents and Trinidad and Tobago's ranked in the top ten. Comparing a foreign language to one of the best aphrodisiacs, CNN had this to say, "For fetishists of oddball sexuality, the Caribbean island of Trinidad offers an undulating, melodic gumbo of pan-African, French, Spanish, Creole and Hindi dialects that, when adapted for English, is sex on a pogo stick".

Combine our sexy tongue with our unique forms of expression – creolised standard English infused with influences from other languages and modern urban lexicon and you've got a language and accent that are instantly recognisable anywhere we travel.

WORK
Trinidad and Tobago is a land of hard-working people. The labour force is strong, with hundreds of thousands working in private and public sectors including agriculture, construction, manufacturing, mining and quarrying, public utilities and service industries. The main industries for employment are beverage processing, cement, chemicals, cotton textiles, energy (oil and gas), food processing and tourism.

Creative industries are also important in Trinidad and Tobago. The most popular and visible creative product is Carnival, which brings together some of the country's most skilled crafts people and most exciting entertainers to promote local culture on an international stage.

Trinbagonians also have a fierce entrepreneurial spirit that is reflected in our steadily growing cottage industries which are small businesses run from home. Traditionally, cottage industries have always been part of the local economy, with families earning extra money or even supporting themselves by making and selling items (in particular food items and crafts) in their villages, at neighbourhood markets and at community and national fairs.

PLAY
No one plays harder than a Trinbagonian. This is not an idle boast as Trinidad and Tobago invented the art of 'liming' which is the word our people use to describe hanging out and having a good time.

A lime occurs when a group of people, as little as two, congregate for some activity with idle chatter and drinks integral components. What's unique about a lime is that it can happen anywhere at any time, even at work. We are an active people who know how to enjoy ourselves and liming is our symbol of this. While the most popular limes take place at public events such as parties and Carnival fetes, the more traditional limes are still much a part of our lifestyle, including the beach lime, the river lime, the house/family lime and the after-work lime.

Sports and games are also a big part of our play psyche. While the country boasts many renowned professional athletes, the average person on the street is a sportsperson in their own right. In Trinidad and Tobago, youngsters grow up playing a variety of sports, with Cricket and Football being top amongst boys and Lawn Tennis and Netball being most popular amongst girls.

WORSHIP
In Trinidad and Tobago, almost all religions and their respective churches exist and are embraced. Traditionalists at heart, our people believe in and rely on a Higher Power to protect their families and friends, their livelihoods, their country and their way of life.

The largest religious groups are the Catholics and Hindus. The Anglicans, Muslim, Presbyterians and Methodists compose a smaller group, while two African-Caribbean faiths – the Shouter/Spiritual Baptists and Orishas – are steadily growing. Other religious groups include Baha'i, Baptists, Buddhists, Jehovah's Witnesses, Jewish, Pentecostals, Seventh Day Adventists and The Church of Jesus Christ of Latter Day Saints. ∎

Sonja Sinaswee, Founder and Managing Director of The Groovy Image Company and Publisher of the *Dougla Magazine*

Used clay pots (diyas) left over after Diwali celebrations at the Temple in the Sea. *Photo: Salim October*

Religious diversity in Trinidad and Tobago

The rich diversity of the people of Trinidad and Tobago, who originated from various parts of the world, is reflected in the multi-religious nature of the nation's society. According to the 2000 Census, Roman Catholics form 29.6 % of the population, followed by Hindus, 25.6%. There are smaller numbers of Anglicans, Shouter or Spiritual Baptists, American-style Pentecostal sects, Seventh Day Adventists, Muslims, Presbyterians, Jehovah Witnesses, Methodists, Moravians, Orishas, Jews, Buddhists, Bahai's, members of The Church of Jesus Christ of Latter-day Saints and Rastafarians. Shouter or Spiritual Baptists and the Yoruban Orisha faith (formerly called Shangos), two African-Caribbean syncretic faiths, have their origins in West Africa and were brought here by slaves from West Africa. There is also a small but active Bobo Shanti community in Trinidad and Tobago. This is an order /sect of Rastafarianism. Its members practise a fusion of Ethiopian Christianity, Garveyism and Judaism.

With such a wide range of religions originating from Africa, India, Asia, Europe and the Middle East, it is inevitable that religious festivals are held throughout the year. Trinidad and Tobago is a model of cultural and religious harmony. There are 14 public holidays in Trinidad and Tobago – many of these are religious holidays. Everyone joins in celebrations of each other's religious festivals.

Leading up to Christmas when Christians celebrate the birth of Christ, everyone enjoys the sound of sweet Parang sung in Spanish by the Parranderos in their colourful costumes. Spiritual Baptist Liberation Day in March is observed with reverence and thanks is given for freedom to worship in Trinidad and Tobago. At midnight on Carnival Tuesday night, the Christian Lenten season begins – leading to Holy Week which begins on Palm Sunday. People beat ▶

Catholic church service. *Photo: James B. Solomon*

Tassa drummers during the Muslim festival of Hosay. *Photo: Shirley Bahadur*

stuffed effigies of Judas (bobolees) on Good Friday. Easter Sunday is the most important celebration in the Christian calendar. Other events include Corpus Christi and the festival of La Divina Pastora (the Divine Shepherdess) in Siparia. Pilgrims fill the Roman Catholic Church there three weeks after Easter Sunday and join in the procession during which the black wooden statue of the Virgin Mary – La Divina Pastora, is carried through the streets.

The statue has been in the Church since the 18th Century. For over 100 years this statue of the Virgin Mary has been venerated by Roman Catholics as well as Hindus who see her as the Hindu Goddess, Kali, destroyer of evil. The Hindus call her Siparee Mai and their festival in her honour is held in Siparia on Maundy Thursday and Good Friday.

The Hindu spring festival of Holi or Phagwa is celebrated in savannahs across Trinidad and Tobago in March. It has deep religious significance and involves singing of special songs called Chowtal or pichakaree and dancing. Participants are sprayed with a variety of coloured dyes (abeer). It is a joyful occasion.

The 4-day festival of Hosay is observed in St James and Cedros annually by Shi'a Muslims in Trinidad and Tobago to commemorate the martyrdom of Prophet Mohammed's grandsons Hassan and Hussein at the Battle of Karbala in Persia in 680 AD. Colourful miniature temples (tadjahs – depicting Hussein's tomb) – 3-10

metres high, and two shapes of half-moons all made of bamboo, wood and paper and are carried through the streets accompanied by the beating of tassa drums. At the end of the festival the tadjahs/hosays are taken to the sea and broken up.

In November, the Hindu festival of lights, Diwali, is celebrated. It is based on the Hindu epic poem, the Ramayana, and signifies the triumph of light over darkness and good over evil. Hindus commemorate this festival for various reasons. Leading up to Diwali, 'Ramleela', a reenactment of the story of Ram and Sita and the battle with the demon, Rawana, takes place at dusk in many villages. On the night of Diwali, thousands of clay deyas filled with oil and wicks, are lit in the homes of Hindus and in some public places. Prayers are said and special food and sweets are shared with family, friends and neighbours.

The Muslim festival of Eid ul-Fitr is celebrated at the end of Ramadan, the month of fasting. This is a time of great religious significance for Muslims who gather in Mosques across Trinidad and Tobago to say prayers of thanksgiving. Charity (zakat) is given to the needy; families and friends visit each other and exchange gifts. Eid ul-Adha is also a significant observance. ■

Leela Ramdeen, Attorney-at-Law, Education Consultant and Chair of the Catholic Commission for Social Justice

A UNIQUE CULINARY EXPERIENCE

You will never go hungry in Trinidad and Tobago. In fact, you'll be spoilt for choice.

Thanks to the country's rich history, its cuisine is a melting pot of big flavours and bold ingredients. When immigrants from Africa, China, England, France, India, Spain, the Middle East and the Netherlands came to our shores, they brought their culinary traditions with them. Over the last 50 years, other cultures have influenced our gastronomy, the result being a fearless approach to eating and drinking. "When in doubt, curry or stew" is the battle cry. It is a strategy that works every time, with everything from vegetables to wild meat.

Trinidad and Tobago is an epicurean paradise. There are few places on earth where you can enjoy wickedly delicious food served riverside by a group of convivial nationals in the day, followed at night by a spectacular gourmet meal prepared by an internationally recognised chef. There are even fewer places you can have a series of foodgasms roadside, thanks to the "sweet han" of street vendors serving up national delicacies.

Such a sharp contrast between gastronomic experiences may seem hard to imagine when you consider the country is but a speck on the world map but if the vast culinary adventures offered in Trinidad and Tobago could be bottled and sold, what a delicious and genuinely unique product it would be!

Photo: Queen's Park Savannah by Ian Brierley
Words: Sonja Sinaswee, founder and Managing Director of The Groovy Image Company and publisher of the 'Dougla Magazine'.

Cutting a green coconut
to obtain coconut water.
Photo: Ian Brierley

Clockwise from top left – Bake & shark. *Photo: Shirley Bahadur*; cassava fries. *Photo: Elizabeth Desiree Chung;* coconu~
~ake. *Photo: Shirley Bahadur;* curry crab. *Photo: Alex Smailes;* Homemade pepper sauce. *Photo: Ian Brierley;* accra. *Photo~
Shirley Bahadur, Creole coo coo & callaloo. *Photo courtesy Tourism Development Company;* oil down. *Photo: Shirley Bahadu~

Clockwise from top – Preparing dough to make roti; once rolled out, the dough is fried on a tawah; turned; then ready to serve. *Photos: Ian Brierley*; an alternative serving of roti is 'buss-up-shut', where the roti is broken up before removing from the tawah. *Photo: Shirley Bahadur*

RECIPES TO WHET THE APPETITE

Recipes taken from *The Multicultural Cuisine of Trinidad and Tobago & the Caribbean: Naparima Girls' High School Cookbook*. This cookbook, which was first published in 1998 as a fundraiser, has become the most commercially successful cookbook produced in the Caribbean. Highly respected among home cooks and professional chefs alike, it is widely regarded as the quintessential guide to the region's cuisine. *Recipes reprinted with the school's permission.*

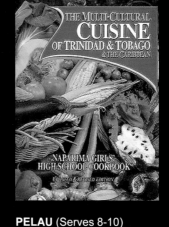

DOUBLES (Serves 8)

Ingredients: 2 cups flour; ½ tsp salt; 1 tsp turmeric powder; ½ tsp ground cumin (geera); ¼ tsp sugar; 1 tsp instant yeast; ½ lb channa (chick peas), soaked overnight; 1 tbsp vegetable oil; 3 cloves garlic, minced; 1 onion, sliced; 2 tbsp curry powder; 1 ¼ cups water; Pinch of ground geera (cumin); 1 tsp salt; hot pepper to taste; 1 cup oil for frying

In a large bowl combine flour, salt, turmeric, geera, sugar and yeast. Add enough lukewarm water to make a soft dough: mix well, cover and let rise for 1 ½ hours. Boil soaked channa in salted water until tender. Drain well. Heat oil in a heavy skillet or iron pot, add garlic, onion and curry powder mixed with ¼ cup water; sauté for a few minutes. Add channa (chick peas), stir to coat well and cook for 5 minutes, add 1 cup water, geera, salt and pepper. Cover, lower heat and simmer until peas are soft, add more water if necessary. When channa is finished, it should be soft and moist; adjust seasoning. Punch down dough and allow to relax for 10-15 minutes. To shape bara, take about 1 tbsp of dough, pat with both hands to flatten to a circle 4-5 inches diameter; use water to moisten the palms to stop dough sticking. Fry a few at a time in hot oil, turn once and drain on kitchen paper. Make a sandwich by placing 2 tbsp cooked channa between 2 baras. Pepper sauce or mango chutney goes well with it.

PELAU (Serves 8-10)

Ingredients: 3 lbs chicken pieces, skinned; 1 tsp salt; ½ tsp black pepper; 2 tbsp mixed green seasoning; 2 tsp minced garlic; 1 tsp Worcestershire sauce; 1 tsp soy sauce; 1 tbsp tomato ketchup; 2 tbsp vegetable oil; 2-3 tbsp brown sugar; 2 cups parboiled rice; ½ cup chopped onion; ½ cup chopped sweet or pimento peppers; 1 ½ cups cooked pigeon peas; 1 tbsp salt; 1 whole hot pepper with the stem; 2 cups coconut milk; 2 cups chicken broth or water

Season chicken with salt, pepper, green seasoning, minced garlic, Worcestershire sauce, soy sauce and ketchup. Heat oil in a large heavy iron pot or skillet. Add sugar and allow to burn until brown. Add seasoned chicken and stir until pieces are well coated with the burnt sugar; brown for 5 minutes. Add rice and turn often until well mixed, cook for 3 minutes more. Add salt, hot pepper, coconut milk and broth. Bring to boil; lower heat, cover and simmer until rice is cooked and all liquid is evaporated (about 25-30 minutes). Add more liquid if rice is still hard and continue to cook for a few minutes. N.B. Pelau could also be baked in an oven. Cover pot with tin foil and bake at 350°F for 30-35 minutes. Chopped carrots could also be added pelau.

RUM, GLORIOUS RUM

In 1797, when the British fought for and wrested the island of Trinidad from Spain, sugar cane was being cultivated on a large scale and rum (ron) manufactured from molasses. One of the main manufacturers was Dr J.G.B. Siegert & Sons who moved from Venezuela to Trinidad in 1875. At first producing Angostura aromatic bitters at their premises in Port of Spain, Siegert entered the rum industry, in the early 1900s, buying bulk rum from other distillers and blending under brand names like Seigert's Bouquet.

By 1949, Angostura was blending and bottling its own brands.

Today, many years and many dramatic milestones later, the House of Angostura has six ageing warehouses and 65,000 casks in stock.

They produce rums that are among the most premium rums in the world and have brought home medals celebrating its expertise in every field, from every international rum festival.

Certainly among the best, Angostura 1824 premium rum honours the tradition of excellence established by the House of Angostura almost two centuries ago. Seductively rich in colour and flavour, it is expertly blended after having been aged in charred oak barrels for a minimum of 12 years.

Whilst in Trinidad and Tobago, do not miss the opportunity to savour this rum. Then continue by trying Angostura 1919 and Angostura Single Barrel Reserve. Then you could boast to have tasted the best that the country has to offer.

Giselle Laronde-West

Independent women of the nation

In the last 50 years, women of Trinidad and Tobago have benefited from two parallel social movements. The first was the shift to greater self-sovereignty as an independent nation. The second was the greater global acceptance of gender equality. Although there continues to be moot acceptance of the latter, the growing visibility of women in many spheres from the mid-20th century to the present is evidence of this marriage of two liberation movements – nationalism and feminism. Perhaps the best signifier of this society's growth is the election of the first female Prime Minister, Kamla Persad-Bissessar, in this 5th decade of Independence. A law attorney by profession, Persad-Bissessar is one of a generation of women who came of age at the dawn of this society's independence. Women like her, although not in similar political leadership capacities, are now contributing evenly with men to the society's continued growth and development.

In 1962, a handful of pioneering women were recognised in the arts, industry, commerce, professions and political leadership. During the subsequent 50 years, we begin to see them recognised for sterling contributions, providing role models for younger women as well as shifting perceptions of femininity. In 1989 Beryl McBurnie, dancer and founder of the Little Carib Theatre received the Trinity Cross, the highest national award in Trinidad and Tobago for promotion of the arts, as did Pat Bishop in 1995 for her pursuit of scholarship, culture and the arts.

Despite the once largely male dominated arena of calypso, from the 1960s a succession of women changed the face of the music industry and forced a society to listen to women's concerns. In 1966 Calypso Rose (Rose McArtha Lewis) wrote the song *Fire in Me Wire*, a blatant expression of female sexuality. In 1977, Rose was the first female to win the Trinidad Road March competition with *Tempo*, with others like Singing Sandra (Sandra Des Vignes) winning the 1999 Calypso Crown. Singing Sandra's eloquent plea for women to preserve their agency in the face of sexual harassment struck the ▶

Singing Sandra
Photo: Shirley Bahadur

PHOTO: WENDELL STEPHEN JAY REYES

right note when in the song *Die with meh Dignity* she advises women: "They (men) could keep their money, I go keep my honey and die with meh dignity."

The blue-eyed daughter of a white father and black mother, Denyse Plummer initially faced significant prejudice in a genre traditionally seen as African-Caribbean and went on to win the Calypso Queen crown in 2001. One of her songs, *Woman Is Boss*, established another moment of consciousness which women were gaining over this period.

In 1988, Indian singer Drupatie Ramgoonai denuded yet another ethnic barrier and claimed a visibility for this group of women with her crossover chutney soca, piling up major hits such as *Hotter than a chulha* and *Roll up the Tassa*,

(Mr Bissessar), with the latter almost winning her the road march title for that year. Contemporary female soca artistes Fay Ann Lyons, Destra Garcia and Sanelle Dempster have widened the musical range and present a deliberately provocative sexual persona on stage that is again ground-breaking, if challenging, to the constantly changing definitions of womanhood.

Women have also been blazing the trail in other areas. In commerce, the first female President of the Trinidad Chamber of Commerce, Angela Persad and prominent businesswoman and philanthropist Helen Bhagwansingh have been making their mark. Medically, accomplished Professors Phyllis Pitt-Miller and Zulaikha Ali are present. In the ▶

Kamla Persad-Bissessar, pictured with her grandson, Kristiano, is one of a generation of women who came of age at the dawn of Trinidad and Tobago's independence. *Photo: Gary Jordan*

legal world, an early pioneer in legislative reform for women, Stephanie Daly has been joined by Occah Seepaul, Dana Seetahal and Gaietry Pargass. Glenda Morean-Phillip SC has the distinction of being the first Trinidad and Tobago born woman in her country to qualify as a solicitor and being the first female to hold the position of President of the Law Association of Trinidad and Tobago. Others like Gillian Lucky have joined Kamla Persad-Bissessar to become active in politics and their professions today.

The present leadership in all these areas have benefitted from the early female politicians like Isabel Teshea and Muriel Donawa McDavidson who, in the 1960s, battled the age old resistance to women in leadership, from the controversial Gene Miles who took a tragic but fearless stand on anti-corruption and more recently Joan Yuille-Williams who championed, though unsuccessfully, the passage of a national policy on gender equality and equity for the society.

As women continue to strive for greater freedoms alongside men in the next 50 years, the legacy of the first half a century of Independence is indeed a hopeful one. It has provided a sense of gender equality and the possibility for a future, which, if not limitless, is certainly more open and challenging for the generation of men and women ahead. ∎

Patricia Mohammed is Professor of Gender and Cultural Studies and Chair, Graduate Studies and Research at the University of the West Indies, Trinidad

The United Kingdom Diaspora

According to the UK Office for National Statistics, Trinbagonians living in the United Kingdom in 2009 was estimated at 24,000. This presence is concentrated mainly in the capital city of London and the impact of this community on British society is significant and noteworthy as members of the Diaspora organised themselves into communal organisations, achieved national and international recognition in their own fields of endeavour and occupied prestigious positions in British society.

The roll call of luminaries from Trinidad and Tobago officially recognised for their contributions to British society is just too long to list here but a notable indication of achievement is the 'gongs' awarded by the Queen. Her Majesty awarded titles to Baron Learie Constantine (cricketer), Baroness Floella Benjamin (broadcaster and writer), Lord Waheed Alli (media entrepreneur and politician), Sir Trevor MacDonald (newscaster), Dame Jocelyn Barrow (educationalist) and Sir V. S. Naipaul TC (writer). Gongs were awarded to scores of others including Greer Sandra Kerrigan CB, Professor Emmanuel Ciprian Amoroso CBE and Horace Ové CBE.

There have been many reconfigurations and reinterpretations of Trinidad and Tobago culture in the UK including the ubiquitous Carnival, Steel Band and Calypso. These cultural retentions have been nourished and sustained by their representative organisations – Association of British Calypsonians, British Association of Steelbands, British Association of Sound Systems, The Caribbean Music Association, Carnival Arts and Masquerade Foundation and the London Notting Hill Carnival Limited. Several individuals within each of these 'arts arenas' have helped to develop and promote their specific arts sector and notable among these are Leslie Palmer, Vijay Ramlal, Claire Holder and Victor Crichlow (Governance); Clary Salandy, Larry Forde, Lincoln Rahamut, Keith Khan and Ray Mahabir (Mas); Pepe Francis, Russell Henderson, Sterling Betancourt, Terry Noel and Frank Rollock (Steelband); Lord Cloak, The Mighty Tiger, Tobago Crusoe, Alexander D Great and D'Alberto (calypso) and Lord Sam, Smokey Joe and Soca Massive (DJs).

The imprimatur of Trinidad and Tobago is etched on the consciousness of the British public through Carnival – a classic reconfiguration of Trinidad and Tobago culture that is celebrated in almost every major British town with Notting Hill leading the way. In fact, with over two million participants over two days of festivities, Notting Hill Carnival has the bragging rights of being the largest Carnival in the world.

To help fan the fires of home, there are a number of restaurants where one could buy roti, doubles and a Carib beer – Bee Wee's, Hummingbird and Quashie's Roti Shop to name a few plus celebrity chefs Brian Danclair and Hasan De Four.

In the arts, Trinidad and Tobago is well represented with Mustapha Matura (dramatist), Lakshmi Persaud (poet), Jacqui Chan (dance), Ainsely Yearwood (painting), Monique Rossey (novelist) and Althea McNish (textiles). In the theatre, Corrine Skinner-Carter, Malcolm Frederick, Martina Laird, Ramjohn Holder, Rudolph Walker, Stephan Kalipha and Nina Baden-Semper fly the flag, whilst Neil Latchman, Faye Clinton and Ronald Samm continue to pack the concert halls.

The late John La Rose and his publishing house New Beacon Books were the hub of social, political and artistic activism around which Caribbean intellectuals congregated.

On the sporting field, Danny Cipriani, Kenwynne Jones and Delon Armitage are our current sporting luminaries in the top divisions walking in the pathway paved by Neil "Shaka" Hislop and Dwight Yorke, among others.

In the legal profession, Leonard Woodley QC and High Court judge, Dr Kameel Khan and several leading advocates, principal among them Jessica Learmond-Criqui together with academicians Heidi Mirza, Colin Prescod and Jacqueline Sealey, complete the tapestry of British society on which is inextricably woven members of the Trinidad and Tobago Diaspora.

Trinidad and Tobago can be proud of the significant contributions made then and now by its sons and daughters of the soil – by heritage and lineage – as there has been a long tradition of success and achievement from George Padmore and Henry Sylvester Williams via Claudia Jones and Bert Achong to the recently departed Edmundo Ros and Geraldine Connor.

Josephine Learmond-Criqui has worked in the City of London

The North American Diaspora

Wherever you find Trinbagonians, you will find attempts at recreating and reinterpreting the nation's art forms and life styles – Calypso, Carnival, liming, for example. North America is no exception. The settlements of Trinidad and Tobago's descendants are in the major conurbations of the continent – New York, Toronto and Miami. And in each city you will find the celebration of Carnival with Toronto's Caribbean Carnival (formally Caribana), Miami's Carnival and the biggest, New York's Labour Day Carnival (started by Tunapuna-born migrant Jessie Waddell in 1967).

Yet the influence of migrants from these islands spreads far wider than the cultural export of Carnival alone.

Migration to North America can be traced back to the 17th century but the first major wave was sparked by bleak work prospects following World War I; the second came when the 1960s American Civil Rights Movement helped loosen racist and restrictive immigration policies and subsequent flows included direct recruitment to jobs, students gaining scholarships to Universities and family members joining parents. Today there are 165,000 people of Trinbagonian ancestry residing in the USA, half of these reside in New York with the second largest concentration in Florida.

Many have risen to prominence in the political arena such as Mervyn Dymally (the first foreign-born US Congressman), veteran Brooklyn politician Maurice Gumbs and Florida's first female Lieutenant Governor, Jennifer Carroll. All are Trinidadian-born as was Stokely Carmichael (Kwame Ture), civil rights activist and Black Panther leader.

In film and television the list of performers with Trinidadian lineage is extensive; beginning with 1930s movie actress Marian Marsh (born in Port of Spain) it includes Lorraine Toussaint, Austin Stoker, Aki Aleong, Hazelle Goodman, Stephen Hadeed Jr, Tony Craig and perhaps best known, the multi-talented Tony Award-winning actor, dancer and designer Geoffrey Holder (Baron Samedi in *Live and Let Die*). Prominent amongst first generation Trinidadian-Americans are Alphonso Ribeiro (grandson of calypsonian Roaring Lion), Nia Long and Tatyana Ali.

With music being such a central part of Trinbagonian society it is little surprise that talented singers and DJs abound in the Diaspora. Tony and Grammy-award winning Heather Headley, gospel singing US Dream Academy founder Wintley Phipps, DJ Bad Lad of Toronto, rappers Aaron Fresh, Foxy Brown, Phife Dawg, The Mad Stuntman, MF Doom, Angel Melaku, Nicki Minaj (born Onika Tanya Maraj in St James) and SW Storm have all excelled in their field.

Food is another subject close to Caribbean hearts and New York's plethora of Trinidadian restaurants means those hankering for the home comforts of roti, bake and doubles are not disappointed. And one New York author of Trinidadian-descent, Ramin Ganeshram, has gone a step further with the publication of *Sweet Hands: Island Cooking from Trinidad and Tobago*.

Mainstream writers born in Trinidad include New York-based *Prospero's Daughter* author Elizabeth Nunez, V.S. Naipaul's nephew Neil Bissoondath, children's author Lynn Joseph, Canadian-based writer, Rabindranath Maharaj and novelist Harold 'Sonny' Ladoo (*No Pain like this Body* & *Yesterdays*).

The list of notable achievers with Trinbagonian heritage and lineage is extensive including Dr Maya Angelou (Trinidadian grandfather), Natalie Rogers-Cropper, director with Garth Fagan Dance, Pearl Primus – dancer, choreographer and anthropologist who was honoured in 1991 by President George H.W. Bush with the National Medal of Arts, David Hochoy, dancer and Collin Abraham who planned Beyonce's wedding.

In other areas young conceptual artist Graham Goddard is gaining a growing reputation; whilst in sport, all-time great basketballer Kareem Abdul-Jabbar, world champion sprinter Lauryn Williams, volleyballer Gabrielle Reece and US soccer player Ricardo Clark all have parents from the twin-island.

It is a proud roll-call leading to the inescapable conclusion that wherever Trinbagonians have settled they have excelled, utilising the talents shaped by their ancestry to influence and enhance their new homelands.

James Fuller is an award-winning freelance journalist and author

The white-fronted capuchin is one of the country's two native primates, the other being the red howler monkey. *Photo: Stephen Broadbridge*

Trinidad and Tobago may be one republic but these sister islands have vastly different and fascinating natural environments, both of which have been influenced by the Amerindians, who sailed over in their humble canoes from the South American continent to the first European settlers who charted new waters in their impressive ships seeking gold.

The country's rich biodiversity is best reflected in the number of natural ecosystems that exist, notably:

- Forests;
- Inland freshwater systems;
- Coastal and marine ecosystems;
- Savannahs;
- Karst landforms and
- Manmade or man-induced systems.

The landscape of both islands altered even further because of development, Trinidad in particular because of its oil and natural gas resources. Thankfully, most of the natural environment has been spared the level of degradation that has occurred on other Caribbean islands. Still, ecosystems have been placed under great stress because of pollution, overharvesting of natural resources and lax enforcement of environmental laws.

Trinidad and Tobago is one of the first Caribbean islands to promote environmental awareness. Tobago's Main Ridge Forest Reserve, which is a mountainous rainforest that covers the length of the island, is considered to be the oldest protected forest in the Western World. Home to impressive concentrations of biodiversity, it was designated a Protected Crown Reserve in 1776. In 1891, the Trinidad and Tobago Field Naturalists' Club was formed to study the islands' natural history and environment. Probably the country's oldest environmental club and definitely one of the first societies on

PHOTO: STEPHEN BROADBRIDGE

Clockwise from top – The silky anteater is known locally as 'poor-me-one'. *Photo: Stephen Broadbridge*; The gold tegu, o̶r
matte', as it is known locally. *Photo: Ian Brierley*; Prehensile-tailed porcupine. *Photo: Stephen Broadbridge*

Clockwise from top – Spectacled caiman. *Photo: Stephen Broadbridge*; Black-eared opossum, known locally as a 'manicou'. *Photo: Stephen Broadbridge*; Phyllodytes auratus tree frog. *Photo: Stephen Broadbridge*; Jack Spaniard wasp. *Photo: Wendell Stephen Jay Reyes*; Copper-rumped hummingbird. *Photo: Oswin Browne*

The red howler monkey is one of the country's two native primates, the other being the white-fronted capuchin: *Photo: Stephen Broadbridge*

The elusive ocelot is known locally as the 'tiger cat' or 'chat tigre'. *Photo: Stephen Broadbridge*

the islands, the club serves its members' varied interests through groups that study ornithology, botany, entomology, herpetology and marine life.

The Red Howler monkey (Alouetta macconnelli) is easily one of our most endearing mammals. They can be frequently seen in Chaguaramas but less so in Nariva Swamp and some parts of South Trinidad. Their primal calls are startling at dusk but their beautiful long red fur offers surprising camouflage in the forest. The less flamboyant Trinidad White fronted capuchin (Cebus albifrons trinitatis) or weeping monkeys require an even larger range and this critically endangered sub-species is at risk of disease and population inbreeding. A third primate, the Tufted capuchin (Cebus apella) found only in the Chaguaramas National Park area, was introduced in the 1940s -1970s by the US military and is considered a non-native species. Other

reminders of Amazonia include the Silky anteater (Cyclopes didactylus), the elusive Ocelot (Leopardus pardalis melanurus) and the critically endangered West Indian manatee (Trichechus manatus manatus).

Since becoming an Independent nation, numerous organisations and clubs have been formed to bring the issues of the natural environment to the fore. Three bodies that have led the way in preservation of the natural world and raising environmental awareness are the Pointe-a-Pierre Wildfowl Trust, the world famous Asa Wright Nature Centre and Nature Seekers.

Forty-five years old, the Wildfowl Trust makes its home on 25 hectares of land and two manmade lakes in the middle of an oil refinery. The Trust is home to three endangered species of wild native ducks, numerous wetland and terrestrial birds and opens its doors daily to visitors and school children.

Clockwise from top – Rainbow (or Colombian rainbow) boa. *Photo: Stephen Broadbridge*; Boa constrictor. *Photo: Stephen Broadbridge; Adenomera hylaedactyla* is a species of frog in the *leptodactylidae* family. *Photo: Wendell Stephen Jay Raye*

Clockwise from top – Sprawling root of a rainforest tree. *Photo: Stephen Broadbridge*; Anolis lizard. *Photo: Wendell Stephen Jay Reyes*; Crested oropendola *Photo: Ian Brierley*; Yellow-banded dart butterfly. *Photo: Wendell Stephen Jay Reyes*; One of the country's more colourful species of spider. *Photo: Ryan P. Mannette*

Turtle-watching is rapidly emerging as a tourist attraction, particularly c
the east and north-east coasts of Trinidad. *Photo: Stephen Broadbridg*

Asa Wright Nature Centre
Photo: Stephen Broadbridge

Clockwise from top left – Sphinx caterpillar. *Photo: Wendell Stephen Jay Reyes*; Silver-beaked tanager. *Photo: Stephen Broadbridge*; The *anartia amathia* is one of the nation's more common butterflies. *Photo: Wendell Stephen Jay Reyes*; Green honeycreeper. *Photo: Stephen Broadbridge*

Secluded in Trinidad's Northern Range mountains, the Asa Wright Nature Centre, established in 1967, boasts 1,500 acres of natural and secondary rainforest and is home to approximately 159 bird species, including the most accessible oilbird colony (Dunston's cave) in the world.

Nature Seekers is best known as the community that made the transformation from hunting a national treasure, the giant Leatherback turtle (Dermochelys coriacea), to becoming its most passionate protector. Established in 1990, this grassroots organisation has become an inspiration to a new generation of young conservationists.

In addition to being home to so many respected environmental organisations, over the last five decades, the contributions of several remarkable individuals have left an indelible mark on the collective environmental consciousness of citizens. Particularly

noteworthy for their national and international contributions are Professor John Agard, Professor Peter Bacon, Angela Cropper, John Cropper, Molly Gaskin, Dr Carol James, Akilah Jaramogi, Professor Julian Kenny, Susan Lackan, Karilyn Shephard and Asa Wright.

It is fair to say that the passionate work of a few have sent urgent signals to our fossil-fuel dependant nationals, stressing the definitive link between promoting sustainable green enterprise, preserving precious natural resources and striking a balance for economical development and the social wellbeing of our people.

Despite the worrying trend in human population growth, the islands of Trinidad and Tobago continue to work toward a safer and healthier outlook for all who call these beautiful islands home.

Alana Jute is an environmental conservationist who has worked in the environmental field for nine years.

Blue-crowned motmot. *Photo: Ryan P. Mannette*

Clockwise from top left – Tufted coquette hummingbird. *Photo: Wendell Stephen Jay Reyes*; White-necked jacobin hummingbird. *Photo: Marcus Gonzales*; Collared trogon. *Photo: Stephen Broadbridge*; Barred antshrike. *Photo: Oswin Browne*; Red-crowned woodpecker. *Photo: Stephen Broadbridge*

BIRDWATCHING IN TRINIDAD AND TOBAGO

For decades the stunning twin-islands of Trinidad and Tobago have been an international bird-watching mecca. Little wonder, as those in the know can tick off as many species in a single day as it would take a week to see in other parts of the neo-tropics. There are over 470 species in Trinidad alone.

The secret is in the incredible mix of habitats present including montane rainforest, palm forest, mangrove swamp, coastal reaches and savannah.

Trinidad is the home to the world-famous Asa Wright Nature Centre where an easy day's viewing can yield dozens of exotic species. These include beautiful hummingbirds and honeycreepers which zip about in blurs of colour, battling for control of the nectar feeders.

Pointe-a-Pierre's Wildfowl Trust offers a unique opportunity to see birds like the endangered black-bellied whistling duck and the patriotic looking red-capped cardinal from the

There are wet-land tours available to the Oropouche, Caroni and Nariva swamps in Trinidad where soaring ospreys, raucous blue and gold macaws and flocks of carmine-coloured scarlet ibis flitting and swooping into roost are prominent species respectively.

Whilst in Tobago, spot the rare white-tailed sabrewing at the Main Ridge Forest Reserve or a host of herons, waders and ducks at the Buccoo Reef/Bon Accord Lagoon Complex.

Rest assured, which ever bird watching fantasies you harbour, they can be indulged on a trip to Trinidad and Tobago: toucans, trogans, hummingbirds, flamingos, tanagers, falcons, vultures, parrots, oilbirds, flycatchers, woodpeckers and bellbirds all form part of a mesmeric array of avifauna few nations in the world can rival.

Farah Gopaul-Fuller developed education programmes for children at the Asa Wright Nature Centre and Pointe-a-Pierre Wildfowl Trust

Violaceous trogon
Photo: Stephen Broadbridge

Purple honeycreeper
Photo: Stephen Broadbridge

Clockwise from top – Channel-billed toucan. *Photo: Stephen Broadbridge*; Turquoise tanager. *Photo: Stephen Broadbridge*; American pygmy kingfisher. *Photo: Stephen Broadbridge*; Yellow-hooded blackbird. *Photo: Stephen Broadbridge*; Rufous-tailed jacamar. *Photo: Stephen Broadbridge*; White-chested emerald hummingbird. *Photo: Wendell Stephen Jay Reyes*

Scarlett ibis take flight at the Caroni Swamp. *Photo: Ian Brierley*

A walk through the forest to Pirate's Bay, Tobago
Photo: Stephen Broadbridge

Welcome to Tobago

When Europeans first encountered Tobago in 1498, the Spanish expedition did not even land here. Instead, the island was named as the expedition passed on its way north. At that time, the island was just an abandoned piece of land, and interestingly, remained so for more than one hundred years, even as other parts of the Caribbean were being developed. The real irony of the situation was that this very island became the most hotly contested piece of land, changing hands no fewer than twenty-six times as colonising powers, including the Eastern European country of Latvia, sought to take control in this part of the New World. We have come a very long way since then.

In the early days, the survival and indeed success of Tobago depended on agriculture. This thrust was so significant that it gave rise to the saying it was a credit to be as "rich as a Tobago farmer". This thrust declined as time and natural disasters took their toll, particularly following the hurricane of 1847. Eventually, in 1898 the island was joined to Trinidad which was under British rule by this time. Since then, there have been several steps on the road to development but Trinidad and Tobago remained a Unitary State through Crown Colony status to Independence in 1962 and Republican status in 1976.

By the end of the 1970s, and especially with the inauguration of the Tobago House of Assembly in 1980, attention had to be turned to finding new ways to ensure Tobago made its contribution to the national economy and, more particularly, to life on the island and enhanced the fortunes of Tobagonians. Tourism became the focus because of an environment offering peace, quiet, relaxation and safety. The industry was boosted by the island's natural beauty consisting of but not limited to, the flora and fauna, beaches, the coral reef, a world renowned rain-forest, the culture and the hospitality of the people.

A look at Tobago today will demonstrate there have been leaps and bounds in its development process. The island boasts a sound and stable administration, a well developed infrastructure, dependable utilities, a sound ferry service on the sea bridge with Trinidad and an international airport connecting it with the rest of the region and the world.

Today's Tobago, however, is at a crossroad in its development and with the exploding expansion, a serious effort has had to be made to diversify the island's economic base. In recent times, attention has been turned to the establishment of 'Cove Eco-Industrial Estate and Business Park'. This initiative is the brainchild of the Tobago House of Assembly and really offers a virgin business environment to entrepreneurs. The Estate offers opportunities to investors to get involved in light industry. It will accommodate knowledge-based industries including information technology, light manufacturing, agro-processing and export as well as selected downstream activities related to natural gas. It will also house receiving and metering facilities for natural gas from Trinidad.

Investment at this park is encouraged through a series of tax holidays, incentives and exemptions. What is even more significant is the fact that, in 2008, there was a natural gas discovery on the island's North West. This will definitely result in the provision of a secure energy base which will drive the Estate initiative and make investment on the island a promise that will be fulfilled.

Rawle Winston Titus, anthropologist and lecturer

Tobago is renowned for its diverse variety of beaches – from the most secluded bays to the most beautiful stretches of white-sand shoreline. *Photo: Gary Jordan*

The nation's bustling capital. *Photo: Stephen Broadbridge*

PORT OF SPAIN

A national and regional capital, a global and globalised city, Port of Spain is the energetic heart of a youthful and ambitious nation with its eyes on the future. It is an ambition which takes physical form in glass and steel edifices like the Nicholas Tower, the Hyatt Regency and the lenticular lines of the National Academy for Performing Arts (NAPA) and in a political form with the hosting of events such as the Fifth Summit of the Americas in 2009.

Yet as development continues its inexorable march there is still room for the architecture of yesteryear and nowhere is this juxtaposition of styles and epochs better displayed than on the fringes of the city's 260-acre green lung, the Queen's Park Savannah. To the south sits NAPA and the imposing corporate offices of petrochemical giants such as bpTT, whilst to the west the flamboyant Victorian grandeur of the aptly-named 'Magnificent Seven' sit in stately repose.

The city stretches its arms out into suburbs such as Woodbrook, St Ann's, St James, Belmont and Laventille and all are overlooked by the rainforest-clad slopes of the Northern Range. Home to 50,000 residents and a transient daily population of 250,000, moves are being made towards decentralisation but for now Port of Spain remains the nation's economic and administrative epicentre.

For many multinationals it doubles as their Caribbean operations capital, typical of which is the headquarters of the Royal Bank of Canada (RBC). It remains a cultural and entertainment focal point: where Carnival was born and continues to proclaim itself; where international stars such as Beyonce, Rihanna and Sean Paul perform; and where you will find a culinary smorgasbord from fine dining restaurants to streetside vendors. Ariapita Avenue is *the* stretch for bars and clubs but for something a little earthier try Smokey and Bunty's in St James.

For shoppers the choice is broad, from plush air-conditioned shopping malls and the upmarket boutiques of Woodbrook to the eclectic pandemonium of Frederick Street. Or for the all-in-one experience of cinema, mall, restaurants and arcades there's the MovieTowne complex, located on reclaimed land adjacent to the Hasely Crawford Stadium.

Also sitting on land reclaimed from tidal mangrove swamps is the port, the country's busiest, which as well as commercial shipping accommodates cruise ships, the Tobago fast ferry and commuter water taxis from San Fernando.

Meandering through this vibrant cauldron of life it is hard to conceive that it began on the site of an old Arawak fishing village, Cu-Mucurapo (Place of the Silk Cotton Trees). Or that in its first incarnation as a capital in the 18th century, what stood where towering structures now thrust skywards was little more than a few homes of mud-and-grass plastered walls, lime-whitewashed and topped with thatched roofs.

James Fuller is an award-winning freelance journalist and author

Naparima Hill. *Photo: Ian Brierley*

SAN FERNANDO

Known as Trinidad's 'industrial capital' and colloquially as 'Sando', the nation's second city, San Fernando, has flourished as a hub of great industry.

Rising impressively, if somewhat reconfigured by old quarrying activity, the area's most recognisable landmark is Naparima Hill. Naparima translates as 'single hill' yet anyone driving San Fernando's seesawing, handbrake-testing roads might be forgiven for feeling they are traversing a continuous series of hills.

It was Naparima which Sir Walter Raleigh first spotted in 1595 and from where, nearly 200 years later, Spanish Governor Don Jose Maria Chacon issued land grants for the construction of a new town. In 1792 it was named San Fernando (after the Spanish king's son); five years later it was second only to Port of Spain in terms of population and was already blessed with eyebrow-raising industry: 28 cotton mills, 25 coffee mills, 20 sugar mills and eight rum distilleries.

During the 19th century, San Fernando became the focal point of the South's enormous sugarcane industry. The sugar factory at nearby Usine St Madeleine was the world's largest. The money flowing from sugar underpinned development and expansion continued apace: 1859 a tramway linking the sugar estates out to Princes Town opened; 1882 rail links established; 1899 piped water introduced; 1900 telephone service introduced; 1915 Palace Cinema opened; 1919 Carnegie Free Library opened; 1923 municipal electricity supply starts.

Yet it was the extension of the rail down to Siparia in 1913 which positioned San Fernando to take advantage of the 20th century's cash crops of oil and natural gas. Over the last 100 years the development of the petrochemical industry and others serviced by it, has seen refineries, smelters and vast industrial plants established at Pointe-a-Pierre, Point Fortin, Point Lisas and La Brea, all of which find their natural gateway in San Fernando.

Shoppers in South Trinidad also gravitate to San Fernando, which became a city in 1988, and normally to High Street or the massive Gulf City shopping centre. For entertainment, the Naparima Bowl stages major concerts, theatre and trade shows; sports enthusiasts can choose from Skinner Park, the Mannie Ramjohn Stadium and Guaracara Park; whilst the Pitch Lake at La Brea is the South's biggest tourist attraction.

Famous sons of San Fernando include Prime Ministers Basdeo Panday and Patrick Manning; Presidents Maxwell Richards and Noor Hassanali; broadcaster Sir Trevor MacDonald; and athletes Hasely Crawford and Mannie Ramjohn.

James Fuller is an award-winning freelance journalist and author

Main street through Couva. *Photo: James B. Solomon*

COUVA

Once synonymous with the nation's oldest industry, Couva is now more closely-linked with those of the future and is the proposed site of a new airport.

An old sugar village near Trinidad's west coast, built on the foundations of the expansive sugarcane fields which once surrounded it, Couva grew rapidly with the coming of the railway in 1880. As motor vehicles rose to pre-eminence in the 20th century, being on the route of the Southern Main Road meant economic benefits from those travelling from San Fernando to Port of Spain and points in-between.

However, with the demise of the railways in 1965, the completion of the Solomon Hochoy Highway diverting north-south traffic, the declining sugar industry and the dramatic rise of its neighbour Chaguanas, the future looked uncertain.

But where once Couva residents looked to sugar, and Caroni 1975 Ltd in particular, as principal employer now their eyes alight on the world-renowned Point Lisas Industrial Estate and its 103 petrochemical and downstream industry companies, to the Petrotrin oil refinery at Pointe-a-Pierre, and to its own environs as a significant commercial and administrative

centre (it is home to the Couva-Tabaquite-Talparo Regional Corporation).

A hangover from the sugar years is the conspicuous number of cyclists on Couva's streets; this is a bicycle town and has been ever since workers rode out to work each morning over the area's gently undulating land. Many modern-day cycling clubs continue to take advantage of this ideal topography.

Religion is also prominent with Anglican (at the famous Roops Junction), Roman Catholic and Presbyterian Churches in short walking distance of one another and uniquely a Mosque and a Mandir sharing the same compound. It adds to Couva's charming old-world nature as a friendly market town which, despite the changes down the years, has remained remarkably constant.

There is development though and upscale housing estates such as Roystonia on its northern fringe have brought new families to the area. And another potentially huge change looms if proposals, currently on hold, for Camden Base on Couva's outskirts – a 4,000ft airstrip home to helicopters and light aircraft – get the go-ahead to become the nation's third airport.

James Fuller is an award-winning freelance journalist and author

The Policy Research and Development Institute building is a dominant edifice in Scarborough
Photo: Stephen Broadbridge

SCARBOROUGH

A charmingly unpretentious mix of new and old, Scarborough's friendly and welcoming ambience belies its bloody past. First settled by Dutch merchants as Lampsinsburg in 1654, Tobago's capital has changed names and ownership a dizzying number of times as it ping-ponged back and forth between the Dutch, French and British for 150 years.

In a sense, Scarborough is still characterised by frenetic activity. The deepwater harbour established in 1991 has allowed greater access to shipping, including cruise ships and the fast ferries which provide excellent service to-and-from Port of Spain, and visitor numbers have increased as a result.

Passengers spill onto jostling streets filled with noise and colour and where vendors selling everything from leather goods to fresh fruit and vegetables sit cheek-by-jowl with international food chains. Tin-roofed homes and modern shops cling to the surrounding hillsides in clustered streets which tumble down towards the waterfront.

Leaving the hustle, bustle and heat, a snaking road leads up to the beautifully-preserved Fort King George which sits regally overlooking the

town and Rockly Bay 450ft below. The fort's ramparts afford cool breezes and stunning views of the coastline and Atlantic Ocean. Here you will also find the superb Tobago Museum which charts the island's colourful history from Amerindian times.

Scarborough has been Tobago's capital since 1769 and is home to around a third of the island's 50,000 residents, as well as its semi-autonomous seat of governance, the Tobago House of Assembly (reinstituted in 1980 after abolition in 1876).

Shoppers will find all they're looking for, and a few things they weren't, in the capital's shops, markets, streetside stalls and Scarborough Mall, but if you're looking for the conveniences of larger-scale mall shopping head to nearby Gulf City Lowlands Mall, which includes a MovieTowne multiplex cinema.

Those staging theatrical and cultural events are eagerly anticipating the completion of the 5,000-capacity Shaw Park Cultural Complex, whilst major sporting events are held at the Dwight Yorke Stadium, a short drive from town.

James Fuller is an award-winning freelance journalist and author

Scarborough's deep-water harbour was built in 1991 and accommodates cruise ships as well as the inter-island ferry service. *Photo: Ian Brierley*

PHOTO: SALIM OCTOBER

The Arima Dial. *Photo: James B. Solomon*

Statue of Hyarima, the last leader of the Amerinians. *Photo: Ryan P. Mannette*

Statue of renowned calypsonian Lord Kitchener. *Photo: Ryan P. Mannette*

ARIMA

Stand on an Arima street corner and the rich cultural history of the nation's fourth largest town reveals itself in the faces of passersby. This bustling town of 35,000 on the banks of the Arima River, with its thriving business community and daily produce market, grew from a Capuchin mission established to convert local Amerindians to Catholicism in the mid-1780s. This indigenous culture lives on proudly in the Santa Rosa Carib Community and its annual Santa Rosa Festival.

The bountiful slopes of the Northern Range which rise above the town were once the epicentre of a booming national cocoa industry, a business which looks set for revival with Trinidad and Tobago's cocoa recognised as some of the finest in the world.

The construction of the nearby US Waller Air Force Base, during World War Two, and the workers and airmen employed there, brought much prosperity and colourful times. And today

it is a vibrant town still with the O'Meara Industrial Park and the University of Trinidad and Tobago's O'Meara Campus located just off O'Meara Road, the Santa Rosa Park horse racing track across the Churchill Roosevelt Highway and the internationally-renowned Asa Wright Nature Centre a short drive up into the mountains.

Horse racing once took place on the town's central savannah each August, during a festival month which culminated with a Grand Ball held at the Town Hall. Also in the town centre is the 'Arima Dial' – a much-loved tower clock at the crossroads of Queen Street and Broadway that residents still navigate by.

Famous sons of Arima, known as the gateway to the East, include legendary calypsonian Lord Kitchener (Aldwyn Roberts), the 'King of Latin American Music', singer, musician and bandleader Edmundo Ros and West Indies batsman Larry Gomes, in whose name an all-purpose sports stadium was built on the edge of town.

TUNAPUNA

One of the country's oldest habitations, Tunapuna was already established during Spanish occupation in the 18th century. It lay then at the apex of an embryonic road system, with tracks heading east to the Capuchin mission at Arima and south to another at Savana Grande (Princes Town).

Sitting at the heart of the Eastern Main Road, Tunapuna has always been a transport hub along the East-West corridor. In 1876, when that corridor was linked by rail its population stood 2,000, just five years after the arrival of the train this had doubled.

A rich agricultural area with cotton, coffee, cocoa and sugar cane grown in the verdant hills above and around, its success inevitably led to growth. In 1881 Canadian missionaries established the Tunapuna Presbyterian School and by 1898, with the construction of a Police Station, Courthouse, new Government School and a waterworks bringing piped water to residents, Tunapuna was declared a town. It quickly became the administrative and services centre for the area, something it remains to this day.

The largest of all the regional corporations, by population, Tunapuna-Piarco Regional Corporation, is headquartered here administering some 275,000 people. It draws from that catchment area each Easter to continue a proud century-old tradition of being one of the largest centres for Carnival outside Port of Spain – featuring traditional and contemporary mas, steelbands and stick fighting.

It is also the location for the annual Tassarama competition, showcasing the country's top tassa groups and the infectious rhythm of tassa drums fills the air as the groups pass along the East Main Road to be judged.

Tunapuna has many famous sons and daughters including one of the West Indies first great cricketers in Learie Constantine; one of the Caribbean's foremost political writers in CLR James, who was not only born here but is buried here; the renowned pianist, Winifred Atwell who enjoyed great success and popularity in Britain from the 1950s and was the first Black artist to have a number one hit in the UK singles chart; Professor Andrew Ramroop who is the only Black bespoke tailor on London's famous Savile Row; and Peter Kanhai who is a past President of the Greater Tunapuna Chamber of Industry and Commerce.

James Fuller is an award-winning freelance journalist and author

PHOTO: SALIM OCTOBER

Named after the founder of Pakistan, the Mohammed Ali Jinnah Memorial Mosque in St Joseph was built in 1954. *Photo: Salim October*

ST JOSEPH

The history of St Joseph reads like a film script; the nation's oldest town and first capital, established by a Spaniard seeking a mythical city of gold, it was sacked three times and ravaged by earthquake, witnessed a revolt and is a tale which incorporates buccaneers, explorers, colonialism, religion and revenge.

The fretwork and colonial architecture of several buildings, as well as St Joseph's gothic-style Catholic Church dating to 1815, hint at venerability but you have to look ever more closely as development along the throbbing Eastern Main Road threatens to swallow the past.

A century after Christopher Columbus first set eyes on Trinidad, Don Antonio de Berrio y Oruna gained a charter from the Spanish crown to search for El Dorado and, after three failures, chose St Joseph to establish a base from which to explore the South American mainland. Founded in 1592 by his second-in-command, Domingo de Vera, San Jose de Oruna (as it was first known) served as the island's capital between 1592 and 1783, whereupon the seat of

St Joseph did not have a happy time of it, being burned to the ground by Sir Walter Raleigh in 1595 (because of a personal vendetta with De Berrio) levelled again in 1637 by the Dutch, by local Caribs in 1640 and then by earthquake in 1766.

When the British claimed Trinidad in 1797 the name was anglicised to St Joseph and they found an industrious little town with sugar, coffee and cotton mills as well as rum distilleries but upheaval was just around the corner. In 1837 Daaga, an African chief who had refused to be cowed by slavery, invoked fellow African members of the Third West India Regiment to mutiny in an ultimately unsuccessful rising.

Today St Joseph, home to Trinidad's first railway service in 1876, is a centre of commerce once more and is well-regarded for its schools, St Joseph's Convent and St Xavier's Preparatory to name a few. The stunning Maracas-St Joseph Valley is also a popular locale for homebuyers with some beautiful developments offering easy access to Port of Spain.

James Fuller is an award-winning freelance journalist and author

PHOTO: IAN BRIERLEY

CHAGUANAS

The fastest-growing town in the country can also stake a claim to being its shopping capital. With a rising population of 100,000 and housing and business developments continuing apace, Chaguanas is far removed from the sleepy locale which over two hundred years ago was named after local Amerindians.

The initial kindling beneath the expansion fire was agricultural success, predominantly sugarcane but also cocoa and coconut, and this was ignited with the establishment of rail links in 1880. Economically-motivated, it nevertheless connected the town to the wider world and it has never looked back.

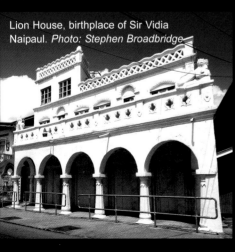

Lion House, birthplace of Sir Vidia Naipaul. *Photo: Stephen Broadbridge*

With its popular markets Chaguanas has long-held a crowded, bazaar-town feel and its central location – rendering it accessible to commuters and shoppers from Port of Spain in the north to San Fernando in the South – allied to cheaper house prices fuelled rapid growth in the late 20th century. Big business moved in with the construction of a series of shopping malls (Centre City, Mid Centre, Centre Point and later Price Plaza) and banking and insurance companies followed suit with many establishing major corporate offices.

A traditionally Indo-Trinidadian area (large-scale indentured Indian labour was utilised on the colonial sugarcane estates) the influx of new arrivals has seen a shift in the cultural mix. East Indian culture remains highly visible though and the Diwali Nagar site, with its 12-metre high Swami Vivekananda statue, attracts droves of visitors during the spectacular annual Diwali festival.

Sitting cheek-by-jowl with all this modern-day development is one of the country's biggest eco attractions, Caroni Swamp, where evening boat tours can be taken to watch flocks of vividly-coloured Scarlet Ibis, the national bird, sweeping in to roost in the expansive mangrove forests.

Chaguanas is also the birthplace of Nobel Prize-winning author Sir Vidia Naipaul and his former home, the Lion House, stands on the Main Road.

James Fuller is an award-winning freelance journalist and author

The natural asphalt from the Pitch Lake was used by the US for its first paved road – Pennsylvania Avenue in Washington in 1872. *Photo: Ian Brierley*

POINT FORTIN

The nation's smallest borough was founded on, and has been inextricably-linked with, the fluctuating fortunes of oil but Point Fortin is now as well-known for its creativity and independent spirit as its connection with black gold.

Bearing the name of an 18th century French settler named Fortin, whose land grant included an important headland (Point), the original coastal settlement enjoyed no road access; being accessible only by ocean steamer. Dotted with sugar estates, the region's remote and wild nature allied to labour shortages following the 1838 abolition of slavery made early commercial life challenging. That all changed when prospectors, attracted by the nearby Pitch Lake at La Brea, made good on their hunch and struck oil in 1906.

With money to be made development followed rapidly and oilfield workers were drawn from far and wide, including other Caribbean nationals and Western expatriates, who merged with the largely religious and conservative locals to create a unique cultural mix. Such a fusion carried implicit tensions and this, together with

the 1970s increased socio-political awareness and a drive for local autonomy, provided abundant material for calypsonians like the late great Mighty Duke (Kelvin Pope). This creative bent continues with soca artistes including Superblue (Austin Lyons) and Fay-Ann Lyons-Alvarez, whilst in the sporting arena English Premier League striker Kenwyne Jones also calls this south-west town home.

Point Fortin achieved a measure of self-governance when declared a borough in 1980, an achievement celebrated royally each year on Borough Day. Assuming the guise of a mini-Carnival, the day begins at 4am with J'Ouvert and goes on to feature masqueraders in traditional costume as well as steel pan players vying for supremacy.

Oil and gas, in the shape of Petrotrin and Atlantic LNG (Liquefied Natural Gas), remain dominant employers, though efforts are being made at agricultural diversification.

James Fuller is an award-winning freelance journalist and author

POINT LISAS INDUSTRIAL ESTATE AND PORT

Point Lisas is spectacular commercial success story, a driving force in the nation's conversion to a gas-based economy and a location pivotal to future diversification plans. It has witnessed an incredible journey from derided pipedream to a backbone of today's economy.

Since its inception, over US$2billion has been invested in the sprawling 860-acre industrial complex and port which gazes out on the Gulf of Paria halfway down Trinidad's west coast. Referred to as the 'Gateway to the Americas', it is home to 103 companies, comprising a mix of methanol (the M5000 plant is the world's largest),

ammonia and urea plants, two steel plants (including ArcelorMittal the Caribbean's biggest steelmaking plant), two power plants, a reverse osmosis water desalination plant and smaller light manufacturing and service companies.

The port itself consists of six general cargo and container berths and handles everything from containers to break bulk, lumber, paper, consumables, dry bulk and DRI (Direct Reduced Iron). Both port and estate are overseen by Point Lisas Industrial Port Development Corporation Limited (PLIPDECO) which is 51 per cent state-owned and 49 per cent private stakeholders.

Successful it maybe now but today's achievements mask years of struggle and a story which has its roots in a north-south rivalry.

Entering the 20th century, Trinidad had no deepwater harbours and the ports at Port of Spain and San Fernando operated in similar fashion; container ships mooring offshore and being unloaded by 'lighters' shuttling cargo to land. That dynamic changed in the late 1930s when the Port of Spain harbour was dredged, making it accessible to merchant shipping. A group of San Fernando businessmen, formed as the South Trinidad Chamber of Industry and Commerce (STCIC), recognised the danger to local business and in the 1950s began investigating the creation of a deepwater harbour in the south supported by, and linked to, an industrial complex concentrating on heavy industries utilising the nation's abundant natural gas. The location of

the harbour was chosen, large areas of undeveloped land purchased and in the late 1960s investors sought.

Yet the vision of men like inaugural STCIC Chairman Bobby Montano was not immediately appreciated and issues with financing the reclamation of land almost led to the collapse of the nascent complex. The Government stepped in to take a controlling share in PLIPDECO and the advent of significant state investment from 1976 has proved the catalyst for Point Lisas' phenomenal success.

Photo: Stephen Broadbridge

Trinidad and Tobago tourism

Trinidad and Tobago is a primary Caribbean destination that has everything to offer – from traditional sun, sea and sand holidays in Tobago to adventure and ecotourism on both islands, or business tourism and meetings, incentives, conferences and exhibitions in Trinidad. Moreover, the country remains relatively inexpensive.

The country has a strong advantage over many of its neighbours in that it has largely escaped the devastating natural disasters which have hit the region in recent years.

The government intends to fully develop the potential of the tourism industry in an effort to successfully diversify the energy-based economy. By 2019 the World Travel and Tourism Council (WTTC) forecasts the industry's share of GDP to rise to 12.7%.

The three government agencies responsible for the development of the tourism sector are the Ministry of Tourism, which sets the policy framework for the sector; the Tobago House of Assembly (THA); and the Tourism Development Company Limited (TDC) which implement government's policy. The guiding principles upon which the sector is being developed are:

- Sustainable Tourism
- Festivals and Events
- Contribution to Social Development
- Placing Trinidad and Tobago on the World Stage
- Contribution to the Economy (Economic Linkages, Jobs and Foreign Exchange)

▶

PHOTO: STEPHEN BROADBRIDGE

With its long stretch of white sand, Pigeon Point is considered to be Tobago's most beautiful beach. The resort area has excellent facilities including bars, a restaurant, souvenir shops, furniture hire and water sports shops. The thatched-roof jetty has become an internationally recognised icon of Tobago. *Photo: Ian Brierley*

Caroni Swamp. *Photo: Stephen Broadbridge*

Scarborough became the capital of Tobago in 1769 and has a population of around 17,000. Its deep-water harbour was built in 1991 and accommodates cruise ships as well as the inter-island ferry service. *Photo: Oswin Browne*

Coco Reef resort in Tobago. *Photo: Ian Brierley*

Trinidad and Tobago has identified and is actively promoting the development of the following tourism niche markets:

- Cruise
- Festivals and Events
- Dive
- Ecotourism
- Weddings and Honeymoons
- Meetings, Incentives, Conferences and Exhibitions (MICE)
- Shopping
- Sports
- Yachting
- Culinary Arts

The booming energy, manufacturing and financial services sectors in Trinidad and Tobago have resulted in a steady growth in business arrivals to the island of Trinidad. Port of Spain in particular, has the potential to become one of the region's busiest business destinations. Its central location in relation to the rest of the Americas puts the country in an ideal position to host the regional headquarters of international organisations and some of the largest multinational corporations in

CRUISE

While Trinidad and Tobago's location – a mere seven miles from Venezuela – has translated to less cruise ship visits than its neighbours to the north, this market is poised for growth. The satisfaction rating among cruise visitors to Trinidad and Tobago is high. Several cruise lines offer itineraries that include a stop in one of the two cruise ports in Trinidad and Tobago. Facilities at Port of Spain's Cruise Ship Complex, which houses a customs hall, car rental agencies, taxi service, shopping, tour guides and modern communications services for disembarking cruise ship passengers.

Trinidad and Tobago offers the added value of its location outside the hurricane belt and competitive fuel prices. At present, cruise ships dock at the south side of Port of Spain, offering cruise visitors easy access to the city's financial and shopping districts, entertainment venues, museums and restaurants. A multi-million dollar International Waterfront Project, which includes the 428 room Hyatt Regency Hotel and Conference Centre, waterfront esplanade, public plaza and

The Nylon Pool is an area of shallow, crystal clear water at Buccoo Reef. Trips to the reef in glass-bottom boats and bathing are popular activities. *Photo: Oswin Browne*

Tobago is one of the world's leading dive destinations
Photo courtesy Tourism Development Company

Whale-watching has become increasingly
more popular. *Photo: Stephen Broadbridge*

Trinidad and Tobago as an exciting new
cruise tourism destination.

DIVE

The dive sector in this country is centred
on the island of Tobago. Tobago's marine
treasures include shipwrecks, over 300
species of coral, Whale Sharks, Giant
Atlantic Manta Rays and Marine Turtles.
Dive has rapidly emerged as a mainstay of
the island's tourism product. Fed by the
nutrient rich currents of the Orinoco River,
Atlantic Ocean and Caribbean Sea, the
underwater diversity of Tobago's
northeast and southwest coast, has made
the island the premiere location for divers
from the United States and United
Kingdom. Accommodation properties in
Tobago, and a few of the airlines that
service the island, have begun catering to
the dive market. Certified dive operators
and instructors are plentiful and the island
is equipped with a recompression
chamber for cases of decompression
sickness.

ECOTOURISM

The country's ecological diversity and
abundance of natural assets has made

ecotourism a successful niche. In the last
ten years, many new properties have been
developed as eco-lodges, alongside
growth in ecotourism attractions, tours
and packages. Emphasis on natural
resource tourism is generally focused on
five products: Asa Wright Nature Centre,
Caroni Swamp and Pitch Lake in Trinidad
and in Tobago the Nylon Pool, Buccoo
Reef and the Forest Reserve.

There are also many new eco-tourism
sites in development including Paramin,
Brasso Seco, Blanchisseuse and Muruga.

Rapidly emerging as an international
quality product is turtle watching,
particularly on the East and North East
coasts of Trinidad.

WEDDINGS AND HONEYMOONS

The Honeymoons and Weddings sector is
a growing niche market, especially in
Tobago, and with a marked improvement
in airlift to the island, this sector will
receive an added boost. Recognising the
growth potential in this sector, many of
the island's hotels offer special wedding
packages. The island's wedding planners
can also recommend a wide range of
products, including wedding locations,

PHOTO COURTESY TOURISM DEVELOPMENT COMPANY

PHOTO: MARCUS GONZALES

PHOTO: STEPHEN BROADBRIDGE

and honeymoon accommodation ranging from the traditional to unorthodox. The amended Marriage Act of 1996 makes it possible for non-resident couples to get married in as little as three days with a Special Marriage Licence.

The turquoise seas, secluded beaches and golden sunsets of unspoilt Tobago and exciting nightlife and eco-adventure of Trinidad, have set the islands apart as a mecca for couples seeking a dream wedding and honeymoon.

PHOTO: GARY JORDAN

MEETINGS, INCENTIVES, CONFERENCES AND EXHIBITIONS (MICE)

It is the stated intention of the Government to position and establish Port of Spain as the meetings and conference capital of the southern Caribbean. That process is well underway with the opening of the Hyatt Regency Trinidad with a conference centre containing 50,000 sq. ft. of flexible meeting space. The Trinidad and Tobago Convention Bureau was established in 2009 as a department within the Tourism Development Company Limited with a mandate to position Port of Spain as the meetings, conferences, incentives and events capital of the Southern Caribbean.

The main focus of the Trinidad and Tobago Convention Bureau will be the effective marketing of Trinidad and Tobago as the destination of choice for regional and international meeting planners.

Port of Spain's impressive waterfront is home to the Hyatt Regency Trinidad, which is the largest conference centre in the English-speaking Caribbean. *Photo: Salim October*

Trinidad has become known as the shopping capital of the Caribbean.
Photo: Ian Brierley

The Trinidad and Tobago Convention Bureau (TTCB) works closely with meeting and event planners to offer the perfect programme. Specific services are targeted to meeting planners, association members and other groups which include the provision of promotional literature, site inspections, assistance with official bids, information and quotations from suppliers and conference marketing. The TTCB can also operate as a liaison and coordinator for hoteliers and tour operators while providing information kits for delegates and arranging tours and spouse programmes.

In 2011, the TTCB facilitated more than 30 meetings and conferences, including the Caribbean Development Bank Board of Governors Annual General Meeting, the International Project Management Conference, the Trade and Investment Conference – which drew exhibitors from as far as China – and the Trinidad and Tobago Energy Conference, which attracted the industry's most influential names and decision makers.

In 2012, Trinidad and Tobago will host the International Press Institute World Congress on Press Freedom in June, which is expected to attract more than 400 delegates, including top media houses and journalists, from around the world.

With a talent for making the ordinary extraordinary, the Trinidad & Tobago Convention Bureau continues to build an impressive reputation for successfully facilitating major international events.

SHOPPING

Trinidad has become known over the last several years as the Shopping Capital of the Caribbean. Indeed, the price and variety of items that can be obtained here rivals many of the urban centres of North America and clearly surpasses what is available in the rest of the Caribbean. In addition to a modern retail sector, the country produces high quality craft, jewellery, art, housewares and fashion.

To complement the vibrant shopping centres of downtown Port of Spain, San Fernando and Chaguanas there are seven major malls carrying a mix of both local and foreign goods.

SPORTS

Sporting activities such as golfing, yachting, boating, cricket, horse racing, archery, powerboat racing, tennis, cycling and football are popular and events related to these take place on an on-going basis. The country has an excellent infrastructure for sporting events and hosts many international tournaments in

The annual Tobago Carnival Regatta attracts yacht racers from throughout the Caribbean and the rest of the world. *Photo: Oswin Browne*

tennis, football and cricket, among others.

The sporting events area offers a substantial growth potential, given the country's capacity to plan and host these ventures. Several modern stadia in both islands, built to host the FIFA Under-17 World Youth Championships, have helped to make the country's sporting infrastructure second to none in the Caribbean.

YACHTING
The country enjoys a clear competitive advantage by way of the availability of hurricane safe moorage and for yachting enthusiasts operating in these waters for extended periods of time, substantially lower insurance rates. The western peninsula of Trinidad, in particular the Chaguaramas area, has had a surge of investment in Outhauling, Boat building and Chandlery and directly or indirectly related businesses. The result is an array of facilities and services in Trinidad which has made it very desirable to the North American and Caribbean yachting community.

Trinidad's cost structure in this field is also lower than other locations and thus this improves competitiveness.

INCENTIVES FOR TOURISM INVESTMENT

- Tax Holidays of up to seven years
- Tax exemption on profits from the initial sale of villas, condominiums and sites thereof within an Integrated Resort Development
- Carry-over of losses from tax exemption period
- Duty concessions on vehicles
- Duty exemption for building materials and articles of tourism equipment
- Capital Allowances
- Accelerated depreciation

EXCITING AND DIVERSE
The country has an exciting and diversified product mix. The Trinidad and Tobago tourism product potential is extraordinary, especially when considered in a Caribbean context. It offers the warm traditional Caribbean experience as well as a cosmopolitan atmosphere, business savvy, exciting festivals, adventures in nature, pulsating music, exotic foods and so much more. ■

Source: Tourism Development Company Limited

PHOTO: STEPHEN BROADBRIDGE

MORE GOOD REASONS TO VISIT TRINIDAD AND TOBAGO

- Trinidad and Tobago was awarded 'World Best Tourism Destination: 2012" by the European Union Council on Tourism and Trade (ECTT)
- The lead Caribbean destination for eco-tourism; Tobago has the oldest protected rainforest in the Western Hemisphere (designated on 17 April 1776); Three sites designated as Wetlands of International Importance – Tobago's Buccoo Reef and The Bon Accord Lagoon Complex and Trinidad's Caroni & Nariva Swamps
- Tobago has pristine beaches and best dive sites in the Eastern Caribbean
- The major nesting sites of the critically endangered leatherback sea turtle. Hundreds of these majestic animals come ashore to deposit their eggs between March and September every year
- Unique opportunities to see rare and exotic species of flora and fauna – Oncidium citrinum orchids, leatherback turtles and bats
- Trinidad is home to the largest Caribbean Carnival; it is the birthplace of soca and calypso music and the steel pan (the only musical instrument invented in the 20th century)
- Two contrasting and complimentary destinations with a range of offers of leisure, event, conference, festival and heritage tourism

- Trinidad and Tobago's religious and cultural diversity is unrivalled in the Caribbean. The contributions of the different ethnic groups have created a rich heritage of dance, music, art, cuisine and festivals making Trinidad and Tobago a truly unique Caribbean destination
- An international variety of culinary delights await, alongside a mixture of indigenous and fusion cuisine that no other destination can boast
- Trinidad features a natural ecological phenomenon known as the Pitch Lake. The natural asphalt lake is about 250 feet deep and is estimated to have reserves in excess of 6 million tons
- Regarded as the 'business capital' of the southern Caribbean, the country hosted the 5th Summit of the Americas Conference and also the 21st Commonwealth Heads of Government Meeting
- Planned investments include a championship golf course, and an eco-tourism theme park and entertainment centre offering world class facilities
- Enhanced safety and security services at all beaches and tourism sites
- Trained and experienced service/hospitality personnel
- The home of Nobel Laureate V.S. Naipaul; Miss Universe 1998, Wendy Fitzwilliam; four-time Olympic medal winner, Ato Boldon; and world record breaking international cricketer, Brian Lara

'El Cerro Del Aripo' at NAPA Fest. *Photo courtesy Ministry of Arts and Multiculturalism*

Stewards of heritage

The Ministry of the Arts and Multiculturalism was established out of the need to more fully recognise and celebrate the cultural diversity of the people of Trinidad and Tobago. In line with government's strategic plan for sustainable development is the Ministry's mandate to promote the richness and beauty of our nation's diverse cultural expressions and nurture a more humane and cohesive society. As such, the Ministry is responsible for providing support to the cultural sector, strengthening our individual and collective identity as we build nationhood, ensuring the administration and care of all public records and material culture and serving the library and information needs of the nation.

In carrying out its tasks, the Ministry of the Arts and Multiculturalism is bolstered by its several agencies that promote both the tangible and intangible cultural heritage of Trinidad and Tobago. In many regards, these organs provide access that is often geared toward enlightening and enriching the public about our prized traditions, legacies and history.

THE DIVISION OF CULTURE

Aspects of our heritage that cannot be physically touched are surely as important as their tangible counterparts. The games we played as children, like 'Brown Girl in the Ring', folkloric stories that have been passed down orally and folk medicine are all examples of our intangible heritage. The Ministry's Culture Division holds a valued collection of these aspects of our culture which are available in audio / visual format. In the very near future, this organ of the Ministry will establish a permanent repository of such material in ▶

The Ministry was established to celebrate the cultural diversity of Trinidad and Tobago. *Photo courtesy Ministry of Arts and Multiculturalism*

African drumming

Calypso Rose at NAPA Fest

Traditional Indian music

A blend of musical influences

M'Fede Ruben at NAPA Fest

Carnival costume designer, Brian MacFarlane. *Photo: Shirley Bahadur*

the Remember When Institute. This facility will allow members of the public to view the digital versions of such material in their entirety and learn how these intangible aspects of our culture can teach us about ourselves and inspire nostalgia for many. Collecting and disseminating material on a regular basis continues to hold the attention of the Division of Culture.

THE NATIONAL ARCHIVES

Much can be told from the study of official documents. Quite apart from the facts that are recorded, official documentation connotes the values of the existing power of the time. In this regard, the National Archives collects, holds and restores this aspect of the nation's collective past. Original contracts of Chinese indentured labourers, The Ship's Register of the Fatal Razack – the vessel that brought the first East Indian indentured labourers and the Slave Registry are all sources that hold deep connections to our past.

THE NATIONAL CARNIVAL COMMISSION

Our Carnival is often described as the greatest show on earth. Full of our unique rhythms, colourful and creative costumes and the local propensity to fully enjoy all the pleasures of life, many tourists who visit at this time conclude that there truly is no other festival quite like Trinidad and Tobago's Carnival. The Ministry's National Carnival Commission (NCC) is the agency responsible for making Carnival a viable, national, cultural and commercial enterprise. The NCC also provides guidance in presenting and marketing our cultural products such as calypso, soca and steel pan music, the costumes and festivals. It also encourages research that will help to preserve and permanently display the annual accumulation of Carnival creations made each year by the passionate craftsmen, musicians, composers and designers of Carnival.

THE NATIONAL LIBRARY AND INFORMATION SYSTEM AUTHORITY (NALIS)

Its Heritage Library holds a unique literary collection that is distinctly Trinbagonian. In addition to this collection, NALIS manages all libraries in Trinidad and Tobago and is actively enhancing our library system throughout Trinidad and Tobago by carrying out refurbishments and building new facilities.

Buildings such as Queen's Royal College are properties that fall under the purview of the National Trust. *Photo: Ian Brierley*

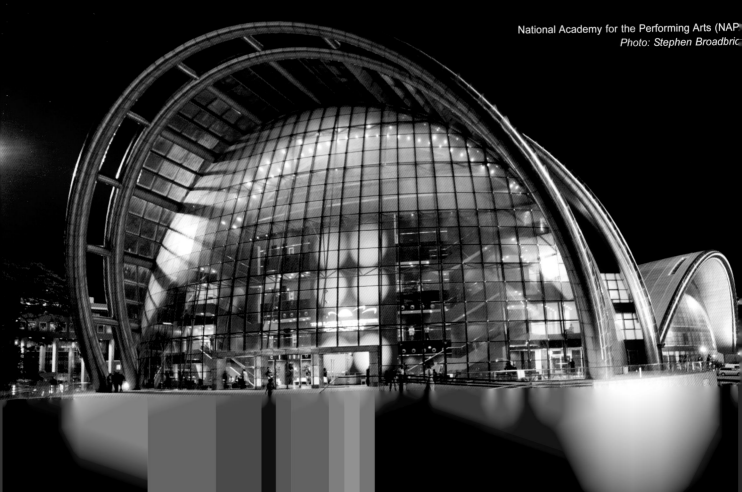

National Academy for the Performing Arts (NAP
Photo: Stephen Broadbri

Trinidad and Tobago Youth Philharmonic Orchestra performing at Queen's Hall. *Photo: Ryan P. Mannette*

THE NATIONAL MUSEUM AND ART GALLERY

Our National Museum and Art Gallery is responsible for our material culture. The Museum manages a collection of some 10,000 items. Along with its seven major galleries, the National Museum often hosts specially themed exhibitions. Its more recent displays have included "A Spirited Butterfly", a history of Trinidad and Tobago's fashion with displays of clothing that date back over a century and "The Enemy Within: Reflections on the 1970 Revolt" which was a display of artful photographs by Apoesho Mutope. The latter is a talented photographer who was closely involved with the revolutionary activities at the time and recorded many of the public demonstrations and related events.

THE NATIONAL TRUST

There are many sites throughout our twin islands that hold much historical significance. Many of them point toward our colonial past and help us remember that era when European rule prevailed so strongly. The National Trust is entrusted with the responsibility for safeguarding our built heritage; ensuring that these tangible testaments to our past retain the integrity of their time. Buildings such as Queen's Royal College and Stollmeyer's Castle are properties that fall under the purview of the National Trust. In addition to preservation, the National Trust hosts tours throughout the year and arranges public lectures that give insight into the significance of these historical sites. Examples of such excursions include a tour of Nelson Island and a tour of the various railway sites throughout Trinidad.

The Ministry of the Arts and Multiculturalism remains committed to promoting and protecting our unique cultural products and safeguarding our legacy as a nation. In so doing, it holds responsibility for Naparima Bowl, National Academies for the Performing Arts, National Theatre Arts Company, Queen's Hall and the Trinidad and Tobago National Steel Symphony Orchestra. ■

Source: Ministry of Arts and Multiculturalism

Handmade leather goods in Scarborough, Tobago. *Photo: Ian Brierley*

Cultural Industries

Ask any Trinbagonian expat what they miss most about home and you will be met with wistful faraway looks and a plaintive whisper: 'The food'. The quantities of frozen doubles and layered roti skins secreted in suitcases bound for North America and London bear testament to the fact and a growing realisation of the commercial potential of the twin-island's culinary heritage has led to investment and promotion in the area.

Port of Spain's *Taste Trinidad and Tobago*, labelled the festival of flavours, has become established on the regional tourism calendar as a showcase for the foods derived from the unique cultural mix of these islands. Tobago's Blue Food Festival acts as a similar medium for the sister isle and proves that seemingly the only limit to what you can make with dasheen is your imagination.

Entertainment, and music in particular, has long been one of Trinidad and Tobago's greatest cultural exports and receives its global shop window each year during Carnival. The Trinidad and Tobago Entertainment Company Ltd was established in 2007 with the remit of building a sustainable, globally competitive entertainment industry' and says significant opportunities exist in the hosting of events in the mould of the Tobago Jazz Festival. The Trinidad and Tobago Film Company was created in 2006 with similar goals for the burgeoning local film industry.

Artworks depicting local scenes, traditions and people have always been a favourite with locals and visitors alike, and some of the finest in the field are Martin Superville, of the Tobago Art Gallery, and landscape painter Karen Sylvester. Horizons Art Gallery is also an established supporter and promoter of local artists and exhibits their work at its gallery in St James.

Amongst cottage industries pottery is popular. At the celebrated Chaguanas potteries, including Radika's Pottery, you can watch the adroit artisans at work using traditional methods.

If your inclination is beautiful batik work infused with a Trinbagonian flavour then two of the best locations to source it are Poui Designs/Batik in Ellerslie Plaza and Sapodilla in Trincity Mall.

On a smaller scale, handmade leather goods, calabash carvings and jewellery are widely available but Tobago's Store Bay and Pigeon Point are locations with a concentration of kiosks and stalls.

James Fuller is an award-winning freelance journalist and author

Calabash carvings. Photo: Marcus Gonzales

PHOTO: JAMES B. SOLOMON

PHOTO: SALIM OCTOBER

PHOTO: JAMES B. SOLOMON

op three pictures – Port of Spain's *Taste Trinidad and Tobago*, labelled the festival of flavours, has become established n the regional tourism calendar as a showcase for the foods derived from the unique cultural mix of these islands ottom Colourful beach-side displays of local handiwork is a common sight. *Photo: Marcus Gonzales*

Traditional pottery is a popular cottage industry. *Photo: Ian Brierley*

From catching 'flims', to making them

We've come a long way from the days of 'catching a flim', and while the charming mispronunciation of the word is still an indelible part of the Trini dialect, the meaning of the word has expanded exponentially. Fifty years ago, sitting in the fancy Globe cinema was the ultimate night on the town as you took in the glamorous shenanigans of Hollywood (…and a great deal of cigarette smoke). Today, the only thing smoking in Cinemas is on screen and Hollywood no longer has a monopoly on the electronic storytelling business.

The lay of cinema land in Trinidad and Tobago is quite different today than it was half a century ago. There are now two Cineplex's – MovieTowne, with three branches and twenty two screens and Caribbean Cinemas 8 with, you guessed it, eight screens. Additionally the ubiquitous Globe is still standing and there is the spanking new Digicel IMAX Digital 3D Theatre. On any given day, you can still catch a kung-fu kick up, a Bollywood saga (be prepared for three hours), a major motion picture, an animated feature, even a foreign independent film – so what's

The Digicel IMAX Digital 3D theatre is the latest venue for film-goers. *Photo: Salim October*

changed really? Nowadays, you can also catch locally produced full-length films, shorts, documentaries, animated features, both on the big screen and on TV. And, the world out there can catch our local actors, locations and locally produced films on the international big screen.

For filmmakers, these shores have always been a superb geographic location but now a resource base including consultants, experienced actors, screen writers, directors and production crews as well as financial incentives represent an exciting opportunity for the local and foreign film industries alike. The most recent example of this is Indian National TV, Door Darshan, filming a documentary on the history and progress of the Indian Diaspora in Trinidad & Tobago, advised by Dr Brinsley Samaroo.

The Trinidad and Tobago Film Company Ltd. (TTFC) has played a pivotal role in this ongoing evolution of the local film industry. Founded in 2006, the TTFC is a state agency with a single purpose – to facilitate the development of this nation's film (audio-visual) industry. TTFC provides logistical support and core services to the local and international film/audio-visual industry, functioning as an essential networker for film makers and the many entities they must liaise with, in the course of production.

The TTFC manages several highly successful Film Funding and Development Programmes and facilitates dozens of film productions and multiple film festivals. Celebrating the best in regional film, the Trinidad and Tobago Film Festival began in 2006 and has proved to be an excellent vehicle for showcasing the work and increasing the profile of, filmmakers. Films examining the nation's social, cultural and political history have figured highly amongst its award winners as is reflected by the 2011 Best Local Feature,

Elizabeth Topp's 70: Remembering a Revolution.

To date, ninety seven locally produced projects have come to life on screen thanks to the Production Assistance and Script Development Programme. This is not just great news for culture but for the economic sector as well. Between 2006 and 2010, one hundred and sixty two crews chose Trinidad and Tobago as their location, injecting TT $13.5 million into the economy and generating hundreds of jobs in a variety of sectors.

With the future in mind, the TTFC took over the management of the Secondary Schools Short Film Festival in 2010 from founder MovieTowne and was able to expand the programme to as far as Roxborough (Tobago) and Matelot – training over (600) students cumulatively in the last two years in the rudiments of filmmaking. Some of these students have gone on to pursue tertiary education in

film either through the B.A. in Film Studies at the UWI or internationally.

Just some of the attractive incentives from the TTFC that beckon local and international film crews include; up to 35% on-location production expenditure rebate, assistance with Customs and the importation of equipment and/or the waiver of duties on same, as well as facilitation of permits, accreditation and copyright issues. But even if you were not entirely convinced, once you actually touch down on these beautiful islands, the decision to shoot in Trinidad and Tobago becomes as clear as the kaleidoscopic sunset over the blue, blue waters. Location, location, location…

A great place to catch a 'flim'… or to make one! ■

Patti-Anne Ali has worked in the Performing Arts and Advertising Industries

Eric Williams was Chief Minister of Trinidad and Tobago from 28 October 1956 until 9 July 1959, whereupon he became the nation's first Premier, a position he held until December 1961. In the same month, he became Trinidad and Tobago's first Prime Minister and held the position until his death on 29 March 1981

The nation's first Prime Minister

Trinidad and Tobago came of age historically with the emergence of a transformational figure in Dr Eric Eustace Williams. Both he and the young nation's future were inextricably intertwined in this grand transformational effort. But it was history that would play a central role in the evolution of both the country and Williams himself.

Eric Williams, as the first Prime Minister of Trinidad and Tobago, is considered by many, the Father of the Nation. Born on 25 September 1911, he attended Queens Royal College in Port of Spain (1922) and was an avid sports enthusiast. He obtained a prestigious Island Scholarship in 1932 to study at Oxford University where he achieved a First Class Honours degree and later a doctorate in History in 1938.

His thesis, *The Economic Aspects of the Abolition and Emancipation of Slavery in the British West Indies* later spawned his seminal work *Capitalism and Slavery*, first published in 1944. This work posited the view that the rise of British Capitalism coincided with rising profits from slavery and that it was economic expediency more than anything else which forced the abolition of slavery in the West Indies.

In 1939, Dr Williams left England for the United States where he taught at Howard University, where in 1947, he became a full Professor in Social and Political Science. In 1948, he resigned from the University to work at the Anglo-American Caribbean Commission where he headed their Research Department. His departure from the Commission (1955) was turbulent to say the least, plagued with ongoing and unresolved conflicts in policy he detailed in his speech, 'My Relations with the Caribbean Commission'.

In Trinidad, his historic transformational efforts resulted in the formation of the People's National Movement (PNM) (January 1956) when he became the party's first political leader. Many of his speeches were delivered at Woodford Square, which was considered the "Hyde Park" of Port of Spain and known for heated didactic exchanges among the people for which it was dubbed the "University of Woodford Square".

At the time, Trinidad and Tobago were still island colonies of Britain, ruled from the Colonial Office through the Secretary of State for the Colonies and its appointed Governor (Sir Edward Beetham).

Dr Williams, with others, began the fight for full self governance and Independence which saw him elected as Chief Minister of the country (1956) in control of the Legislative Council and then in 1959, as first Premier with significant plurality. After the failure of the West Indian Federation, he negotiated the peaceful independence of Trinidad and Tobago from Great Britain, saw the new nation's flag hoisted and the Union Jack lowered on 31st August 1962.

Constitutional reform then led the twin-island state to become a republic, in 1972, with its own President as Head of State, instead of the hitherto British monarch, Queen Elizabeth II.

Under his leadership, until his death in office in 1981, Trinidad and Tobago moved from being a backward country to take its rightful place among world nations. Today, the country enjoys relative prosperity and political stability. However, the "Doc" would be the first to admit that there are problems that still need to be resolved. But during his tenure as Prime Minister, he had placed his country firmly in control of its destiny. ■

Dr Michael Belcon is an educator, scholar and health professional

Kamla Persad-Bissessar has challenged herself "with the mission to build a society through a leadership style where everyone felt valued, appreciated and invited to make a meaningful contribution to the development of our nation." *Photo: Calvin French*

The nation's first female Prime Minister

It was on the 24th of May 2010 that Trinidad and Tobago, after forty eight years of Independence, got its first female Prime Minister in the person of Kamla Persad-Bissessar. Prior to becoming Prime Minister in a victory that gave her a Constitutional majority, she had acted as Prime Minister as well as has the distinction of being the country's first female Attorney General. She also served as Minister of Legal Affairs and as Minister of Education during which period she introduced universal secondary school education. Kamla Persad-Bissessar is a successful Attorney at Law and holds academic qualifications in Education and a Masters in Business Administration. She has taught at both the secondary and tertiary levels and brings these experiences to bear upon her Prime Ministership.

As Prime Minister, she has continued to pursue her objective of ensuring that women and girls are afforded equal opportunities to participate in political decision making and to serve in the Parliament. As Chair in Office of the Commonwealth (May 2010- November 2011), she vigorously pursued this goal by holding the first Regional colloquium of Caribbean women leaders in a year in which the Commonwealth had as its theme "Women as Agents of Change." She successfully mounted a meeting of women leaders on the margins of the 66th Session of the UNGA. This was supported by the President of Brazil, Her Excellency Dilma Roussef, as well as Secretary of State Hilary Clinton, Head of the UNDP, Helen Clarke and Michelle Bacchelet of UN Women. The outcome of these efforts was the signing of a Declaration on Political Participation by Women which was supported by Commonwealth Leaders at CHOGM 2011 in Perth, Australia.

In her desire to ensure that children in Trinidad and Tobago are afforded life saving surgery which cannot be obtained locally, Mrs Bissessar has pioneered the Children's Life Fund for which legislation was successfully introduced in the Parliament. This ensures that the poorest child has the same opportunity for advanced medical care as the richest.

She believes that the way out of poverty is through education and in her desire to build a knowledge based society and improve global competitiveness every child entering secondary school since 2010 is given a fully loaded lap top computer.

Long before the Arab Spring, in a lecture delivered at Harvard University in 2010 she asserted that "the paradigm of governance has shifted from one of authoritarianism or different degrees of the same to one where the people view themselves as employers of the government with the right to fire as much as they hire through the democratic process of the vote."

She further asserted that "we are clear in our minds that successful nations today will only be built through the channeling of intellectual power to meaningful ends. Democracy and the spirit of cooperation are the only channels through which this can be accomplished. It may take longer to arrive at decisions but because of consensus, commitment will be higher and subsequent progress faster."

As Prime Minister of Trinidad and Tobago and as Trinidad and Tobago looks to its 50th Year of Independence in 2012, she is very clear as to her vision for her country. In her own words we get a delightful and insightful picture of her thoughts in this regard.

"I was born a Hindu, attended a Presbyterian secondary school. I was baptised as a Spiritual Baptist. I studied, lived and worked in Jamaica. I studied law in Barbados. I went to school in England. These experiences taught me to value diverse cultures and peoples and the success that can be achieved from synthesising the richness of this diversity. It created for me an understanding of the importance of being open to all peoples and the realisation that everyone is capable of contributing to the whole. I challenged myself with the mission to build a society through a leadership style where everyone felt valued, appreciated and invited to make a meaningful contribution to the development of our nation. If I were to answer as to my leadership philosophy, I would answer in one word, inclusiveness. My country had suffered enough from people who lived on the margins of national life. It truncated creativity and stymied nationalism. You cannot become a competitive nation with only half of the talent and energy of your people." ■

Suruj Rambachan, Minister for Local Government

Governing Trinidad and Tobago

Serious party government in Trinidad and Tobago was established by Dr Eric Eustace Williams and the People's National Movement (PNM) from 1956, when it first came to power. The PNM governed for 30 continuous years comprising of six 5-year administrations until 1986. This included 24 years and five consecutive administrations as an independent country. During this period various political parties emerged in an attempt to establish a viable opposition. As a party of government in the formative years of the nation, the PNM became something of a monolith while the parties in opposition struggled to come up with an appropriate formula for effective challenge.

Trinidad and Tobago became an Independent country with its own constitution in 1962 following the collapse of the Federation of the West Indies in 1959 with the withdrawal of, first Jamaica and then, Trinidad and Tobago. Once full internal self government was achieved both Jamaica and Trinidad and Tobago pursued a path to Independence.

The path to Independence was peaceful but not without its challenges in Trinidad and Tobago. The main opposition party, the Democratic Labour Party (DLP), walked out of the consultation on the proposed Independence constitution at Queen's Hall and so the draft that was taken to London to negotiate the terms of Independence lacked input from the official opposition. Ultimately, differences were resolved at

Marlborough House, London and on May 28th, 1962, under the Chairmanship of the Secretary of State for the Colonies the Honourable Reginald Maudling, it was agreed that 31st August 1962 would be Independence Day in Trinidad and Tobago. Dr Eric Williams served as Prime Minister of Trinidad and Tobago until his death in 1980.

In 1976 Dr Williams led the debate for a new constitution following the report of a Constitution Commission, and Trinidad and Tobago became a Republic in that year. Since 1961, there had been concerted attempts to establish a two party system in Trinidad and Tobago.

George Chambers had succeeded Eric Williams as Prime Minister in 1980 and went on to win elections in 1981 with the largest majority up to that time. In 1986, however, the National Alliance for Reconstruction won all but three seats in the House of Representatives and Arthur Napoleon Raymond Robinson became Prime Minister.

From 1986 to 2010 (a period of 24 years), after 30 years of one party rule, the government has changed hands seven times and in the decade 2000 to 2010, five times. This period has seen the opposition forces configuring and reconfiguring themselves in a range of forms. The main opposition emerged as the United National Congress (UNC) after 1991 and its leader Basdeo Panday emerged as Prime Minister in 1995. Panday was able to secure a narrow victory again in 2000 but internal party problems forced an ▶

George Michael Chambers (b.1928 - d.1997)
George Chambers became Trinidad and Tobago's second Prime Minister, serving from on 30 March 1981 to 18 December 1986. Having worked his way up from the grass roots of the People's National Movement (PNM), Chambers was able to build close support with ordinary folks who formed the bulk of his support. Among his major achievements as Prime Minister was the election of Ms Muriel Green as his party's first female deputy leader and his decision to purchase the assets of the oil giant Texaco. Sadly for him, the 1980s was a period of drastic reduction in oil prices which adversely affected the nation which was too dependent on one resource.

election within a year of office. Since 1991 the Prime Minister of Trinidad and Tobago has either been Patrick Manning (PNM) or Basdeo Panday (UNC). All of this changed in 2010.

In 2010, Kamla Persad-Bissessar, beat Basdeo Panday by a phenomenally large margin to become the first female leader of the UNC and of any political party in Trinidad and Tobago. On May 24th, 2010, Mrs Persad-Bissessar became the first woman Prime Minister of Trinidad and Tobago.

She led a strong UNC to form a coalition with the other significant political party at that time, the Congress of the People (COP) but significantly, the broad coalition that she established included the Movement for Social Justice (MSJ), an umbrella organisation of trade unions and worker interests, the National Joint Action Committee (NJAC) which had led a peoples' protest movement in 1970 calling for unity of Africans and Indians and an end to ethnically divisive politics, together with a range of civil society groups including a broad coalition of women's interests.

This broad coalition started tentatively at first, but after two years in office, seems solid and purposeful having taken care to avoid a confrontational approach on issues with regard to interests in society and having agreed to disagree on issues within its ranks, without resorting to open conflict and without approaching anything close to rupture. ∎

Dr Bhoendradatt Tewarie, Senator and Minister o Planning and the Economy

Basdeo Panday (b.1933 -)

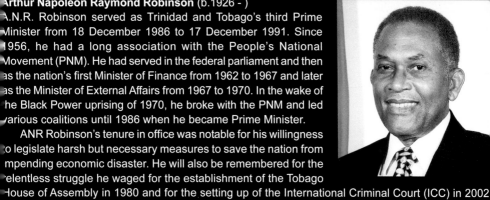

Basdeo Panday was elected as Trinidad and Tobago's fifth Prime Minister and served from 9 November 1995 to 24 Decemebr 2001. He is the only Prime Minister to come directly out of the trade union movement.

From 1966, he became legal advisor to a number of trade unions and using his sugar union base, he founded, with others, the United Labour Front (ULF) in 1975 and emerged as its undisputed leader.

In October 1988, Basdeo Panday formed the United National Congress (UNC). In the elections of 1995 he became Prime Minister in alliance with the National Alliance for Reconstruction (NAR) which had won the two Tobago seats. He served one full term from 1995 to 2000 and another short term from 2000 to 2002.

Panday's ascendancy was a source of deep inspiration to the labour movement and the East Indian community. His administration continued the dream of Eric Williams to make education available to all by abolishing the common entrance examination so that every child could receive a free education, and the Shouter Baptists, a hitherto neglected group, were given a national holiday (30 March) and land where they could build a school and establish their headquarters. *Photo courtesy Government Information Services Ltd*

Arthur Napoleon Raymond Robinson (b.1926 -)

A.N.R. Robinson served as Trinidad and Tobago's third Prime Minister from 18 December 1986 to 17 December 1991. Since 1956, he had a long association with the People's National Movement (PNM). He had served in the federal parliament and then as the nation's first Minister of Finance from 1962 to 1967 and later as the Minister of External Affairs from 1967 to 1970. In the wake of the Black Power uprising of 1970, he broke with the PNM and led various coalitions until 1986 when he became Prime Minister.

ANR Robinson's tenure in office was notable for his willingness to legislate harsh but necessary measures to save the nation from impending economic disaster. He will also be remembered for the relentless struggle he waged for the establishment of the Tobago House of Assembly in 1980 and for the setting up of the International Criminal Court (ICC) in 2002 He became President of Trinidad and Tobago on 18 March 1997 and served until 17 March 2003.

Robinson is the only person to have held the country's three highest public offices – Chairman of the Tobago House of Assembly, Prime Minister and President. In 2011, he was awarded the

Harmonious and exemplary democracy

Trinidad and Tobago's political landscape is indelibly linked to its ethnic diversity and has an equally rich history of colour and characters.

In the 1956 elections, the African-based People's National Movement and Indian-based Democratic Labour Party emerged as the two main political forces, led by noted scholars, Dr Eric Williams and Dr Rudranath Capildeo, respectively. The country gained Independence in 1962, functioning since as unitary State, regulated by a Parliamentary democracy modelled on the UK's Westminster system, comprising 31 selected members of the Senate and, since 2009, 41 elected members of the House of Representatives. General elections are held every five years and Government rests with the Cabinet, led by the Prime Minister.

Trinidad and Tobago was made the first Presidential Republic within the Commonwealth in 1976. In 1980, Tobago was made semi-autonomous via the Tobago House of Assembly. From 1956-1986, the PNM won every general election, with George Chambers being made Prime Minister in 1981 upon Williams' death.

In 1970, the country underwent another major political upheaval with the Black Power Revolution led by several other labour and social activists lobbying for equality for the majority non-white population. Fifteen of its leaders were arrested, causing a short lived mutiny of a section of the army led by Raffique Shah and Rex Lasalle.

Dr Keith Rowley is the current Leader of the Opposition PNM party

Basdeo Panday and his United Labour Front party then emerged as the main Opposition faction.

In 1986, amid allegations of massive Government corruption, the NAR union of all opposing political elements, led by Tobagonian ANR Robinson, won the elections. By 1988, Panday broke ranks with the Government and formed the United National Congress. In 1990, the Jamaat Al Muslimeen, a black extremist Muslim group, failed to overthrow the Government and by 1991, the Patrick Manning-led PNM won the elections.

The UNC/NAR coalition secured victory in the 1995 polls and Panday was elected the country's first ever Indian-Trinbigonian Prime Minister. The UNC won the 2000 general elections, but the defection of three MPs resulted in a return to the polls in 2001, where, for the first time ever, the results were deadlocked – 18-18. Then President ANR Robinson appointed Patrick Manning as Prime Minister despite the UNC being the incumbent and having the majority of the popular vote. The PNM won the 2002 and 2007 polls.

In the 2010 elections, the coalition People's Partnership secured victory with Kamla Persad-Bissessar elected as the first female Prime Minister.

The country is a member of the Commonwealth and United Nations, and its highest court remains the London-based Privy Council. The country is signatory to numerous international treaties and protocols, and today, is regarded to be one of the most harmonious, exemplary democracies on the globe. ∎

Sasha Mohammed

Patrick Augustus Mervyn Manning (b.1946 -)
Patrick Manning served three terms as Prime Minister. His first term in office (as Trinidad and Tobago's fourth Prime Minister) was from 17 December 1991 to 9 November 1995. He was re-elected on 24 December 2001 and served two terms until 26 May 2010.

In a political career which started in 1971 and which continues today, Patrick Manning held many ministerial positions. From 1971 to 1979, he served as Parliamentary Secretary in various ministries and from 1981 to 1986, he was Minister of Energy and Natural Resources.

As a trained geologist he was able to personally oversee the expansion of the petro-chemical industry, leading to enhanced oil and natural gas exports. His government launched an array of social programs aimed at assisting, training and employing citizens.

His administration rebuilt aging primary and secondary schools, complete with school feeding programs. They set up the University of Trinidad and Tobago (UTT) as well as the College of Science, Technology and Applied Arts (COSTAATT). Under Manning's administration, the public service transport was improved with more routes to rural places. He is the longest-serving member of the national parliament.
Photo courtesy Government Information Services Ltd

HISTORY OF THE PRESIDENCY

Prior to Trinidad and Tobago gaining its independence from Great Britain, it was a crown colony and the Queen of England was the nation's Head of State, represented by the Governor.

Upon becoming independent on the 31st August 1962, the Queen remained titular Head of State but a Governor-General now governed the country's affairs.

On 1st August 1976, Trinidad and Tobago became a republic within the Commonwealth and the Republican Constitution provided for a President who is the Head of State and Commander in Chief of the armed forces. The President is also the repository of all Executive Authority whose powers are exercisable within certain constitutional limits and most of the constitutional acts must be performed in accordance with the advice of, or after consultation with, another authority, usually the Cabinet, the Prime Minister or the Leader of the Opposition.

A person is qualified to be nominated for election as President if they are a citizen of Trinidad and Tobago of age thirty-five years or upwards who, at the date of their nomination as President, has been ordinarily resident in Trinidad and Tobago for ten years immediately preceding their nomination.

The Constitution provides for an Electoral College consisting of all the Members of the Senate and all the Members of the House of Representatives assembled together and convened and presided over by the Speaker of the House. The President is elected by the Electoral College voting by secret ballot. Ten Senators, the Speaker and twelve other Members of the House of Representatives constitute a quorum of the Electoral College. The President so elected shall normally hold office for a term of five years.

Sir Solomon Hochoy
(b.1905 - d.1983)
Solomon Hochoy was the last Governor of Trinidad and Tobago and held the post from 4 July 1960 to 31 August 1962. He became the nation's first Governor-General, also on 31 August 1962, and remained in that position until 15 September 1972.

Ellis Emmanuel Innocent Clarke
(b.1917 - d.2010)
24 September 1976 to 19 March 1987
Ellis Clarke succeeded Solomon Hochoy as Governor-General in 1972, becoming the second and last Governor-General

(1972-1976). He was unanimously elected as the first President of Trinidad and Tobago when the nation became a Republic in 1976.

Noor Mohamed Hassanali
(b.1918 - d.2006)
20 March 1987 to 17 March 1997
The second President of the Republic of Trinidad and Tobago, Noor Hassanali served two terms between 1987 and 1997. He was a retired High Court Judge, the first Indo-Trinidadian to hold the office of President and the first Muslim Head of State in the Americas.

Arthur Napoleon Raymond Robinson
(b.1926 -)
18 March 1997 to 16 March 2003
Arthur N.R. Robinson succeeded Noor Hassanali as President of the Republic of Trinidad and Tobago and served in office from 1997-2003. He was previously Prime Minister from 1986-1991, during which time he was a member of the National Alliance for Reconstruction. Mr Robinson was the first active politician to be elected to the Presidency and was the first presidential candidate who was elected unopposed.

George Maxwell Richards
(b.1931 -)
17 March 2003 to present
Professor Richards, the country's fourth President, is currently serving a second term as President (appointed 1 February 2008). He is the first Head of State in the Anglophone Caribbean of Amerindian ancestry.

Political pioneers

The development of Trinidad and Tobago was achieved on the backs of many notable individuals, among them Cipriani, Butler, Rienzi, Weekes, Maharaj and Williams to name a few. Many have received well-deserved accolades for their significant contributions to the cause of Trinidad and Tobago Nationalism. We highlight here two such pioneering individuals – Albert Gomes and George Weekes.

ALBERT MARIA GOMES

Born Albert Maria Gomes in Belmont of Portuguese parents on 25th March 1911, 'Bertie' grew up straddling the hinterland of the elite and the lower class. This "portogee" and his family were never embraced by the British expatriates or the influential French Creole high society. With his father's business a stone throw from "behind the bridge", Bertie would embrace the suppressed culture and oppressed people of the "real" Trinidad and Tobago. He would later champion the cause of calypsonians, steelbandsmen and Shouter Baptists with the same vigour of disenfranchised workers.

He established *"The Beacon"*, a literary magazine that published the works of radical notables like CLR James, Alfred Mendes, Quintin O'Connor, Hugh Stollmeyer and Ralph de Boissière. They offered an irreverent view of the Colonial establishment.

The so called "Labour Riots" in 1937 was a turning point for Trinidad and Tobago Nationalism. Butler and Cipriani were engaged in representing the oil workers and dock workers respectively. Gomes became President of the Federated Workers' Trade Union (FWTU) representing Railroad and Construction workers. The labour movement was on the move and inevitably, their leaders would make forays into politics. Gomes was no exception.

He was elected to the Port of Spain City Council in 1938 where he served for nine years as a Councilor and Deputy Mayor for three of those years. He then founded the first Political Progress Groups, the forerunner of Party of Political Progress Groups (POPPG) and was later elected to the Legislative Council in 1945.

Gomes continued to represent Port of Spain North until 1956. In the 1950 election the POPPG won 2 seats and the Butler party won 6 seats. Despite the Butler Party's success the Governor was in no mood to appoint Butler to lead the country. So it was Gomes and his Party with only two seats who was asked to form a government. He thus became the country's First Chief Minister of Trinidad and Tobago from 1950 to 1956.

Gomes worked tirelessly for the working man in and out of the labour movement. With Cipriani, he advocated for adult suffrage, workers' pension, eight hour work days, overtime pay, minimum wage, compulsory education, women's rights and an end to child labour and the Crown Colony System.

A lover of the arts, he helped define the movement of budding independent thinkers of the day that saw the emergence of the West Indian novel and poetry. The elites shunned and suppressed the steelband, carnival and calypso. Together with our folk art and dance, Gomes instead embraced them and helped propel these art forms from the back water to the forefront of Trinidad and Tobago culture.

Beyond his publishing and writing experiences, Gomes championed the cause of literacy in colonial Trinidad and Tobago and as chairman of the Management Committee of the Public Library opened up access to the library to all and sundry.

Gomes was a quintessential Caribbean man long before that post colonial movement surged. His entry and victory in federal politics was probably the most satisfying for him. The demise of the federation was likely his most disappointing. This was the final "crick-crack that broke the monkey's back" as he left for England to join other Caribbean cultural castaways in exile adrift in a sea of self-doubt and uncertainty.

While Gomes will be remembered most for his political successes and was instrumental in transitioning the country from a dependent colonial entity to an independent state, it is the scope and breadth of his influence shaping the emergence of a self confident and optimistic people of Trinidad and Tobago that will be his lasting legacy.

Gomes died in Europe in 1978 in exile barely remembered by his compatriots.

GEORGE WEEKES

Any serious analysis of the labour movement and the role it played in the development of Trinidad and Tobago would be incomplete without recognising the contribution of George Weekes. That he led the most powerful trade union in the country for 25 years during some of the most turbulent times in the history of the country speaks volumes for his tenacity and leadership abilities.

Born 9th March 1921, Weekes joined the Caribbean Regiment fighting for the British during WWII. He returned to Trinidad in 1945 and registered as a member of the British Empire Workers, Peasants and Rate Payers Union established by Tubal Uriah "Buzz" Butler. But very early Weekes recognised the merits of political action in the fight for "home rule" and became a member of the West Indian Independence Party (WIIP).

Fate will play a decisive role in the evolution of George Weekes when he joined the staff of Texaco in 1960, becoming a member of the Oilfield Workers Trade Union (OWTU) that same year. Within two years, 25th June 1962, he was elected President General of the most powerful union in the country.

He spearheaded democracy in the union with the introduction of the "one man one vote" rule and successfully agitated for a reduction in the length of the work week. With his power base firmly in industrial South Trinidad he moved to expand the membership of his union to include workers from Federation Chemicals, the Dunlop Company, Trinidad Cement Ltd and T&TEC.

Weekes realised that the fight for workers rights went beyond the struggle for better wages and working conditions. He recognised that political action was a necessary adjunct to attain freedom, dignity and justice for all. Consequently, he joined CLR James and Stephen Maharaj to form the Workers and Farmers Party in 1965. At the time James was perceived as a major threat to Williams' grip on the country and a formidable foe with the intellectual prowess to match Williams' own.

In response to Weekes calling for general strikes in 1965, the Williams government introduced the *Industrial Stabilisation Act* (ISA), which banned strike action in the public service and restricted the use of strikes and lock-outs in private industry. The establishment of the Industrial Court was considered a dagger to the heart of collective bargaining and trade unionism. Many considered its successful implementation and the trade union movement's inability to stop it, a fatal failing of Weekes' leadership. It implied that Williams had ultimately outsmarted the wily union leader.

It will not be the last time that Weekes will lock horns with Williams in the struggle for workers rights. Weekes was jailed twice following the declaration of States of Emergencies, first on 20th April 1970 and then again in November 1971. It was only after Williams' death in 1981 that Weekes would finally make his mark in the political arena when he was appointed to the Senate.

In the end George Weekes served his union and the labour movement well and his efforts to use political action to advance the cause of social justice and dignity for all the people of Trinidad and Tobago must never be forgotten. ■

Michael C. Belcon, MD, MPH

Kelly-Ann Baptiste celebrates her 100m bronze medal at the IAAF World Athletics Championships in South Korea in 2011.
Photo: Andy Lyons/Getty Images

A varied sporting calendar

Witness a tight finish to a cricket match at the Queens Park Oval or a sub-par performance by the Soca Warriors at the Hasely Crawford Stadium, and you will know few things raise Trinbagonian blood pressures like sport; even if adherence to the credo of "Party – win, lose or draw" is still strictly observed.

While cricket – with incomparable batting phenomenon Brian Lara – and football – where stars such as Dwight Yorke and Russell Latapy helped Trinidad and Tobago become the smallest World Cup qualifying nation in 2006 – still dominate, the sporting tastes of these twin-islands are diverse.

In 1948, Rodney Wilkes became the country's first Olympic medallist by winning silver in weightlifting at the London games; and in 1984, Rachael Marshall became the country's first and only Paralympic medallist, winning two gold medals (javelin and shot put) and a bronze medal for the 100m freestyle swimming.

Until the 2012 Olympic games in London, the only other gold medal-winning performance was Hasely Crawford's storming 100m victory in 1976, which sent a nation into delirium. In recent years, four-time Olympic medallist and former 200m world champion, Ato Boldon has come close, as has Richard Thompson in Beijing in 2008 with 100m and 4 x 100m relay silver medals.

However, in 2012, London would again set the stage for another of the nation's sons to enter the Olympic record books. Nineteen-year-old Keshorn Walcott's gold medal performance in the javelin secured Trinidad and Tobago's second gold in Olympic history. The teenager simultaneously became the first non-European to win the men's javelin since 1952.

The London 2012 Games also saw bronze medal performances from Trinidad and Tobago's men's 4 x 100m relay team (Richard Thompson, Keston Bledman,

▶

Nicknamed "The Prince of Port of Spain", cricketer Brian Lara holds many batting records including the highest individual score in a Test match innings (400 not out, for the West Indies against England in Antigua, 2004) and the highest first-class score of 501 not out for Warwickshire against Durham at Edgbaston in 1994. He retired from international cricket in April 2007 and is pictured during his final match for the West Indies against England in Barbados. *Photo: Tom Shaw/Getty Images*

Keshorn Walcott celebrates his gold medal-winning performance in the javelin at the London 2012 Olympics. *Photo: Alexander Hassenstein/Getty Images*

The Hasely Crawford Stadium in Port of Spain was opened in 1980 and is named after Hasely Crawford, the first athlete from Trinidad and Tobago to win an Olympic gold medal. *Photo: Marcus Gonzales*

The Great Race powerboat contest to Tobago has been a regular feature for over forty years.
Photo: Shirley Bahadur

Marc Burns, Emmanuel Callender), and its men's 4 x 400m relay (Lalonde Gordon, Ade Alleyne-Forte, Deon Lendore, Jarrin Solomon). Lalonde Gordon also achieved a second individual bronze in the men's 400m.

For the women, Tobago's rising star, Kelly-Ann Baptiste took 100m bronze in the 2011 World Championships but missed out on a medal in the final of the 100m at the London 2012 Olympics.

In the pool, George Bovell III's bronze in 2004 helped raise the sport's profile and prompted the construction of a National Aquatic Centre. And in 1994, Trinidad and Tobago competed at a Winter Olympics for the first time with its two-man bobsled team of Gregory Sun and Curtis Harry.

Trinidad and Tobago has punched above its weight with world champion boxers in Claude Noel (1981 WBA Lightweight), Leslie Stewart (1987 WBA Light-Heavyweight) and 21-year-old light-middleweight Giselle Salandy, who held six world titles and looked set to rule women's boxing before she was tragically killed in a car crash in 2009.

Others have tasted success – mostly regional – in sports including basketball, archery, hockey, taekwondo, netball, golf, rugby union, volleyball, triathlon, cycling, tennis, surfing and bodybuilding; and in martial arts Professor Don Jacob's Purple Dragon School has spawned multiple world champions.

Chaguaramas is a hub for many sporting activities including kayaking, yachting, sailing, mountain biking and Chinese dragon boat racing (with an annual festival now instituted); whilst in powerboating the celebrated Great Race to Tobago has been blasting away from the area for over forty years.

Beneath the waves, angling enthusiasts will find superb big game fishing in Tobago whilst Trinidad is world-renowned for tarpon.

Motorsports like rallying, drag racing and gravel-track racing in Caroni continue to gain in popularity whereas, for lovers of natural horsepower, there is top-class weekly horse racing, on turf and all-weather, at Arima's Santa Rosa Park. And for something completely different, but taken nonetheless seriously by its combatants, Buccoo in Tobago, at Easter, is the venue for the hugely popular sport of goat racing! ∎

Goat racing! *Photo: Stephen Broadbridge*

A taste for the high octane

Motorsport activities have been present in Trinidad and Tobago since the late 1960s with circuit racing legends Selbourne Clarke, Frankie Boodram, Mike Baboolal, Tom Miller, the Amars, James Fifi, Greg Solis and Gordon Gonsalves. Trinidad also hosted formula-car races in the 1970s and drivers of this era represented the country at racing meets in Guyana, Barbados, Jamaica and the USA. New names like Tanko Baboolal, Ravi Singh and Gerrard Carrington have now emerged to take the baton. In the discipline of drag racing however, Trinidadian Sheldon Bissessar is well known throughout the USA where he competes in the IHRA (International Hot Rod Association) Top Dragster category. Sheldon has reset the IHRA World record in this class three times from 2007-2011.

The sport of rally has developed quite independently through the Trinidad and Tobago Rally Club which has steadily been refining its annual five-day Rally Trinidad high-speed gravel stages event. Along with Barbados and Jamaica, the top drivers in the Caribbean like Doug Gore, Geoffrey Panton, Paul Bourne and Roger Skeete compete against local heroes like Ainsley Lochan and Jamaican-born John Powell for the unofficial title of the Caribbean Rally Champion each year. Trinidad has now become the premier venue in the Caribbean for gravel stage rallies, thanks to the high standard of stage preparation and the extreme level of difficulty. There has also been the more recent development of Rally Tobago, which combines the rally experience with vacation discount packages for a weekend guaranteed to satisfy any motorsport fan.

The Trinidad and Tobago Karting Club has also been active since 1978 when three circuit racers decided to introduce the sport after a Grand Prix trip in the USA. Since then many racers have represented

Group 4 Formula cars on the grid at Wallerfield Raceway, Trinidad. *Photo: Ian Abraham*

Clockwise from top: Ainsley Lochan and co-driver Robert Dumas catch some air at Rally Trinidad 2010 in their Mitsubishi Evolution IX. *Photo: Narend Sooknarine*; Karting stars Brandon Steele and Bridget Singh pose with newcomer Shane Pinheiro in his 100cc go kart. *Photo: Narend Sooknarine*; Sheldon Bissessar launches his Trinidad Rocket down the dragstrip at Palm Beach International Raceway, Florida, USA. *Photo: Narend Sooknarine*; Frankie Boodram and Gordon Gonsalves battle in the rain at Wallerfield. *Photo: Ian Abraham*

Trinidad and Tobago regionally and internationally, including Roger Sooknarine, Gary Hunt and more recently, teen racing star Brandon Steele and young female champion Bridget Singh.

With motorsport events held almost every weekend of the year, the Ministry of Sport and Youth Affairs has recently announced the approval of a major new motorsport facility. Along with signature events like Rally Trinidad, which is held at various locations in Trinidad, this new facility will provide spectators, sponsors and tourists looking for excitement with competitive racing action, marketing opportunities and outstanding amenities. The facility will also be used to teach drivers accident avoidance techniques and advanced car control on various surfaces as part of obtaining or upgrading their driver's licence in accordance with the UN Decade of Action for Road Safety 2011-2020.

Motorsport in Trinidad and Tobago also has spawned dedicated media houses over the last decade like Zorce Magazine, Trinituner.com, Paradise Motorsports TV and I Love My Ride TV that produce event coverage and automotive and motorsport-related content for Trinidad and Tobago and the region. ■

Narend Sooknarine is Editor of Zorce Magazine

Trinidad lies south of the hurricane belt and, therefore, offers excellent safety from storms.
Photo: Stephen Broadbridge

Yachting in Trinidad and Tobago

Any visiting cruiser arriving in Trinidad and Tobago is met with a warm welcome and safe harbour. For those of you who have not been here before, there are significant differences between Tobago and Trinidad and once you have spent some time here you will surely know about them!

Tobago is relatively laid back and tranquil with lovely clear seas, beautiful sandy beaches and gorgeous bays tucked away amongst the lush greenery of the mountains that rise quickly up from the sea. The frigate birds circle high in the skies and the pelicans dive deep into the seas. The snorkelling and diving are wonderful, especially in the north eastern areas. The people are conservative but friendly and welcoming. Today or tomorrow? It's not that important, it's bound to get done eventually. The services available specifically for cruisers are limited but that is part of the charm. Tobago remains unspoilt.

Trinidad is much more industrial and hectic. It is vibrant. It brims with sporting and cultural events, theatre, calypso shows and a host of festivals: Hosay, Diwali and of course, Carnival. It is the place for liming and laughing, for business and bacchanal, for rum and roti, for calypso… and confusion! Trinidad is a melting pot of races and religions, of culinary intrigue. It's the birthplace of steel pan and nothing could be sweeter than the gentle sound of a soft melody ringing in the hills surrounding Port of Spain on a quiet night. Trinidad is the home of the most wonderful bird sanctuaries in the Caribbean, of rivers and streams and hikes and walks, of the two longest beaches in the Caribbean, of coconut trees that seem to stretch forever into the distance, and a lake made of natural pitch, the only one in the world. And of course… Chaguaramas in Trinidad is the home of the yacht service industry.

Our own Harold and Kwailan La Borde were pioneers of yachting, building their own yachts and sailing around the world twice. Over the last two decades, our yacht service industry has developed hugely and today it is the most comprehensive one in the Southern Caribbean. In only one mile of Chaguaramas coastline, cruisers will find an incredible array of yachting supplies and services – a true economic cluster. A huge spectrum of boats can be accommodated on land in Chaguaramas. The total capacity of the boat yards stands at about nine hundred boats on the hard with marine hoists that range from 15 tons to 150 tons. Extra wide catamarans can also be lifted. Importantly, being south of the well beaten hurricane belt, Trinidad offers excellent safety from storms and because Chaguaramas lies inside the Gulf of Paria, it is particularly well protected. During the Second World War, the Gulf of Paria was by far the most important assembly point in the Caribbean for convoys heading out of the Caribbean.

The Yacht Services Association of Trinidad and Tobago (YSATT) is the umbrella body of the yacht services cluster. Our office is located in Crews Inn and is open in the mornings to visiting cruisers, so please drop in to have a chat and find out more about our home and what we do. We are constantly developing and we welcome your suggestions. We invite you to come, to experience, to take part and to enjoy! ■

Donald Stollmeyer, President, Yacht Services Association of Trinidad and Tobago (YSATT)

The development of education in Trinidad and Tobago is driven by the society's need to develop its human capital and an educated, skilled and knowledgeable citizenry. *Photo: Stephen Broadbridge*

Education in Trinidad and Tobago

At a World Teachers' Day function in 2011, Trinidad and Tobago's Education Minister, Dr Tim Gopeesingh, touched many hearts when he said: "I'll tell you today about the story of a young boy, growing up in rural Trinidad in the 1950s, whose parents were too poor to send him to primary school…. But a woman called Mabel Nathasingh kept a school under her house, where poor children could still get the chance to learn, instead of remaining illiterate and falling victim to the cruel cycle of poverty. That little boy went to school there until his father could finally afford to send him to the Fyzabad Intermediate EC School where he met another dedicated teacher, Oliver Defour. Secondary education was not free then and students got a rare chance of a State sponsored scholarship if they topped the Exhibition exam. That little boy won one of these prestigious scholarships and got the chance to attend Naparima Boys College. He is standing before you today."

Dr Gopeesingh's life's experiences reflect the impressive historical strides and significance of Trinidad and Tobago's

education sector which, just half a century ago, was chiefly designed to empower its tiny elite population.

Today the education landscape is totally different, despite some of the features from half a century ago still evident but the Ministry has initiated reform programmes with an emphasis on curricula, teacher training, education administration, methods of learning, basic literacy and numeracy, ICT and the adoption of new teaching technologies to create a strong education system that is seamless and relevant to the development needs of both learners and the country.

The development of education in Trinidad and Tobago is driven by the society's need to develop its human capital and an educated, skilled and knowledgeable citizenry able to interact and compete on the world stage underpins this development. The goal is to achieve Universal Early Childhood Education by 2015 at one end and at the other to have education and training systems delivering a human talent pool that is rooted in knowledge, skills, experiences and attitudes necessary for personal success and national development.

For the investor, Trinidad and Tobago has a workforce of 99% literacy, enterprising, self-motivated and able to be responsive to the challenges of new roles and together with the Government's incentives to employers to train employees, Trinidad and Tobago is a destination of first choice for investors.

With the promotion of values and attitudes, through education and training, such as civic responsibility and pride, the visitor to these shores will be accorded a warm welcome from a workforce that is knowledgeable, efficient and committed to service delivery. ∎

Education Minister, Dr Tim Gopeesingh meeting students. *Photo: Shirley Bahadur*

Sasha Mohammed

Rededicated UWI Administration
Building, St Augustine Campus

Five decades of academic excellence

On the 12th October 1960, the Imperial College of Tropical Agriculture (ICTA) merged with the University College of the West Indies (UCWI), formally establishing the University of the West Indies (UWI) St Augustine Campus. The Premier of Trinidad and Tobago at that time, Dr Eric Williams, envisioned a university that would be "the conscience of the nation" and would allow for all persons in Trinidad and Tobago of diverse backgrounds and talents to have access to a university education. And so came into being the St Augustine Campus, the second Campus of the University of the West Indies, with an established Faculty of Agriculture which was soon followed by a Faculty of Engineering.

As we celebrated our 50th anniversary in 2010, we noted with great appreciation the growth and expansion of our Campus. For what began as a single Faculty Campus with 39 undergraduate students, 28 graduate students and a few staff members has blossomed into a diverse and vibrant Campus today, with five Faculties (and a sixth, the Faculty of Law, on the horizon) and over 17,500 students and 3,000 staff members; a Campus that this year produced nearly 4,000 Doctoral, Masters and Bachelor degree graduates.

Our Campus did not only expand physically, but it also assumed its place in society as an intellectual leader, a driver of national and regional development and a shaper of Caribbean identity.

Over the past five decades, we have built an extensive community of alumni, academics, partners, supporters, friends and well-wishers and it is through their collective efforts and support that this Campus has withstood the test of time. We salute Trinidad and Tobago on the attainment of its 50th anniversary and are thankful to the successive government administrations that have nurtured the UWI St Augustine Campus. Our 50-year-old journey, as an institution, and that of our beloved country, has been a synergistic one.

We are pleased to have contributed to the country's post-independence evolution and are proud of the leadership produced by the UWI in all our spheres of human endeavour and critical thought. We are one of the few post-federation and post-independence regional symbols that still proudly stand tall and we pledge to continue to build this institution in service of the development of Trinidad and Tobago and our region. ∎

Prof. Clement K. Sankat, Pro Vice-Chancellor, University of the West Indies, St Augustine

UWI Administration Building in the 1960s

Trinidad and Tobago has a skilled and educated population and the resources to achieve quality affordable healthcare for all segments of the population.
Photo: Stephen Broadbridge

Healthcare in Trinidad and Tobago

Trinidad and Tobago inherited a British colonial system of healthcare where the direction and control was centrally vested in the Ministry of Health. By 1994 the public system was devolved to Regional Health Authorities with governmental input channelled through policy directives and funding mechanisms.

Post independence, the provision of healthcare had a wider focus, not just on medical, surgical and dental care but also the provision of adequate food and nutrition, water supply, housing, education and environmental health (including the proper handling of wastes). This shift in focus resulted in a significant improvement in the health of the population.

The country's Public Health Departments have had a major impact on the health of the population. Trinidad and Tobago continues to experience consistently high rates of immunisation coverage (greater than 95%) with the result that polio, diphtheria, tetanus, pertussis, mumps, measles and tetanus, once very common, are now decidedly rare among the younger population. Widening the use of other vaccines (such as HPV, meningococus, pneumococcus, hepatitis B, etc.) will undoubtedly prove to be a cost-effective approach to increasing life expectancy and tempering morbidity and mortality in Trinidad and Tobago.

The role of proper nutrition in reducing maternal and perinatal mortality is recognised and successive government administrations have set adequate food provision for all as a major priority with much success.

Trinidad and Tobago relies on its own resources to feed the nation and does so quite successfully. The national school-feeding program which was expanded to include children in both primary and secondary schools is an exemplary program that has significantly benefitted the health of children. As a result of this success, adequate calorie intake is now less of a problem than is the proper allocation of these calories which perversely is now leading to a significant obesity problem.

Studies have shown that improvement in socioeconomic status is associated with significant improvement in the health of populations – chief among these are education, housing and employment.

In education, Trinidad and Tobago has achieved a level of literacy comparable to many developed countries. A sustained achievement level over the decade from 1970 to 1980 saw a rise in literacy rates from 94% to 96% culminating with a literacy rate of 98.6% (99.1% male and 98% female) in 2003. An educated population has contributed to a healthier one.

Expansion of private and public housing and a diversified economy have also led to substantial improvements in the standard of living for nationals that are the envy of the entire Caribbean region. However, the pace of the economic expansion and industrialisation can be expected to adversely impact on the pristine environment of Trinidad and Tobago but the Environmental Management Authority (EMA) has been charged with co-ordinating all environment-related agencies and implementing the provisions of the EMA Act in an attempt at preserving the fragile environment. The Water and Sewerage Authority (WASA) is the main facilitator of these environmental services and has the exclusive legislative responsibility to supply potable water to the nation and to collect and dispose of liquid waste. Eighty seven percent of the total population has house water connections in urban areas with the other 13% having access to standpipes. Visitors to Trinidad and Tobago should be aware that much like developed countries the water supply in urban areas of Trinidad and Tobago meets the WHO high standards of quality.

Despite all these successes, Trinidad and Tobago still faces many health challenges including adequate provision of mental health, dental care, cancer treatment and help for the disabled. The mismatch in medical personnel (especially doctors, nurses and technicians) and population-needs has garnered greater focus of successive governments. The bulk of medical care services in the country have been provided by both public and private sector-entities with some contributions from NGOs, industrial corporations and the national security services.

Care is mainly provided by institutions such as hospitals, health centres and outreach centres throughout the country including the Port of Spain General Hospital, the San Fernando General Hospital and the tertiary care facility at the Eric Williams Medical Complex at Mount Hope. The state of the art Scarborough General Hospital in Tobago is close to completion. In addition to the two main general hospitals a comprehensive range of diagnostic and treatment services is also available at District or regional hospitals and private clinics throughout Trinidad and Tobago. These include diagnostic services such as CAT scans, MRI scans, coronary angiography, ultrasonography and modern laboratory facilities. Specialised units also provide services in women's health, psychiatric, chest disease, substance abuse, geriatric, oncology and physical therapy services.

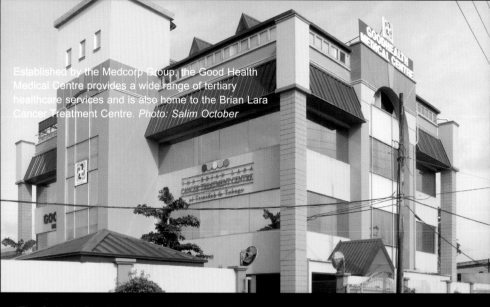
Established by the Medcorp Group, the Good Health Medical Centre provides a wide range of tertiary healthcare services and is also home to the Brian Lara Cancer Treatment Centre. *Photo: Salim October*

The St Ann's Psychiatric Hospital is the only hospital providing specialised mental health care in the country and the St James Medical Complex now provides specialised care in Oncology, including chemotherapy and radiation treatment, gerontology, physical medicine and rehabilitation. It is proposed that a new Oncology Center located at Mount Hope will be the flagship institution providing cancer care, including screening, diagnosis, treatment and palliative care.

Pharmacy dispensaries located in many hospitals have traditionally provided pharmaceuticals for in- and outpatients patients and a special drug program, the chronic disease assistance program (CDAP) provides free prescription drugs for the treatment of chronic conditions such as diabetes mellitus, hypertension, heart disease, glaucoma, asthma, arthritic conditions, depression, benign prostate conditions, HIV, etc. Private pharmacies also provide much of the pharmaceuticals for the nation.

Currently there is about 1 physician per 1,200 populations in Trinidad and Tobago. Government has quickly established new medical and dental schools and the importation of foreign doctors to help close this gap. In the 2011-2012 fiscal year government has allocated 4.7 billion dollars TT to the health sector. This will go a long way towards providing the infrastructure, equipment and training of healthcare personnel.

While the country trains its own nurses at the two main hospitals it still has difficulty keeping up with attrition and population demands. The education of other health personnel is concentrated at the Eric Williams Medical Sciences Complex including undergraduate and postgraduate education programs for physicians, dentists and veterinarians.

Despite these challenges the future of healthcare in Trinidad appears bright. Trinidad and Tobago has the skilled and educated population, the wherewithal and the resources to overcome all challenges on its way to achieving quality affordable healthcare for all segments of the population. ∎

Michael C. Belcon, MD, MPH

TRANSFORMING HEALTHCARE

To counteract the heavy dependence on revenues from the energy sector, Trinidad and Tobago is seeking to change the structure of the economy, explore new investment and economic spaces and facilitate private sector investments. A major focus is on new investments that will promote business competitiveness and create industries that will fuel diversification of the economy.

The Tertiary Health Sector is being targeted as a new investment area with plans to establish a first world cardiac, vascular and oncology services centre in Trinidad, supported by sophisticated diagnostics and servicing both the local and regional market places.

This centre will contribute to the diversification of the economy as it is not dependent on revenues from the energy sector and is expected to provide significant benefits such as:

- A catalyst for transformation of the health sector
- The reduction and effective treatment of diseases that are the leading causes of death in Trinidad and Tobago and the region
- The removal of the need for citizens to seek access to first world services from abroad
- The creation of a platform for Trinidad and Tobago to be involved in the wider regional and international health services market and to build the country as a destination of first choice in medical tourism.
- As a centre of excellence, reduce the migration of professionals from the country and at the same time attract external professionals and practitioners to Trinidad and Tobago
- Increase foreign exchange earnings
- Contribute to clinical tertiary education and research and create an unprecedented body of knowledge, both locally and the region

Jewan Ramcharitar is a Fellow of the Institute of Consulting (UK) and the Association of the Chartered Certified Accountants (UK)

The Scarborough Health Centre was officially opened in March 2011. *Photo: Ian Brierley*

EFFICIENT, ACCESSIBLE AND AFFORDABLE HEALTHCARE

The Health System of Trinidad and Tobago consists of government funded and private hospitals, private medical practitioners and clinics throughout the country. Working in these facilities are qualified specialists in gynaecology, paediatrics, radiology, physiotherapy, cardiology, gastrology, urology and orthopaedics. Medical services are free at the government-funded institutions and clinics but fees are charged at all others. There are 24-hour emergency services at both government and private medical facilities and a 24-hour Emergency Air Ambulance Service.

The government has set health care services and hospitals as major features of its drive to socially and economically transform the society. Its vision for the health sector is to create a health system of the highest standard by promoting healthy lifestyles; providing quality health care; modernising the physical infrastructure by upgrading and expanding hospitals and specialist units; updating the legislative and policy framework governing the sector; developing the capacity to respond effectively, timely and comprehensively to current and emerging health issues; providing qualified and experienced health care professionals through international recruitment, capacity building and attractive remuneration packages; digitising patient records and administrative systems; positioning the sector, together with other services, to respond to health emergencies and capitalising on the growing medical tourism market.

This new vision for the health sector will see the transformation of major areas and services of the health sector that, once realised, will deliver first class health care to meet the needs of every tier in the population.

This transformation will include health centres offering 24 hours services including Radiology Services, Pharmaceutical Services, same day surgery services and Emergency Surgeries.

Additionally, a first for the Caribbean, will be the construction of a Children's Hospital and a National Oncology Centre at Mount Hope.

There will be an aggressive plan to upgrade and repair existing hospitals as well as the construction of more hospitals in Point Fortin, Arima, Sangre Grande and Chaguanas.

Private clinics offer quality care in a range of services, including on-site testing for ultra-sound, MRI scans, X-ray, colposcopy and bone densitometry. For the relocating family with children, quality paediatric and dental services are available.

In addition to the physical infrastructure, emphasis is also being placed on the training and retaining of medical personnel with plans to increase the population ratio of physician and medical professionals.

Developing the skills base of staff includes incentive learning programmes, the development of health related curricula and the promotion of medical careers through schools outreach programmes.

The country is thus well poised to confront and meet the many challenges it faces. This is a comprehensive approach to achieving operational, institutional and managerial excellence based on efficiency, accessibility and affordability. ∎

Sheldon Yearwood is a Senior Producer and Presenter at Win Communications

Port of Spain's skyline reflects a highly developed industrial and social infrastructure.
Photo: Salim October

National progress and development

In nation-years, 50 is a small number for development of a country, but 50 years since Independence, there is clear evidence that Trinidad and Tobago is coming of age and into its own in economics, politics and civic participation.

The challenge of independence was integrating the masses of different groups whom, by the time Britain was ready to let go, were an endemic part of the national population. The collective of peoples, indigenous population along with Europeans, Africans, Chinese, Arabs and Indians, all demanded a national whole be created from the disparate elements of culture, ethnicities, religion, colours, beliefs, habits and practices. Thus began the steady trek towards forming a nation.

As the colonial rulers withdrew, they left the former colonists independent, to shape the country in their own image.

Trinidad and Tobago, as with other new-born free and independent societies in the once-Empire, moving from colonial rule to self-governance, was intoxicated by the limitless possibilities of choosing its leaders, managing its affairs and shaping its destiny. As elsewhere, potential leaders came to the population full of promise and with hyperboles of promises. To the willing-to-be-led masses, no dream seemed too impossible, no manifesto unachievable.

It is on the basis of this, much has come to be expected of politicians and such expectations have at times been the root of tremendous disappointment.

It is within this knowledge, the progress and achievements of independence ought to be judged. Other than in comparative terms of what was expected post Independence, how much in real terms have we achieved?

When one thinks of achievement, Trinidad and Tobago's economic success is what has most often been touted. An economy buoyed on products of the energy sector that has contributed to some of the most developed industrial and social infrastructure in the region with port and airport facilities, roads and highways forming an intricate network of linkages within the islands while an expanding infrastructure for virtual connectivity, positions it on the cutting edge of 21st century developments.

Add to this, a seamless education system providing almost universal pre-, primary ▶

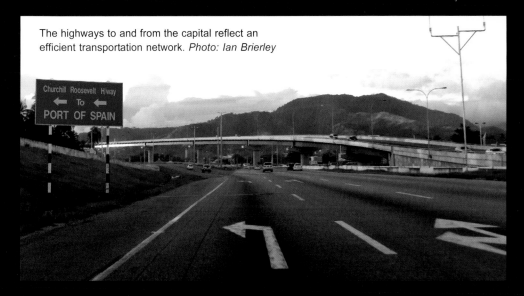

The highways to and from the capital reflect an efficient transportation network. *Photo: Ian Brierley*

Well developed roads and highways form an intricate network of linkages within the islands. *Photo: James B. Solomon*

Trinidad and Tobago has some of the most developed industrial and social infrastructure in the Caribbean region including state-of-the-art port facilities. *Photo: Marcus Gonzales*

Trinidad and Tobago's economic success is buoyed on products of the energy sector, such as oil. *Photo: Marcus Gonzales*

and secondary level education and easy access to tertiary and technical vocational disciplines, make the country a net generator of intellectual and creative capital.

But, it is this capacity for accommodating diversity which makes this small twin-island state exemplary among nations. In a world that is shrinking as a global village, where the real challenge is managing relations between and among peoples of diverse backgrounds, ethnicities, cultures and identities, Trinidad and Tobago can boast of a society in which such social strife is absent.

At 50, the people of Trinidad and Tobago recognise and embrace their diversity within the national mould.

The cultural repertoire of song, music, craft, storytelling, literary and oral arts has been the fabric of the country's underpinnings in camaraderie and social cohesion. Our festivals, integrated into national life and representative of all migrant and ethnic streams have been the safety valve through which tensions are released and relinquished and providing the social stability – the necessary precondition for business and tourism activities. ∎

Dr Kris Rampersad specialises in the comparative analysis of Caribbean development issues in culture, education, literature, gender and media in global contexts

Investment opportunities
to support lasting prosperity

The Ministry of Planning and the Economy has the mandate to provide Government's national strategic direction for Trinidad and Tobago. To this end the Ministry of Planning and the Economy has prepared the country's Medium Term Planning Framework 2011-2014 entitled "*Innovation for Lasting Prosperity*" to guide investment and development strategy over the three-year period.

Innovation for Lasting Prosperity is built on seven pillars identified in the 2010 Manifesto of the People's Partnership which has been adopted as Government policy by Cabinet.

These seven pillars are: people-centred development; poverty eradication and social justice; national and personal security; information and communication technologies; a more diversified, knowledge-intensive economy; good governance; and a foreign policy approach to support the achievement of strategic national goals.

Within the framework of these seven pillars, five priorities have been identified going forward:

1. Crime and Law and Order
2. Agriculture and Food Security
3. Health Care Services and Hospitals
4. Economic Growth, Job creation, Competitiveness and Innovation
5. Poverty Reduction and Human Development

Economic growth, job creation and competitiveness and innovation in the context of integrating with the global economy, require investment support. To this end the following information is relevant:

1. Government has identified five growth poles located in various parts of the country and investment priorities have been identified for each of these growth poles. Each growth pole enjoys a range of incentives as encouragement to investors.
2. In addition to the five growth poles, Chaguaramas on the northwest peninsula has been identified for specific investments related to the tourism and entertainment sectors.
3. The Tamana Intech Park aligned to the University of Trinidad and Tobago has been identified for ICT and other related

Hyatt Regency Trinidad is the largest conference centre in the English-speaking Caribbean. *Photo: Ian Brierley*

Clockwise from top – Pigeon Point beach, Tobago. *Photo: Ian Brierley*; Entrance to Coco Reef resort, Tobago: *Photo: Ian Brierley*; Tobago's golf courses are among the best in the Caribbean. *Photo: Ian Brierley*; Albion Plaza. *Photo: James B. Solomon*; New housing scheme in San Fernando, Trinidad: *Photo: Ian Brierley*

The Inter-American Development Bank has identified Port of Spain for development as one of ten potential sustainable cities in the Western Hemisphere. *Photo: Marcus Gonzales*

Ship repair, servicing and shipbuilding are specific investment areas which have been identified for private sector growth. *Photo: Stephen Broadbridge*

Clockwise from top left – Construction companies such as Mootilal Ramhit & Sons Constructing Ltd will benefit from the government's focus on the construction industry as one of its many areas identified for private sector growth; MovieTown. *Photo: Ian Brierley*; T-rex exhibition at the NAPA building. *Photo: Salim October*; Quarry in Roxborough. *Photo: Ian Brierley*

investments in which research support can be a vital factor.

4. The Port of Spain City Centre is targeted for private sector led construction, business, commercial and residential development. At the same time the Inter-American Development Bank (IDB) has identified Port of Spain for development as one of ten potential sustainable cities in the Western Hemisphere.

5. Specific investment areas identified for private sector growth include:

- Downstream energy projects
- Construction
- Alternative Energy
- Creative Industries
- ICT and High Tech Industries
- Music and Entertainment
- Tourism and Hotel Construction
- Food Production and Agriculture
- Services Industries
- Green Manufacturing
- Golf course development
- Ship repair, servicing and shipbuilding
- Film and Television
- Food and Beverage
- Fashion and Glamour
- The Visual Arts
- Advertising
- Book and Magazine Publishing

Trinidad and Tobago anticipates 2% growth in 2012, enjoyed the lowest rate of inflation in decades in 2011 and is committed to diversification of the energy sector as well as diversification beyond the energy sector.

The current participation rate in the tertiary sector is 40% and a 60% participation rate is the stated target for 2015. Trinidad and Tobago ranks 59 in human development in the world and this is likely to improve over the coming years.

In 2012, 7% of the budget is devoted to public sector investment programmes and the Government is committed to public-private partnership and private sector expansion. ■

Dr Bhoendradatt Tewarie, Senator and Minister of Planning and the Economy

Magdalena Grand Beach Resort

TRANSFORMING THE ECONOMY

Customised investor solutions… this is what Trinidad and Tobago's foremost investment promotion agency, invesTT, has been established to deliver. An agency under the Ministry of Trade and Industry, invesTT is unwavering in its mission to grow the nation's non oil and gas sectors significantly and sustainably, through two clearly defined strategic platforms – Local and Foreign Direct Investment and Sector Eco-system Innovation.

After more than a century of success in industries such as asphalt, petroleum and natural gas, the Government of Trinidad and Tobago has embarked on an aggressive drive to diversify the national economy. invesTT is therefore perfectly positioned to play the lead role in this diversification agenda as the primary contributor to GDP growth, in select non oil & gas sectors. Top among this list of priority sectors targeted for development and investment opportunity are Information Communications Technology, Light Manufacturing, Creative Industries, Transport and Logistics and Clean Technology.

For businesses seeking investment opportunities in Trinidad and Tobago, invesTT is the agency that delivers quality facilitation solutions. The unique combination of internal experts, strategic alliances and network of owned and

managed industrial parks, including Tamana Intech Park, guarantees that investors will find the credible reliable, international expertise they need.

In addition to its lead role in sourcing and facilitation of investment to Trinidad and Tobago and stimulating improvements to the local business ecosystem, invesTT is also making major strides in the re-energising of Tobago's tourism industry specifically with the re-opening of the Magdalena Grand Beach Resort (pictured above). This 4-star oceanfront resort provides the highest standards of quality, luxury and service expected in the region.

The strength of invesTT, coupled with a spectrum of investment incentives, an enabling business environment and access to regional and international markets through trade agreements truly makes doing business in Trinidad and Tobago a compelling investment decision.

For more information on investing in Trinidad and Tobago, please visit www.investtnt.com www.tamana.com or contact us at investtnt@eteck.co.tt or +1.868.638.0038.

Trinidad and Tobago

HIGHLY-RATED FINANCIAL SERVICES

Trinidad and Tobago's globally recognised industrial strength in the hydrocarbon and manufacturing sectors is underpinned by a strong, dynamic and diversified range of financial institutions and services. It could not have been any other way. Correspondent banking, online banking, trade finance, mortgage finance, merchant and investment banking, underwriting, agricultural finance, general and life insurance, credit and debit card facilities and more, are all available at competitive rates. Included among financial institutions are eight commercial banks, over 130 ABMs, 18 non-banking financial institutions and over a dozen insurance companies. Since 1993 there has been a free movement of capital and citizens hold foreign currency accounts.

The country boasts a good mix of institutions, which are foreign-owned, government-owned or privately-held. Several of these companies are traded on the local stock exchange in which some 38 companies participate.

This varied range of service providers are supported by a strong regulatory environment which includes the Central Bank of Trinidad and Tobago, the Deposit Insurance Corporation, the Securities and Exchange Commission and continuously updated financial and company legislation. This is all supported by a strong legal system and long-standing respect for property rights.

The openness of the country is reflected in its membership in major regional and international organisations including the International Monetary Fund, Inter-American Development Bank and World Bank and in trade agreements with North America, Europe and other world bodies such as the World Trade Organisation. A liberalised telecommunications sector, broadband and major air and sea port linkages make the country a clearly superior destination for business.

The country of just about 1.3 million people boasts a GDP per capita of US$17,231 in 2011 and strong foreign exchange reserves amounting to US$11 billion. Additionally, it holds approximately some US$3 billion in its Heritage and Stabilisation Fund and carries an "A" rating from the international rating agency, Standard and Poor's.

Ronald Ramkissoon

BANKING SECTOR SEEN AS THE CARIBBEAN'S BANKER

The Trinidad and Tobago Banking Sector (TTBS) is governed by the Central Bank of Trinidad & Tobago (CBTT) under the Financial Institutions Act, 2008. The enactment of updated governing legislation is imminent.

Confidence in the TTBS was demonstrated during the 2008 global financial crisis when individuals and institutions flocked en masse to the local commercial banks in an attempt to safeguard their cash, a trend referred to as a 'Flight to Quality'. The opposite effect was experienced by some of the top tier banks in the United States and Europe. While inherent confidence in the TTBS facilitated this 'Flight to Quality', the sector was somewhat shielded from the contagion effects of the global financial crisis due to its non-participation in the infamous toxic sub-prime mortgage business and by the fact that local loan portfolios are largely funded by domestic deposits with minimal exposure to wholesale external financing.

In 2011, the Governor of the CBTT reported that regional banks typically maintained Capital Adequacy ratios in the range of 15% to 20%, way above the statutory minimum of 8%. In Trinidad and Tobago, the average is 27% while in the US it is 15%. The Governor also reported that the TTBS, despite recording increases to non-performing loans over the last six years, is still considered highly profitable with Return on Equity averaging 19.5% as compared to the US banks, which averaged 2.35% in 2011. Also, the TTBS maintains significantly higher interest rate spreads, being in excess of 8%, where in the developed world, interest rate spreads are currently in the 2% to 3% range.

The TTBS is considered the region's banker as their traditional and wholesale banking desks have financed sovereigns, corporate entities and projects in every English speaking and most Spanish and Dutch speaking countries in the Caribbean. This regional lending presence attracts the attention of foreign investors.

In 2008, the Royal Bank of Canada re-acquired the local RBTT banking group (which they previously owned) for US $2.2B. In 2007, India's state owned and third largest bank, the Bank of Baroda, opened its first branch in Trinidad. In 2003, Jamaican born billionaire, Michael Lee Chin launched the AIC Financial Group in Trinidad by acquiring a number of local financial institutions. In 1998, Intercommercial Bank was launched by a joint venture between one of Jamaica's leading brokerage houses and well known steel magnate, Lakshmi Mittal of India. Citibank of the US and Scotiabank of Canada have both had a significant presence in Trinidad since 1965 and 1954 respectively. As the Governor of the CBTT recently highlighted, four decades ago, the Government of Trinidad and Tobago embarked on localising the banking sector. Today, six of the eight commercial banks operating in Trinidad and Tobago are owned by foreigners.

Angus P. Young, Managing Director, Young and Associates

EXPORTING, TRADING AND INVESTING IN TRINIDAD AND TOBAGO

Trinidad and Tobago is one of the most industrialised countries in the Caribbean and is a regional hub for business, transshipment, investment and finance. Geographically placed at the crossroads of the Caribbean, North and South America, it is ideally positioned as a strategic base for penetrating these markets.

There are significant prospects for exporters in the following priority areas:

- Oil & Gas
- Security & Defence
- Construction & Infrastructure
- Education & Training
- Health
- ICT
- Water & Waste Water
- Finance

In its drive to diversify its economy away from the energy sector, the Government of Trinidad and Tobago has identified the following non-energy sectors for investment:

- Downstream Petrochemicals
- Food & Beverages
- Fishing & Fish Processing
- Film
- Music & Entertainment
- Merchant Marine
- Yachting
- Printing & Packaging

Like any other country, there are challenges to doing business in Trinidad and Tobago but there are few major restrictions or disincentives to trading, exporting, investing or visiting for business.

Trinidad and Tobago is a market driven economy and there are no barriers to doing business. Highlights to note:

- There are no formal restrictions on the number and duration of employment of foreign managers
- There are prohibitions on unfair competition
- The World Trade Organisation certified the country as compliant with the Agreement on Trade-Related Aspects of Intellectual Property Rights in June 2000.
- Intellectual property legislation protects trademarks, patents, copyright, industrial design, integrated circuits, geographical indications and new plant varieties
- There are no restrictions on repatriation of capital, profits, dividends, interest, distributions or gains on investment.
- There are several investment incentives available through various government ministries
- The rates of Custom Duties vary from 0% to 30% on specified items with duties on non-competing Capital Goods at 2.5%.
- The Trinidad and Tobago Bureau of Standards (TTBS) has a statutory responsibility for the quality of all goods and services in the country, except food, drugs and cosmetics which the Chemistry, Food and Drug Division of the Ministry of Health monitor.

Credit is an important feature of the market with many companies using 30 to 90 days with the most common means of payment being cash, credit and debit cards and electronic transfers through Point of Sale terminals, the Automated Clearing House (ACH) and the Real Time Gross Settlement Systems (RTGS).

REASONS TO TRADE WITH AND INVEST IN TRINIDAD AND TOBAGO

- Strategic geographical location: Gateway to South and North America with good access to developing & emerging markets and at the southern tip of the hurricane belt.
- Modern infrastructure – from Port and airport to inland port; ICT Facilities, etc.
- Location of Caribbean Court of Justice (CCJ) and Association of Caribbean States (ACS) Headquarters
- Regulated financial system with competitive fiscal incentives and no foreign exchange controls.
- World class utilities; Highly developed industrial sector as well as oil, petrochemical and steel industries
- Good infrastructure and full range of support services for heavy and secondary industries which includes information technology, telecoms, construction, training, business and accounting, research & testing.
- A strong democratic tradition with a pro-investment business climate and very stable political system.
- Low energy and competitive raw material costs.
- International confidence in economic resilience and positive economic growth with impressive mid-term strategy to achieve lasting prosperity through innovation, diversification and economic transformation.
- Track record of attracting local, regional and international investment and attention.
- Good living standards with modern and accessible leisure activities and facilities for foreign nationals and their families.
- Educated and highly skilled and trained English-speaking workforce with 99% literacy rate
- Developed Private Sector
- Very Stable economy and growth trends

THE ECONOMY

Trinidad and Tobago is the most diversified and industrialised economy in the English-speaking Caribbean and has earned a deserved reputation as a prime investment site for international businesses. There are substantial proven reserves of petroleum and natural gas and heavy industries such as iron and steel, methanol and nitrogenous fertilisers are well developed.

Trinidad and Tobago's economic policy over the last 10 years has been one directed towards making the country an open, market-driven economy, fuelled by trade liberalisation, foreign investment and public sector divestment.

In 2011, The Government had published its framework for the economic and social transformation of the country that is based on a strategy for survival, growth and sustainability reflecting the expectation that its petroleum resources are finite.

The country is committed to building a competitive, innovation-driven economy that is knowledge-based and technologically driven within four dimensions:

- Being internationally competitive in the domestic market
- Being competitive in the global market
- Developing locally-based firms with a global presence
- Attracting international firms

ON TOP OF THE WORLD

In addition to its wealth of natural resources, Trinidad and Tobago can lay claim to being top of the world in numerous other areas. These include the following areas of excellence and accolades:

The largest Conference Centre in the English speaking Caribbean – Hyatt Regency Trinidad, 43,000 sq ft.

Trinidad is the "Business Capital of the Caribbean".

The oldest protected forest reserve in the Western Hemisphere – The Tobago Forest Reserve.

The largest brain coral in the world – Speyside Coral Reef in Tobago.

The most stadia and developed sports grounds in the Caribbean.

The largest and most modern transport facility in the Caribbean – Piarco International Airport with Trinidad and Tobago being one of the first five countries in the world to implement the new Communication Navigation Surveillance Air Traffic Management System.

- The "Shopping Capital of the Caribbean" with the most Malls in the Caribbean (7).
- MovieTowne, an entertainment & shopping complex, is the first of its kind in the Caribbean
- The largest GDP in the English-speaking Caribbean
- The largest CARICOM Economy
- Largest single-site exporter of ammonia in the world
- The largest producer and single-site exporter of methanol in the world with 18.5% of global production
- The best cocoa in the world with Tobago Coco (Duane Dove, Tobago Cocoa Estates WI Ltd) winning Gold at the 2011 Guild of Fine Foods in London.

FINANCIALLY VIABLE WORKFORCE

With education up to the tertiary level completely or almost fully subsidised by the Government, Trinidad and Tobago boasts a highly literate and qualified pool of skilled labour.

In 2007 the Central Bank launched the National Financial Literacy Programme (NFLP). A significant thrust of the programme was to offer free courses on the job, taking the financial burden off of employers, helping them mitigate the negative impact of employee financial problems in the workplace.

With the foreign exchange rate of $6.40 Trinidad and Tobago dollars to US$1.00, any international employer would find it easy to provide a competitive range of employee benefits including a private medical plan from any of our top insurers such as Guardian Life and Sagico Life Inc. These companies in addition to the local banks also provide a wide array of choices of employee retirement and savings plans. Also on the menu of these reputable institutions is a broad selection of professionally managed regional and international mutual funds, approved by the Securities and Exchange Commission.

There is also no dearth of highly qualified commissioned or independent financial advisors and brokers including but not limited to: Bourse Securities Limited, West Indies Stock Brokers, RBC Bank Limited, First Citizens and The Financial Coaching Centre Limited.

Nicholas Dean, financial coach and training

Oil: The lifeblood of Trinidad and Tobago

According to the *Petroleum Encyclopedia of Trinidad and Tobago (1993 edition)*, the first commercial oil production started at Point Ligoure, Southern Trinidad in 1907.

Since that first commercial venture in Point Fortin, exploration activity spread to virtually all areas of the country both, offshore and onshore. Refining quickly followed, as early as 1910, when a small unit was built at Brighton. Refining would reach its zenith in the 1950s when throughput at the Pointe-a-Pierre Refinery exceeded 350,000 barrels per day.

As a company whose predecessors dated back to 1910, Petroleum Company of Trinidad and Tobago Limited, PETROTRIN, was incorporated on 21 January 1993 as a limited liability company wholly owned by the Government of the Republic of Trinidad and Tobago.

The Company has the only refining operations in Trinidad, located at Pointe-a-Pierre on the West Coast of Trinidad. The refinery encompasses 809 hectares or 2,000 acres of land, approximately 56 kilometres south of Port of Spain. Refinery throughput is approximately 160,000 barrels of oil per day; 70,000 of which is available locally, while the rest is imported from Venezuela, Brazil, West Africa, Russia, Colombia and Ecuador.

Petrotrin enjoys market advantage and customer confidence in the Caribbean and Latin American region. With an inherited reputation as a reliable supplier of petroleum products for many decades, Petrotrin's upgraded refinery will continue to meet the combined challenges of increasingly stringent product specification both diesel and fuel oils as well as the demand for more products in the growing economies of the Caribbean and Latin America.

Started four years ago, the Clean Fuels Program which comprises the Gasoline Optimisation Project and the Ultra Low Sulphur Diesel Project will be completed by mid-2012. This will enhance our ability to provide higher quantities and quality of petroleum products to premium markets.

UPSTREAM CHALLENGES AND INITIATIVES

Total local production of crude oil at one time exceeded 150,000 barrels of oil per

day (bopd) but this has declined to the current levels of under 100,000 bopd. Boosting oil production at Petrotrin after recent years of decline is the Company's and indeed the country's greatest priority.

The Trinmar holdings, located offshore Point Fortin in the Southwest of the island, currently comprise the Petrotrin asset with the greatest short term potential for increased production and consequent enhanced indigenous crude supply to the upgraded refinery at Pointe-a-Pierre.

In March 2011, therefore, Petrotrin resumed an aggressive round of drilling activities in Trinmar's Soldado Fields on Trinidad's West Coast after a hiatus of almost three years. During the first year of the drilling program, a total of 21 wells are carded to be drilled. The production from these new wells is expected to yield a substantial increase in the daily production of crude oil. The Trinmar Forward Drilling Programme is of key strategic importance to Petrotrin and to the country as a whole. Petrotrin is also proud to be one of the first upstream operators to return to active offshore drilling after the steep decline in offshore activity of the last few years.

Petrotrin continues to use joint venture arrangements to conduct most of its exploration activities. It has just completed the largest ever 3D seismic survey of the entire southwest peninsula of the country in an effort to find additional reserves

A wise man once remarked that oil is the lifeblood of the Trinidad and Tobago economy. Petrotrin is indeed the heart. ■

Feature and photos courtesy of Petroleum Company of Trinidad and Tobago

The government has targeted a number of key
initiatives to revitalise the agricultural sector
including the strengthening of entrepreneurship.
Photo: Stephen Broadbridge

The 2010 publication of the World Economic Forum (WEF), *Realising a New Vision for Agriculture: A roadmap for stakeholders* explicitly recognises the major challenges to food and agricultural sustainability and projects a vision of agriculture as a positive contributor to food security, environmental sustainability and economic opportunity. This vision is rolled out in a roadmap and framework for action built on business-led and market-based solutions that are explicitly linked to national development priorities.

The Regional Food and Nutrition Security Policy, which was adopted by the Member States of CARICOM in late 2010, identifies the key issues and provides a holistic framework for addressing food security concerns from a regional perspective. This framework addresses the issue along the lines of the four inter-connected components of food security – availability, accessibility, nutrition and stability.

Recognising these frameworks, the country's agricultural policy was formulated to respond to the challenge of feeding the population in the context of instability in world food markets, from which a large proportion of its food supplies are obtained, and the limitations in the domestic farm-to-market agriculture and food systems. An essential and strategic goal was thus to create a food secure nation.

In a globalised environment, the trend of soaring food prices is of concern to all of the Caribbean, as this situation can affect food security. This reality is further compounded by the effects of climate change, rising sea levels and changing weather patterns which can all impact negatively on the supply of agricultural products.

The Ministry of Food Production, Land and Marine Affairs thus has a critical role to play in developing a productive sector that is modern and competitive and generating income levels as attractive as other sectors of the economy. A major goal is to ensure each citizen of Trinidad and Tobago is secure in his/her 'right to food', which is, according to the Food and Agriculture Organisation of the United Nations (FAO) *"the right to have continuous access to the resources that will enable you to*

Greenhouse technology is being explored. *Photo: Ministry of Agriculture*

The government is determined to revitalise the agricultural sector and create a food-secure nation. *Photo: Stephen Broadbridge*

Cocoa farmer drying a harvest of cocoa beans. *Photo: Stephen Broadbridge*

Clockwise from top – The Valley of Paramin is known as the chive and celery capital of Trinidad and Tobago; Cocoa pods and cocoa beans; A selection of local fruit. *Photos: Ministry of Agriculture*

produce, earn or purchase enough food to not only prevent hunger, but also to ensure health and well-being".

The agriculture sector comprises production, processing and marketing activities in the crop, livestock and fisheries industries. To create a food secure nation, reduce the nation's food import bill and secure this 'right to food', increased investment is required. The government has recognised this and has targeted a number of key initiatives to revitalise the agricultural sector, strengthen entrepreneurship, increase export, protect lands for the exclusive use of agriculture and engage in partnerships with the private sector.

There are therefore many opportunities for investors to participate in all of these key initiatives of the Ministry's strategy for agriculture and food security. As there will be a multi-sectoral approach to agricultural development, investors will be able to integrate or spread their investments over other sectors such as tourism, culture and manufacturing. ∎

Source: Ministry of Food Production, Land and Marine Affairs' Draft Strategic Plan 2011-2015. Yolande Agard-Simmons is Director of Corporate Communications with direct responsibility for the Ministry's Communications and Public Education programmes and activities

The challenge to preserve the heritage of the sugar industry in Trinidad and Tobago was taken up in 2008. *Photo: Ian Brierley*

CARONI LIMITED
BRECHIN CASTLE

Preserving the heritage of the sugar industry

Trinidad and Tobago started its road to development with the sugar industry and the arrival of Roume de St Laurent and his French compatriots and their slaves in 1783 in Northern Trinidad, gradually moving to the Central and Southern areas as slavery continued to provide the necessary labour. After emancipation in 1838 Indian indentured labourers were brought in to replace African workers. But all the Africans did not abandon the plantations; many remained as cartermen, boilers, carpenters, mechanics, cane weighers and policemen. On the plains of Caroni and the Naparimas, the Ganges met the Nile as the two major races struggled to keep the economy on a sound footing. In the process they created a culture of sugar which still dominates the life of the former sugar lands.

In 1937 there were two major developments which occurred on these sugar lands. One was the formation of the All Trinidad Sugar Estates and Factory Workers Trade Union which gave representation to many thousands of sugar workers who had revolted in 1935, 1936 and 1937 against slave conditions on the sugar estates. Under the leadership of Adrian Cola Rienzi they transformed the nature of the industry. At the same time, Caroni (1937) was created when Tate and Lyle, a British multi-national company, bought out Caroni Sugar Estates (Trinidad) Ltd making a conglomerate of Waterloo on the Western coast and Brechin Castle in Couva.

Brechin Castle became the headquarters and by 1940 its landscape was changed by the construction of the factory, the four cooling ponds, the dispensary, Sevilla School, Sevilla Club and residences for the mainly expatriate senior staff. In 1960 Caroni bought out Usine Ste. Madeleine which had grown considerably since its founding in 1870.

In 1975 the State bought the conglomerate, calling it Caroni (1975) Ltd which continued producing sugar but also went into diversification, producing citrus, prawns, large and small ruminants and rice.

By the end of the 20th century as oil became increasingly significant, the sugar industry and agriculture generally sank into a low second place until the state closed down Caroni Ltd in 2003, retrenching 9,000 workers directly and a further 35,000 who were dependant on the industry. Over 75,000 acres of land now became available for other uses.

The need to preserve this heritage was a challenge taken up by The Academy for Arts, Letters, Culture and Public Affairs at the University of Trinidad and Tobago in 2008. The Sugar Museum and Heritage Village is the result – a 560 acre project that includes an archive of books, pamphlets, tapes, and letters; a Museum at Sevilla House; a Heritage Village which will re-create life on the sugar estates; a replica exhibit of the old sugar factory; a living sugar cane museum consisting of all the varieties of canes brought to Trinbago over the centuries and cultural and conference centres with accommodation for visiting researchers and visitors. The Four Ponds area at the back of the factory will be converted into a recreation park, using much of the present landscape but making the resort more people-friendly.

The Sugar Museum and Heritage Village will strive to be a major tourist centre and a valuable resource to educate the nation of our evolution from slavery and indentureship into nationhood. With state support and public co-operation this project will be a major boost to our efforts to make ourselves a truly independent people. ■

MANAGING THE ENVIRONMENT

The Environmental Management Authority (EMA) of Trinidad and Tobago is the only organisation of its kind in the Caribbean region, charged with ensuring environmental considerations to inform economic development. In other Caribbean countries, environmental management functions are usually executed by a department within a government Ministry and not by a statutory body like the EMA.

In 1992, the Government of the Republic of Trinidad and Tobago adopted Agenda 21 at the UN Conference on Environmental and Development (Earth Summit) in Rio de Janeiro, Brazil. Through this agreement, the country committed to take national action in areas where humans impact the environment. Three years later, the Environmental

Management Act, No. 3 of 1995 was enacted and the EMA established in June of that same year. The Act was later repealed and re-enacted in 2000 and is now cited as the Environmental Management (EM) Act, Chap. 35:05

The EM Act provides the primary legal framework for the protection, conservation, enhancement and wise use of the environment of Trinidad and Tobago. It mandates the EMA, inter alia, to develop the National Environmental Policy and draft and enforce subsidiary environmental legislation intended to address specific environmental issues. Subsidiary legislation under the EM Act currently include: The Certificate of Environmental Clearance Rules; the Noise Pollution Control Rules; the Environmentally Sensitive Species Rules; the

Environmentally Sensitive Areas Rules and the Water Pollution Rules.

Under these subsidiary legislation, the EMA acts as a regulatory body to provide for the designation and protection of environmentally sensitive species and areas in Trinidad and Tobago; regulate water pollution from point sources, manage the impacts of noise pollution; and determine applications for Certificates of Environmental Clearance (CEC) for new or significantly modified or expanded activities that may impact the environment, which are designated as requiring a CEC by the Minister with responsibility for the Environment.

Under the EM Act, the EMA is also mandated to implement national education and public awareness programmes since environmental awareness is a strong prerequisite in changing attitudes and behaviours into positive and sustainable actions to benefit the environment.

The EMA is responsible for developing and establishing environmental standards and criteria and also for coordinating environmental functions performed by government agencies, private organisations and non-governmental and community-based organisations. In fulfilling its mandate the EMA is therefore committed to promoting sustainable development in Trinidad and Tobago through co-ordination, education, regulation and enforcement.

Source: The Environmental Management Authority
Photo: Stephen Broadbridge

The Red House is the seat of Parliament in the Republic of Trinidad and Tobago. Located in the centre of Port of Spain, its architectural style is Greek revival. The building is currently undergoing extensive repairs and refurbishment, and Parliament is in temporary premises on the waterfront.
Photo: Robert Lerich/Dreamstime.com

The built environment

The architecture of Trinidad and Tobago is rooted in its vast and varied history. The influences range from the indigenous Amerindian population to alternating Spanish, French and English colonial settlements, through to those from the intercontinental African and East Indian heritage. Today, Trinidad and Tobago's architectural landscape is a vibrant assemblage of its rather eventful history.

The earliest architecture of the twin-island emanates from the Amerindian *Ajoupa* – the early wooden-post structures with thatched roofs, now stylised throughout the Caribbean's most exclusive destinations. Subsequent to Amerindian occupation, colonisation brought the contemporary architectural styles to the island in Spanish Renaissance, Gothic Revival, French Renaissance and Classical forms of architecture. Modern day Trinidad and Tobago is speckled with notable examples of these.

Discerning visitors to the island will notice the fine examples of Spanish Renaissance in the original capital city of San Jose de Oruma.

In the present day capital city of Port of Spain, Gothic Revival is pronounced in many of the churches, with Holy Trinity Cathedral on Woodford Square being a timeless example. Also on Woodford Square, the Red House, home to Trinidad and Tobago's Houses of Parliament, is a classic example of French Renaissance. The old Railway Station, which now serves as *City Gate*, the primary transit hub into the city, is an elegant example of formal Classical architecture.

At the turn of the 20th century, a Glaswegian by the name of George Brown brought cast iron and pre-fabricated mass- ▶

Cutting-edge architecture sits side-by-side with more traditional forms. *Photo: Salim October*

Known for its German Renaissance architecture, Queen's Royal College is the oldest secondary school in Trinidad and Tobago. *Photo: Ian Brierley*

Clockwise from top – Opened in 1902, this building served as the main library for Port of Spain for more than 100 years. *Photo: Salim October*; This elaborate, old fashioned building was designed by George Brown and is now home to the restaurant, Jenny's on the Boulevard. *Photo: Ian Brierley*; Fine examples of traditional architecture can be seen in the churches throughout the nation. *Photo: Stephen Broadbridge*; The National Museum and Art Gallery was originally built to commemorate the Diamond Jubilee of Queen Victoria. *Photo: Ian Brierley*; Known as the Gingerbread House, Boissiere House was designed and built by architect Edward Bowen in 1904. *Photo: Stephen Broadbridge*.

Holy Trinity Anglican Cathedral was completed in 1818 and consecrated on 30 May 1823. *Photo courtesy Tourism Development Company*

Clockwise from top left – Popularly called Stollmeyer's Castle, Killarney was built in 1904. *Photo courtesy Tourism Development Company*; Archbishop's Palace, the official residence of the Roman Catholic Archbishop of Port of Spain, was built in 1903. *Photo: Shirley Bahadur*; Knowsley was built in 1904 and is used as offices for the Ministry of Foreign Affairs. *Photo: Salim October*; Known as 'Roomor', Ambard's House was built in 1904. *Photo: Stephen Broadbridge*

produced building components to Trinidad. This brought the ornate ironwork and fretwork typified in the historic buildings seen along the Queen's Park Savannah. Along the western edge of the Savannah there are the 'Magnificent Seven' – seven eloquently detailed European-styled mansions.

Progressing outward from the capital city, heading south in particular, the architecture becomes distinctly East Indian in origin. Temples, mosques and residences punctuate the lush countryside with domes and cupolas from the pristine to the rudimentary. The Hanuman Murti and Temple-on-the-Sea buildings in Carapichaima are humbling experiences of such architecture.

Today, Trinidad and Tobago continues to build on its prolific architectural heritage. The country has been home to great masterbuilders and architects such as John Newel Lewis, Anthony C. Lewis and Colin Laird. Newel Lewis' seminal

book *Ajoupa: Architecture of the Caribbean*, 1983 gives readers a profound insight into the architecture of the country. Anthony C Lewis' Church of the Assumption built in 1952 is an exemplary model of Trinidadian vernacular, a celebration of simple forms, local materials and climatic sensitivity. Colin Laird's work dapples the city, one of his more outstanding pieces being the National Library, built in 2003. Laird's National Library is a primary expression of Caribbean contextual 'green' architecture using simple yet sophisticated techniques to create a perfectly sustainable building, respectful of its urban, social and climatic context.

It is evident that the architecture of Trinidad and Tobago serves as a dynamic reflection of the country's diversity, prosperity and goodwill. ■

Mandilee Newton is a freelance writer and architect and one of the founding members of the Trinidad and Tobago Green Building Council.

Trinidad and Tobago has an extensive transportation network of paved roads that is constantly being upgraded. Highways link the north and south of the island (Uriah Butler Highway, Solomon Hochoy Highway) and the east and west (Churchill-Roosevelt Highway). However, traffic is extremely heavy during the rush hour periods. *Photo: Stephen Broadbridge*

HIGH QUALITY PUBLIC UTILITIES

The Ministry of Public Utilities (MPU) is the arm of the Government with responsibility for the provision of effective leadership and governance in the delivery of public utilities to the citizens of Trinidad and Tobago. The Ministry has closely partnered with the various state agencies and divisions under its purview to ensure that Trinidad and Tobago's utility sector works towards being modern, customer oriented and technologically capable of providing high quality and cost effective services to all its citizens.

Through this collaborative planning, the MPU has developed a new Five Year Strategic Plan 2011-2015 and Annual Action Plans aimed at ensuring that the nation's basic utility needs for water, sewerage, electricity, post, telecommunications and meteorological services are met. At the end of the first year, the Ministry has seen major improvements in the quality of utility services provided to its citizenry. This improvement has been highlighted in the local July 2011 Mori Opinion Poll, which saw three of the MPU's agencies being rated among the top five in the provision of services to the public.

The MPU through its agency WASA maintains an extensive water distribution network and provides water supply to 92% of the population, although only about 20% of the population receive a 24/7 supply. WASA is working assiduously towards ensuring that the majority of customers attain a 24/7 water supply by 2015.

The electricity sector continues to be a critical engine of socio-economic development in Trinidad and Tobago, through the provision of a safe and reliable supply of electricity for domestic, commercial and industrial use. TTEC currently provides electricity to 98% of the population.

TTPost, provides postal service to 94% of the population with 87% of persons receiving mail by the following day. The Trinidad and Tobago Meteorological Office monitors major weather systems in the region and is the main Meteorological Office in the Eastern Caribbean. It bears responsibility for Trinidad and Tobago and the neighbouring country of Grenada and its dependencies.

The utility sector continues to improve its services not only to the citizenry but has also contributed to Trinidad and Tobago being the prime location for investment in the region. Evidence of this is the Point Lisas Industrial Estate, which is made up of industries which are world class producers of petrochemicals, steel and other heavy industrial products. The estate has an ample water supply for its various plant operations and enjoys one of the most competitive electricity rates in the world and indeed, perhaps the lowest rates in the region. ■

Navet Reservoir, South Trinidad: The Water and Sewerage Authority (WASA) is a state enterprise and the sole provider of water services in Trinidad and Tobago. The supply to hotels and guest houses is reliable and the water is chlorinated and safe to drink.

Trinidad and Tobago has a reliable supply of electricity and its rates are among the lowest in the Caribbean. *Photo: Ian Brierley*

Power to the people

The Trinidad and Tobago Electricity Commission (T&TEC) is the sole entity for the transmission and distribution of electric power throughout Trinidad and Tobago. T&TEC is also responsible for lighting of all highways and public roads throughout the twin-island state.

T&TEC carries out its mandate by designing, constructing, operating and maintaining the country's electrical transmission and distribution networks and also ensuring that the generation capacity is adequate to meet the national electricity demand at all times. Generation is sourced mainly through long term Power Purchase Agreements (PPAs) with Independent Power Producers (IPPs). At present, there are three IPPs supplying T&TEC with bulk power, Powergen, Trinity Power and Trinidad Generation Unlimited (TGU).

T&TEC also owns and operates a 64 MW Power Station at Cove Tobago which although now being diesel-fired, is expected to be fully converted to natural gas by 30 April 2012.

Recently eight new substations and associated transmission lines were constructed, including 220 kV voltage systems for the first time in the English Speaking Caribbean. These complemented T&TEC's pre-existing 33 kV, 66 kV and 132 kV transmission systems.

Through its approximately 3000 employees, T&TEC serves over 423,000 customers spread across five Distribution Areas. Industrial demand is predominant, representing over 60% of annual energy sales. The 37 largest industrial customers (4 MVA and over) alone account for over 35% of annual energy consumption. Energy sales for 2010 were 8,485 GWh and the corresponding maximum demand was 1,222 MW.

Tariffs and quality-of-service standards are set by an independent regulatory body, the Regulated Industries

▶

In August 2011, the Trinidad and Tobago Electricity Commission (T&TEC) started receiving a commercial supply of power from Trinidad Generation Unlimited (seen in the background) at its Union Estate 220/66 kV substation at La Brea (foreground). The substation is the first to be energised at 220 kV in the Commission. *Photo courtesy T&TEC*

Laying of the first submarine cable between Trinidad and Tobago in 1965. The cable, at the time the second longest alternating current undersea cable in the world, carried 33,000v of electricity over a 23-mile distance between the two islands. Prior to the laying of the cable, Tobago's electricity supply was generated from the Tobago Power station, which was converted to a standby facility after the undersea cable was commissioned.
Photo courtesy T&TEC

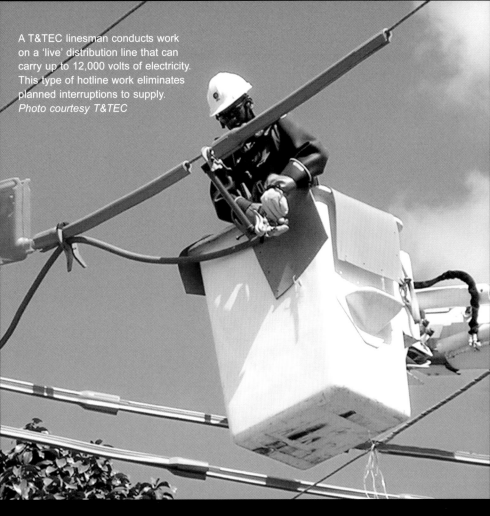

Commission (RIC). Standards of performance have been consistently met despite operating with tariffs that are amongst the lowest for Latin American and Caribbean Electric Utilities.

T&TEC strives to continuously improve the quality of service it provides. In this regard, an Advanced Metering Infrastructure with outage management capabilities was recently deployed, contributing to 98% of all customer meters being remotely read, while a state-of-the-art Distribution System Control and Data Acquisition (SCADA) System and a country wide fibre optic network system have been added to complement the transmission SCADA system. The Southern Distribution Area achieved ISO 9001 certification status in 2010 and the Quality Management System from this Area along with ISO 14001 environmental management systems are currently being rolled out throughout the Commission. Establishment of an OHSAS 18001 management system is also being actively pursued.

An estimated 98% of the population has access to electricity with full deployment of streetlights across the national grid. Several parks and recreational grounds have been illuminated to facilitate night time sporting and leisure activities and also to support crime fighting initiatives. Disaster preparedness capabilities are also being established to facilitate quick restoration of electricity supply in the event of a disaster event.

As the engine for economic growth and development, T&TEC sees itself contributing to making Trinidad and Tobago the most attractive destination for foreign direct investment in the Caribbean and South Americas, moving upward from its present third ranking, according to the FDI's Caribbean and Central American Country of the Future 2011/12 report. ■

Trinidad &Tobago Electricity Commission (T&TEC)

There is a modern telecommunications infrastructure that uses digital and fibre-optic technology. Telecommunications Services of Trinidad and Tobago Limited (TSTT) has been the provider of both landline and mobile telephone services. However, Digicel now offers mobile phone services in both islands and Flow (Columbus Communication) offers cable television, Internet and landline telephone service. International direct-distance dialling is available nationwide and on public payphones. *Photo: Salim October*

TELECOMMUNICATIONS

Telecommunications Services of Trinidad and Tobago Limited is the country's most advanced provider of communications solutions with leading edge products designed around its IP-based core infrastructure and marketed under its BLINK and Bmobile brands.

Catering to the communications needs of those ranging from the youth, to the home-maker, to the business person alike, the company works to provide access to services that are so necessary for productivity and personal time-management in today's fast-paced society. In addition to fixed line and mobile communications, the company has an innovative line of best-in-class devices for consumers and business professionals; Broadband access including mobile 4G technologies to suit all markets; subscription based television service as well as business and home-alarm monitoring and security services.

TSTT is the industry leader deploying both wireless and fiber optic networks to deliver voice, data and multimedia capabilities and is the only local telecom operator poised to deliver true "quintuple-play" services. The continuous evolution of its networks to incorporate leading technologies, allows it to maintain its leadership as one of the more advanced providers of telecommunications within the Caribbean.

While adding value for the ordinary citizen, TSTT's development has also given state agencies, local enterprises and locally based multinational corporations a solid foundation for their own expansion and development strategies. Customers include key industry leaders in the finance, energy, government, manufacturing, education, healthcare and tourism sectors.

TSTT is equally proud of its long-standing history of excellence as a corporate citizen. Its participation in and support for national events has made it one of the most admired corporate citizens in the country. It harnesses the power of its technology and staff resources to make a difference in the lives of the citizens and TSTT remains firm in its commitment to supporting continued business development and economic growth in Trinidad and Tobago. ∎

Source: Telecommunications Services of Trinidad and Tobago Limited

FROM GPO TO TTPOST

In 1999 the Government of the Republic of Trinidad and Tobago (GoRTT), as part of its National Development Plan, decided to embark upon a Postal Sector Reform Programme aimed to significantly improve the efficiency, coverage and security of the postal systems in Trinidad and Tobago.

Consequently, the Trinidad and Tobago Postal Corporation, a statutory Corporation, was established under the Trinidad and Tobago Postal Corporation Act, Chapter 47:02 of 1999. The Act itself puts into place the framework for the reform of the postal service from a Government Department to a sustainable, economically viable corporate enterprise, less dependent on Government subsidy.

Since its inception, the Corporation has set a positive path towards stabilising and solidifying its financial position. Its strategy to increase revenue has included the construction of modern infrastructure, improved operational efficiencies, the introduction of commercial products and services such as, Direct Mail, Unaddressed Mail, Philatelic, Local and International Courier, an international shopping mailbox service (TTPak), a range of merchandise products available at retail locations, as well as the implementation of information and communication systems throughout the organisation.

Furthermore, the transformation has seen the development of a robust retail network comprising 16 corporate shops, 84 franchises and 83 stamp retailers (as at November 2011); an increase in the mail delivery service from 49% of households in 1999 to 94.21% of households and businesses in Trinidad and Tobago (as at November 2011); and improved mail delivery times from six days to next-day delivery for 87% of households. In addition, the Corporation has implemented state of the art x-ray scanning machines for the purpose of ensuring the safety and security of all inbound and outbound parcels.

The most recent initiative, in the ongoing transformation of the postal service, is the implementation of the Postal Code and National Addressing Systems throughout Trinidad and Tobago. These systems facilitate improved acceleration and accuracy with regard to handling, processing and delivery of mail consequently, the citizens and businesses of Trinidad and Tobago will continue to enjoy an improved, on-time mail delivery service to keep abreast of international standards.

In recognition of TTPost's commitment to international standards, it represents Trinidad and Tobago as a Co-Vice Chair of the Council of Administration (CA) of the Universal Postal Union (UPU). The UPU is an international body of postal operators comprising 191 member countries and the CA is the major governing body that administers the work of the UPU.

The Corporation continues to find new ways to serve the citizens and businesses of Trinidad and Tobago and become more efficient at it. Its efforts have resulted in TTPost capturing, for the third consecutive year, the number one position in the 2011 Market and Opinion Research International (MORI) Poll as it relates to the public's satisfaction with the delivery of service across a wide variety of sectors including the public sector, within which TTPost operates.

The TTPost brand has indeed become a very strong brand in Trinidad and Tobago and the region and continues to represent innovation and efficiency.

The Trinidad and Tobago Postal Corporation continues to change the way it operates as it builds on the accomplishments realised thus far and at the same time, embarks on a course of action that best positions the company for the challenges ahead. ■

Regular mail, express mail and courier delivery are reliable and available from the local provider TTPost at reasonable and competitive rates. International courier services from a range of established companies are efficient and readily available.

The Caribbean media market is a thriving industry, with Trinidad and Tobago being a receptacle of pluralistic culture. Some media operatives continue to use basic equipment and marketing techniques, while others have merged and revamped themselves in order to survive locally in the more than ever competitive media industry. Since Independence in 1962, Trinidad and Tobago has undergone notable diversification in its media industry. The dynamic media landscape has altered so that the cultural identities and social life are supported, reflected and to a large extent remade, thus showcasing the various ethnic dimensions that exist in Trinidad and Tobago.

On 31st August 1962, the nation's first TV station, Trinidad & Tobago Television (TTT), was born. AVM and TV6 respectively subsequently joined the industry. Trinidad Express ran its first print in 1967, having been formed by locals to compete with British owned publications, the Daily Mirror and the Guardian.

Established in 1917, the Guardian is the oldest surviving newspaper. Other Newspaper Organisations /Tabloids that existed included the Evening News, the Sun, the Bomb, the Punch, Newsday, the Independent and the Tobago News Express). The privately-run Radio Trinidad was operated by a subsidiary of the British firm Rediffusion. In 1968, previously Canadian owned Radio Guardian was renamed 610 Action Radio (NBN). In conjunction with Trinidad and Tobago Television (TTT) it became part of the state controlled media company, the National Broadcasting Service (NBS). In October 1972, Radio 100, the first frequency on the FM band came into being.

Thus, during the period 1962-1986 there was a small number of media houses operating in Trinidad and Tobago. Then after 1986 the industry opened up through the granting of licenses to television and radio stations; giving birth to the modern day broadcasters such as AVM Channel 4, TV6 and IETV, the first local cable channel in Trinidad and Tobago.

In the mid 1990's, Indian oriented radio stations and state owned media house increased their Indian programming. Previously the two AM frequencies offered approximately 1 hour of Indian music per week, with 610 AM offering much more than Radio Trinidad.

The country has attained major benefits from developments in the media industry. For instance, the introduction of 103 FM, the first Indian radio station in 1993, led to a pivotal period in the growth of public interest. In 2004, WACK 90.1 FM was opened as a community based radio station which plays 100% local music.

Ethnic influences have increased tremendously since independence and the expression of different views transcends the print and broadcast media. Citizens now have a direct intervention in the expression of opinions and influencing decisions in their own education of issues locally, regionally and internationally.

Advanced telecommunications technologies have also helped by making the world a global village. These developments in technology have led to several newspapers, radio and television stations establishing websites and fan bases on several popular international social media sites such as Facebook and Twitter.

After 50 years of independence, the media industry has indeed grown. For a small island developing nation with just over 1.3 million people, the playing field is not only level but extremely large. For its success we must acknowledge the pioneers of yesteryear and those who have kept the industry alive, fulfilling the democratic need to inform, educate and entertain the population and share our thoughts and opinions with the wider world.

Gideon Hanoomansingh

SERVING YOU FOR THE PAST 25 YEARS
Tobago NEWS

the bomb

MIRROR
WEEKEND EDITION

TRINIDAD and TOBAGO
NEWSDAY

$2
Guardian
Trinidad and Tobago

BROADCASTING

There are ten free-to-air television stations and some 37 radio stations, 31 that operate throughout the twin-island Republic of Trinidad and Tobago and six others territorially. And like the rest of the world, social media has also become an integral part of Media and Communications in Trinidad and Tobago, with the wide use of mobile phones, the Internet, Facebook, Twitter, Skype, the blogosphere, BBM and Instant Messenger, especially by the youths in the society.

Just about every workplace and household has computers with internet access. However, some of the elders in the society opt to view the TV or listen to the radio for their own pleasure.

Among the popular television stations that they mostly rely on for news and what's going on locally, as well as local and foreign entertainment are CCN Television Limited (TV6), Caribbean New Media Group Limited (CTV), Guardian Media Limited (CNC3) and IETV Limited.

Then for mostly entertainment, there are the Advance Community Television Network Limited, Synergy Entertainment Network Limited, Mohan Jaikaran and to a much lesser extent, Gayelle Limited. And for those who are interested in strictly politics, the Parliament of the Republic of Trinidad and Tobago can be seen round the clock.

There are also, Subscription Television Broadcasters that facilitate news, sports, entertainment, style, educational, historical and geographical programmes from local and foreign networks and are available nationally via Columbus Communications Trinidad (Flow) Limited, DirecTV Limited, Green Dot Limited, Telecommunications Services of Trinidad and Tobago Limited (Blink Entertainment) and the Independent Cable Network of Trinidad and Tobago (ICNTT), while other niche market providers can be found in mainly southern towns.

The FM Radio broadcasting Service Providers can be found on bandwidth ranging from 90.1 to 107.7 and depending on one's taste, they can find a suitable station to satisfy their needs.

Joan Rampersad, Senior Reporter, Newsday

LAW AND ORDER

Crime, law and order and vandalism have been one of the most formidable challenges facing Trinidad and Tobago and it was the escalation of these that led to the calling of a State of Emergency in 2011 in an attempt to contain and accelerate the process to achieve a reversal of the growing incidences of unlawful activity.

The Government has committed itself to a comprehensive and multi-pronged programme to contain and reduce crime. The key elements of this programme are:

- More effective law enforcement and policy
- Reform of the justice system & the legal framework
- Rehabilitation of offenders
- Social intervention programmes to discourage a lifestyle of crime and violence

It is recognised that these crime-specific programmes must also be supported by the national strategies for economic transformation and recovery aimed at reducing unemployment, fostering greater economic inclusion and targeting young people early to pre-empt their involvement in deviant behaviour.

Some of the concrete measures that are being taken to achieve the Government's goal of reducing and preventing crime and ensuring that everyone feel safe in their homes, offices and communities include:

- Constructing 19 more Police Stations throughout the country
- Increasing vocational and basic skills training for inmates
- Assigning a Police Officer to each school to foster better relations among parents, students and law enforcement officials.
- Constructing and equipping a state-of-the-art Forensic Centre
- Targeting businesses that provide cover for crime and criminal activities
- Increasing penalties by 50% for offences involving a firearm or any prohibited weapon.

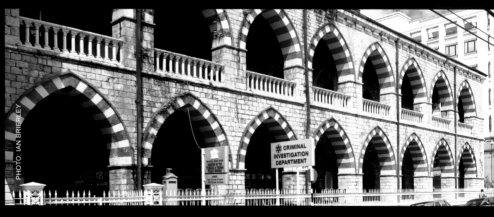

PHOTO: IAN BRIERLEY

Prefacio

El Primer Ministro de Trinidad y Tobago, el Dr. Eric Williams, en su mensaje del Día de Independencia recomendó,

"...cualquiera que sea el desafío que enfrentas, de cualquier lugar, pon primero el interés de la nación y la causa nacional. La fortaleza de la Nación depende de la Fortaleza de sus ciudadanos."

Cincuenta años más tarde, la actual y primera mujer Primera Ministra de Trinidad y Tobago, la Sra. Kamla Persad-Bissessar, ha dedicado su gobierno a construir una sociedad,

"que aprecia la vida, honra la diversidad, genera prosperidad, promueve la innovación y actúa con compasión con los ciudadanos más vulnerables."

Ambos Primer Ministros están al extremo final de los 50 años de la jornada de Trinidad y Tobago como una nación independiente de islas gemelas, con cada una jugando un papel trascendental en la dirección de desarrollo del país, un país cuya diversidad es ampliamente reconocida – diversidad en su historia, en su población, en su flora y fauna, en sus artes, su cultura, su música, en estilos de vida, en religión, en su cocina, en sus oportunidades de inversión, infraestructura y medio ambiente.

Trinidad y Tobago, ahora dirigido por la Sra. Kamla Persad-Bissessar, la primera mujer Primera Ministra de ascendencia Hindú en el Hemisferio Occidental, está a punto de iniciar una transformación económica y social para asegurar la sobrevivencia de la nación, su crecimiento, competitividad y sustentabilidad. Esta nación de islas gemelas, es verdaderamente un dúo dinámico que ofrece dos mercados diferentes –Trinidad, "el lugar para negocios"; y Tobago, un paraíso vacacional que es "limpio, verde y sereno".

El país ha publicado su marco de referencia política a medio plazo para crear prosperidad para todos. El gobierno está estableciendo un programa de acciones a fin de desplazarse por los principales retos de los nuevos escenarios políticos y económicos. Está extendiendo atractivas oportunidades para estimular el comercio y la inversión interna y externa de manera que Trinidad y Tobago llegue a ser el eje central para el Caribe y Latinoamérica, y ser un actor global y un lugar seguro para el comercio y la inversión.

La creatividad del país es una parte integral de este proceso de transformación y las industrias culturales están siendo desarrolladas a los niveles internacionales a fin de mostrar el talento de sus artistas y practicantes a través de la afluencia de visitantes y turistas y a través de sus exportaciones.

En el futuro inmediato, el país continuará fomentando el turismo y la inversión turística con varias áreas destinadas para la inversión y el crecimiento, incluyendo áreas específicas como deportes, relajación, salud, negocios y conferencias, festivales, películas, cultura, eco hoteles y boutique hoteles. El objetivo es crear un destino de calidad de primera elección con servicios a clientes de calidad mundial.

Se están promoviendo los consorcios a fin de crear iniciativas transformativas para aumentar la productividad e incrementar la competitividad, confrontar los obstáculos al desarrollo del éxito industrial y cultural de la nación y crear más riqueza, y al hacer esto, añadir a la economía basada en la energía del país.

Cincuenta años de Independencia, y 35 años como República han marcado la evolución rápida del país de colonia Británica a Estado Soberano. Como Estado soberano, no obstante pequeño, Trinidad y Tobago ha dado al mundo numerosos individuos de destacado mérito, incluyendo a Brian Lara (jugador de Cricket), Dai Ailan ("madre de la danza China"), Edmundo Ros (líder de banda), Peter Minshall (diseñador), Rudranath Capildeo (físico), y Heather Headley (cantante), Sam Mendes (director de cine) y VS Naipaul (escritor), y el lugar de nacimiento del único instrumento musical inventado en el siglo XX – el tambor de acero.

Esta República de islas gemelas es la entrada de oportunidades y experiencias de oro tanto para el inversionista como para el visitante. ∎

Avant-propos

Le premier ministre de Trinité-et-Tobago, Dr Eric Williams, a donné le conseil suivant lors de son discours du Jour de l'Indépendance,

« Quel que soit le défi auquel vous ayez à faire face et quelle qu'en soit l'origine, mettez l'intérêt et la cause de la nation avant toute autre chose. La force de la Nation dépend de la force de ses citoyens. »

Cinquante ans après, l'actuel Premier Ministre de Trinité-et-Tobago, première femme Premier Ministre, Mme Kamla Persad-Bissessar, s'est engagée en tant que Premier Ministre à construire une société

« qui chérit la vie, fait honneur à la diversité, génère la prospérité, encourage l'innovation et agit avec compassion envers ses citoyens les plus vulnérables. »

Ces deux Premiers Ministres sont aux deux extrémités de ce voyage de 50 ans de Trinité-et-Tobago en tant que nation indépendante composée de deux îles sœurs, chacune jouant des rôles déterminants dans la gestion du pays. Il s'agit d'un pays dont la diversité est largement reconnue - diversité dans son histoire, sa population, la faune et la flore, les arts, la culture, la musique, les modes de vie, la religion, la cuisine, les possibilités d'investissement, l'infrastructure et l'environnement.

Désormais mené par Mme Kamla Persad-Bissessar, première femme Premier Ministre d'origine indienne dans l'hémisphère occidental, Trinité-et-Tobago possède l'assurance nécessaire pour lancer une transformation sociale et économique afin d'assurer la survie de la nation, la croissance, la compétitivité, et la durabilité. Cette nation d'îles sœurs est un duo vraiment dynamique offrant deux marchés bien distincts. Trinité, « l'endroit où l'on fait des affaires » et Tobago, un paradis pour les vacances qui est « propre, vert et serein ».

Le pays a publié son cadre d'action à moyen terme afin de tendre vers la prospérité pour tous. Le gouvernement met en place un programme d'actions pour gérer les défis majeurs de la nouvelle économie globale et des nouveaux paysages politiques. Il offre des possibilités attractives pour stimuler le commerce et les investissements internes et externes afin que Trinité-et-Tobago devienne le centre régional de la Caraïbe et l'Amérique Latine, qu'il soit un compétiteur mondial ainsi qu'un lieu privilégié pour le commerce et les investissements.

La créativité du pays fait partie intégrante de ce processus de transformation et les industries culturelles sont en train d'être développées selon des normes internationales afin de démontrer le talent des artistes et praticiens grâce à l'afflux de visiteurs et de touristes et grâce aux exportations.

Dans un futur proche, le pays va continuer à encourager le tourisme et les investissements dans le tourisme grâce à diverses zones ciblées pour l'investissement et la croissance, y compris des créneaux comme le sport, les loisirs, la santé, le commerce et les conférences, les festivals, les films, la culture, les petits hôtels de luxe et les hôtels respectueux de l'environnement. Le but étant de créer une destination de qualité de premier choix avec un service client de classe internationale.

On encourage aussi les partenariats afin de créer des initiatives de transformation pour stimuler la productivité et accroître la compétitivité, afin de faire face aux obstacles à un développement industriel et culturel réussi de la nation et pour créer plus de richesses, et ce faisant, ajouter à l'économie du pays, basée sur l'énergie.

Ces cinquante ans d'Independence et 35 en tant que République ont marqué l'évolution rapide du pays, passant de colonie britannique à état souverain. En tant qu'état souverain, même si petit, Trinité-et-Tobago a offert au monde de nombreux individus talentueux au mérite remarquable, y compris Brian Lara (joueur de cricket), Dai Ailan ("mère de la danse chinoise"), Edmundo Ros (leader de groupe), Peter Minshall (créateur), Rudranath Capildeo (physicien), Heather Headley (chanteuse), Sam Mendes (réalisateur de films), et VS Naipaul (écrivain). C'est aussi le lieu de naissance du seul instrument de musique inventé au 20e siècle, le steel pan.

Cette République des deux îles sœurs est la passerelle vers des opportunités et des expériences en or, à la fois pour l'investisseur et le visiteur. ∎

Prefácio

O primeiro Primeiro-Ministro de Trinidad e Tobago, Dr. Eric Williams, em seu discurso do Dia da Independência, aconselhou:

"...seja qual for o desafio a enfrentar, de qualquer trimestre, coloque na frente o interesse nacional e a causa nacional. A força da nação depende da força de seus cidadãos. "

Cinquenta anos depois, a atual Primeira-Ministra de Trinidad e Tobago, a primeira do sexo feminino, Sra. Kamla Persad-Bissessar, comprometeu-se em seu mandato a construir uma sociedade

"que valorize a vida, honre a diversidade, gere prosperidade, encoraje a inovação e aja com compaixão para com seus cidadãos mais vulneráveis."

Ambos Primeiros-Ministros estão nas extremidades dos 50 anos de jornada de Trinidad e Tobago como uma independente nação de ilhas-gêmeas – cada qual exercendo papel seminal em direção ao desenvolvimento do país; um país cuja diversidade é amplamente reconhecida – diversidade de sua história, população, fauna e flora, arte, cultura, música, estilo de vida, religião, culinária, oportunidades de investimento, infraestrutura e meio ambiente.

Agora, liderada pela Sra. Kamla Persad-Bissessar, a primeira mulher de herança indiana do Hemisfério Ocidental a se tornar Primeira-Ministra, Trinidad e Tobago está preparada para iniciar uma transformação social e econômica que garanta a sobrevivênciam, o crescimento, a competitividade e a sustentabilidade da nação. Esta nação de ilhas-gêmeas é um duo verdadeiramente dinâmico, oferecendo dois mercados distintos – Trinidad, "o lugar para negócios", e Tobago, um paraíso de férias que é "limpo, verde e sereno".

O país tem publicado seu quadro de política de médio prazo para que gere prosperidade para todos. O governo está colocando em prática um programa de ações para abrir caminho para os principais desafios dos novos cenários econômicos e políticos globais. É aumentar as oportunidade atraentes para estimular o comércio interno e externo e os investimentos, a fim de que Trinidad e Tobago se torne um centro regional das atividades do Caribe e da América Latina e seja um protagonista global e um paraíso para comércio e investimento.

A criatividade do país é parte integrante deste processo de transformação e as indústrias culturais estão sendo desenvolvidas para os padrões internacionais a fim de mostrar o talento de seus artistas e profissionais através do fluxo de visitantes e turistas e por meio de exportações.

Em um futuro próximo, o país continuará a impulsionar o turismo e os investimentos turísticos, com diversas áreas dirigidas ao investimento e ao crescimento, inclusive em áreas de nicho, como esporte, lazer, saúde, negócios e conferências, festivais, cinema, cultura, ecologia e boutique hotéis. O objetivo é criar um destino de qualidade de primeira opção com um serviço de padrão internacional ao cliente.

Parcerias estão sendo incentivadas para criar iniciativas transformadoras para aumentar a produtividade e a competitividade, enfrentar os obstáculos ao bem-sucedido desenvolvimento industrial e cultural da nação e criar mais riqueza, e, ao fazê-lo, somar à economia de base energética do país.

Cinquenta anos de Independência, e 35 anos como uma República, marcaram a rápida evolução do país de colônia britânica para Estado soberano. Como um Estado soberano, embora pequeno, Trinidad e Tobago tem presenteado o mundo com numerosos indivíduos de méritos excepcionais, incluindo Brian Lara (jogador de críquete), Dai Ailan ("mãe da dança chinesa"), Edmundo Ros (líder de banda), Peter Minshall (designer), Rudranath Capildeo (físico), Heather Headley (cantora), Sam Mendes (diretor de cinema) e VS Naipaul (escritor), além de ser o local de nascimento do único instrumento musical inventado no século 20 – o tambor de aço.

Esta República de ilhas-gêmeas é a porta de entrada para oportunidades e experiências de ouro tanto para o investidor quanto para o visitante. ∎

Vorwort

In seiner Rede anläßlich des Unabhängigkeitstages berät der erste Premierminister von Trinidad und Tobago, Dr. Eric Williams, unter anderem Folgendes:

"...egal welcher Herausforderung Sie gegenüber stehen, egal aus welcher Richtung, stellen Sie zuerst die Staatsinteressen sowie das nationale Anliegen in den Vordergrund. Die Kraft der Nation ist abhängig von der Kraft seiner Staatsbürger."

Fünfzig Jahre später hat sich die derzeitige und erste Premierministerin von Trinidad und Tobago, Frau Kamla Persad-Bissessar, in ihrer Amtszeit dazu verpflichtet eine Gesellschaft zu schaffen,

"die das Leben schätzt, die Verschiedenartigkeit ehrt, den Wohlstand erzeugt, ein innovationsfreundliches Klima fördert und ihren am meisten schutzbedürftigen Bürgern Mitgefühl zeigen."

Die beiden Premierminister stehen an den äußeren Grenzen der 50-jährigen Reise von Trinidad und Tobago als unabhängiger Doppelinselstaat, wo jeder eine grundlegende Rolle bei der Entwicklungssteuerung des Landes spielt, eines Landes, dessen Vielfalt allgemein anerkannt ist – eine Vielfalt, die in seiner Geschichte, Bevölkerung, Pflanzen und Tiere, Künste, Kultur, Musik, Lebensarten, Religion, Gastronomie, Investitionsmöglichkeiten, Infrastruktur und Umgebung widerspiegelt ist.

Nun steht Trinidad und Tobago bereit, durch die Leitung von Frau Kamla Persad-Bissessar, die erste weibliche Premierministerin indischer Herkunft in der westlichen Hemisphäre, eine soziale und wirtschaftliche Transformation einzuleiten, um das Überleben der Nation, den Wachstum, die Wettbewerbsfähigkeit und Nachhaltigkeit zu gewährleisten. Dieser Doppel-Inselstaat ist ein wahrhaftig dynamisches Duo mit zwei verschiedenen Märkten - Trinidad, „der Staat für Geschäftsangelegenheiten", und Tobago, ein Ferienparadies, das „sauber, grün und ruhig" ist.

Nun wurde ein mittelfristiger politischer Rahmen des Landes veröffentlicht, der den Wohlstand für alle schaffen soll. Die Regierung arbeitet derzeit an einem Aktionsprogramm, um die großen Herausforderungen der neuen globalen wirtschaftlichen und politischen Landschaften zu navigieren. Sie bietet attraktive Möglichkeiten, um den internen und externen Handel und Investitionen zu stimulieren, damit Trinidad und Tobago das regionale Zentrum für die Karibik und Lateinamerika bzw. ein "Global Player" und eine Oase für Handel und Investitionen wird.

Die Kreativität des Landes ist ein wesentlicher Bestandteil dieses Umwandlungsprozesses und die Kulturindustrien werden nach internationalen Standards entwickelt, um die Talente seiner Künstler und Kulturschaffenden durch den Zustrom von Besuchern und Touristen und durch Exporte zu präsentieren.

In der unmittelbaren Zukunft wird das Land weiterhin Tourismus bzw. Tourismusinvestitionen weiterhin fördern, wobei sie auf mehreren Bereichen für die Investitionen und das Wachstum ausgerichtet werden, einschließlich Nischen wie beispielsweise Sport, Freizeit, Gesundheit, Geschäftliches und Konferenzen, Feste, Filme, Kultur, Öko- und Boutique-Hotels. Das Ziel ist es, eine hochwertige Destination erster Wahl mit einer weltklasse Kundenbetreuung herzustellen.

Es werden Partnerschaften gefördert um Umgestaltungsinitiativen zu schaffen, damit Produktivität und Wettbewerbsfähigkeit gesteigert werden, die Hindernisse für die erfolgreichen, industriellen und kulturellen Entwicklung der Nation entgegentreten, zu mehr Wohlstand zu führen, und dabei der energiebezogenen Wirtschaft des Landes beizutragen.

In den 50 Jahren der Unabhängigkeit und 35 Jahren als Republik hat sich das Land von einer britischen Kolonie zu einem souveränen Staat schnell entwickelt. Als souveräner Staat, obwohl sehr klein, hat Trinidad und Tobago zahlreiche begabte Personen, die ausgezeichnete Leistungen hervorgebracht haben, der Welt zur Verfügung gestellt, unter anderem Dai Ailan ("die Mutter des chinesischen Tanzes"), Rudranath Capildeo (Physiker), Heather Headley (Sängerin), Brian Lara (Cricketspieler), Sam Mendes (Filmdirektor), Peter Minshall (Designer), and VS Naipaul (Autor), Edmundo Ros (Bandleader), und ist der Geburtsort des einzigen Musikinstruments, das im 20. Jahrhundert erfunden wurde – der Steel Pan.

Dieser Zwillingsinselrepublik ist das Tor zu einzigartigen Gelegenheiten und Erfahrungen, sowohl für den Investor als auch für den Besucher. ■

त्रिनिडाड एवं टबैगो : अद्भुत और शांतिमय

भूमिका

त्रिनिडाड एवं टबैगो के प्रथम प्रधानमंत्री, डॉ एरिक विलियम्स, ने स्वतंत्रता दिवस पर दिए अपने अभिभाषण में कहा.....................

"....आपके सामने कोई भी चुनौती आए, किसी भी दिशा से आए, आप राष्ट्र हित को सर्वोपरि रखें। किसी भी राष्ट्र की ताकत उसके नागरिकों की ताकत से बनती है"।

आज पचास वर्ष बाद, त्रिनिडाड एवं टबैगो की मौजूदा एवं प्रथम महिला प्रधान मंत्री श्रीमती कमला प्रसाद बिसेसर का कुशल नेतृत्व ऐसा समाज बनाने के प्रति समर्पित है,

"जो जीवंत है, विविधता का आदर करता है, समृद्धि के लिए प्रयत्नशील है, नवीकरण को प्रोत्साहित करता है और अपने सबसे कमज़ोर नागरिकों के साथ उदारता का व्यवहार करता है"।

इस दो-द्वीपीय स्वतंत्र राष्ट्र त्रिनिडाड एवं टबैगो की अब तक की 50 वर्षों की यात्रा के शुरुआती दौर में प्रधान-मंत्री डॉ एरिक विलियम्स ने बागडोर सम्भाली थी और वर्तमान नेता श्रीमती कमला प्रसाद बिसेसर हैं, और दोनों ने ही, अपने-अपने समय में इस विकासशील देश के मार्गदर्शन में अग्रज की भूमिका का निर्वहन किया है, एक ऐसे देश के मार्गदर्शन में, जिसकी विविधता व्यापक रूप से जानी जाती है - विविधता इसके इतिहास में, जनसमुदाय में, वनस्पति और जीवजंतु में, कला,संस्कृति, संगीत, जीवनशैली, धर्म, खान-पान में, निवेश के अवसरों में, बुनियादी संरचना में और पर्यावरण में।

इस समय, पश्चिमी गोलार्ध में भारतीय मूल की प्रथम महिला प्रधान-मंत्री श्रीमती कमला प्रसाद बिसेसर के नेतृत्व में त्रिनिडाड एवं टबैगो, एक राष्ट्र के रूप में अपने अस्तित्व को बनाए रखने, अपना विकास, अपनी प्रतिस्पर्धात्मकता और अपना स्थायित्व सुनिश्चित करने के लिए तत्पर है। इस दो-द्वीपीय राष्ट्र में, वास्तव में, दो बिल्कुल भिन्न प्रकार के बाज़ार उपलब्ध हैं - एक त्रिनिडाड जो उत्तम व्यापारिक केंद्र है, और दूसरा टबैगो, जो "स्वच्छ, हरित (हरा भरा) और शांत होने के कारण छुट्टियाँ मनाने की दृष्टि से स्वर्ग है।

इस देश ने अपने सभी लोगों की समृद्धि के लिए एक मध्यम अवधि की नीति की रूपरेखा तैयार कर ली है। सरकार नए वैश्विक, आर्थिक और राजनैतिक परिदृश्य की प्रमुख चुनौतियों का सामना करने के लिए कार्ययोजना तैयार कर रही है। सरकार घरेलू और अंतरराष्ट्रीय व्यापार और निवेश को

बढ़ावा देने के लिए आकर्षक अवसर प्रदान कर रही है ताकि त्रिनिडाड एवं टबैगो व्यापार और निवेश के लिए कैरिबियाई और लातिन अमरीका क्षेत्र का केंद्र और विश्व स्तर का प्रतिभागी और सुरक्षित स्थान बन सके ।

इस देश की सृजनात्मकता इसकी रूपांतरण प्रक्रिया का अभिन्न अंग है और यहाँ अंतरराष्ट्रीय स्तर के सांस्कृतिक उद्योग विकसित किए जा रहे हैं ताकि आगुंतकों और सैलानियों के आगमन के माध्यम से और निर्यात के माध्यम से इस देश के कलाकार और व्यवसायी अपनी प्रतिभा का प्रदर्शन कर सकें।

निकट भविष्य में, इस देश में पर्यटन और पर्यटन निवेश में वृद्धि जारी रहेगी क्योंकि यहाँ निवेश और विकास के लिए कई क्षेत्र निर्धारित किए गए हैं - इसमें खेलकूद, मनोरंजन, स्वास्थ्य, व्यापार एवं सम्मेलन, पर्व, फिल्म, संस्कृति, किफायती एवं इको बूटीक होटल जैसे क्षेत्र शामिल हैं । उद्देश्य है – एक उत्तम पर्यटक-स्थल का निर्माण जहाँ विश्व स्तरीय सेवाएं अपलब्ध हों और जो लोगों का पसंदीदा स्थान हो।

उत्पादकता और प्रतिस्पर्धात्मकता बढ़ाने के लिए, देश के औद्योगिक और सांस्कृतिक विकास की सफलता के रास्ते में आने वाली बाधाओं का सामना करने के लिए एवं और अधिक आर्थिक सम्पन्नता बढ़ाने के लिए परिवर्तन लाने की क्षमता रखने वाले प्रयास

प्रारम्भ करने के उद्देश्य से भागीदारी को बढ़ावा दिया जा रहा है।

स्वतंत्रता के 50 वर्षों और गणराज्य बनने के 35 वर्षों की अवधि के मध्य इस देश ने ब्रिटिश उपनिवेश से एक प्रभुसत्तासम्पन्न राष्ट्र होने तक की यात्रा तेज़ी से तय की है । छोटा ही सही, एक प्रभुसत्तासम्पन्न राष्ट्र के रूप में त्रिनिडाड एवं टबैगो ने विश्व को अद्वितीय प्रतिभा वाले अनेक व्यक्ति दिए हैं जिनमें शामिल हैं - दाई आइलान (चीनी नृत्य की जननी), रुद्रनाथ कपिलदेव (भौतिक शास्त्री), हीथर हेडली (गायक), ब्रायन लारा (क्रिकेट खिलाड़ी), सैम मेंडेज़ (फिल्म निर्देशक) ,पीटर मिंशल (डिज़ाइनर), वी एस नायपॉल (लेखक) और एड्मुंडो रॉस (बैंड लीडर) और यह वह देश है जहाँ 20वीं शताब्दी के एकमात्र वाद्य - यंत्र - 'स्टील पैन' का अविष्कार हुआ ।

दो द्वीपों के समूह से बना यह गणराज्य निवेशकों और आगुंतकों, दोनों के लिए स्वर्णिम अवसरों और अनुभवों का सुमार्ग है ।

前言
"

埃里克·威廉姆斯博士是特立尼达和多巴哥的第一任总理，在他的独立日演讲中，他说到：
…

位。无一论个你国面家对的什力么量样取的决挑于战她，的也人无民论的这力挑量战。来" 自何处，你永远要将国家利益和目标放在第一

五十年后，特立尼达和多巴哥的现任总理，也是第一位女总理
-

士群体，承的诺社在会她" 的。总理任期内，要建立一个"珍视生命、认同差异、缔造卡繁姆荣拉、·倡帕导萨创德新·并比同塞情萨弱女势

多性物、。样性艺两术的位国、总家文理的化，发、分展音别中乐处扮、于演生特着活立方设尼式计达师、和宗的多教角巴色、哥烹。这饪众个所、双周投岛知资国机，度会特五以立十及尼年基达独础和立设多历施巴程和哥的环在两境历

端等史，、都方种在面族这充、个满动充植多满样

达和持多续现发巴在哥展，力已在经。卡为这姆一个拉场双·社岛帕会国萨和度德经，·济就比的像塞转是萨型一女做场士好生，了动这准的位备二印重。度唱这裔个表的转演西型一半将般球保，首证提位国供女家了总两理生个的存迥领异、导的发下展舞，台、特竞立争尼力
—

尼达特立
-

" 商务场所"；多巴哥
-

" 整洁、绿色而幽静度假天堂"。

全和多球巴新这哥的个成经国济为家和加已政勒经治比公和方布拉面了的美旨挑地在战区促，的进通中全过转面延站繁长，荣优并的惠同中时期在政全以策球刺框激范架围内。外政成贸府易为正一并在个吸推引贸出易投一资和系投，列资从的的而措天使施堂特以立。
应尼对达

方际式水平来国发家现展的。
创而造且力艺是术这家个与转
从型业过者程们中的不才可华
缺与少天的赋一正部在分通。
过特进立入尼国达家和的多来
巴访哥者的和文旅化游产者业
以正及在出向口国的
成闲、为一健特个康立、拥尼
商有达务世和界与多顶会巴级
议哥服、将务节持质日续量、
推的电动首影旅、选游文之业
化地、。旅生游态投与资精以
品带饭动店某。些其特目色标
行在业于的将发特展立，尼包
达括和体多育巴、哥休建
发展，政从府而正在以鼓能励
源多为范主围的经合济作形以
式提的高基生础产上效创率造
、更增多强的竞财争富、。克
服障碍，成功促进工业与文化
的
唱演物迅速，））包发，，在
展括希彼独得瑟布成立·为莱五
一恩海闵十个绍·德年尔利拉主
、权（（成歌国设（立手家板
计共师。球和这和）运国个，
动三主罗员十权德）五兰国，
年家纳戴的爱斯虽历莲然·程卡
（面中" 皮积，中很尔特国小

迪立舞奥，尼蹈但（达之她物
和母已理多经" 学巴）孕家哥
育，）已埃，了经德山诸从姆
蒙多英世国界·蒙的迪罗级一斯
的个（（杰殖电乐出民影人队
地主导
V.S.
奈保尔（作家）。而且，这里
也是钢鼓
—
的乐器的发源地。唯一发明于
二十世纪
这个双岛之国是对投资者和旅
游者提供金色机遇与体验的窗
口。__

و قدرة الوطن الفنية و الإبداعية هي جزء لايتجزأ من هذه العملية التحويلية فيطور الصناعات الثقافية للوصول إلى المعايير الدولية لعرض مواهب الفنانين و الممارسين في المجالات الفنية و هذا العرض يتم من خلال الزيارات المستمرة من الزوار و السياحيين و من خلال تصديرات.

و في المستقبل المباشر سوف يقوم البلد بتدعيم و تعزيز في مجال السياحة و الإستثمار فيها مع المجالات المعينة تنوى فيها الإستثمار و النمو. و من تلك المجالات الركنية مجال الرياضة و النزهات/ وقت الفراغ و المجالات الصحية و التجارية و مؤتمرية و الأعياد و الأفلام و الثقافات و فنادق إيكولوجية و بوتيكية. الحدف هو تصنيع ملجأ ذو جودة فائقة يحل مرتبة الإختيار الأول بخدمة العملاء و الزبائن خدمة تماثل أعلى درجة في العالم.

و يرحب بالشركات و يحث علية لإحداث إبداعات مجددة لتعزيز القدرة الإنتاجية والتنافسية , لمواجهة الموانع والعوائق التي تعمل ضد النجاحات و التطورات الصناعية و الثقافية في الوطن و لجلب أموال زائدة في نفس الحين تضيف إلى إقتصاد البلد الحالي المبني على الوقود و الطاقات.

خمسون عاما في الحالة الإستقلالية و خمسة و ثلاثون كبلد جمهوري و هذا قد خطط سرعة مضي البلد من

إستعمار بريطاني و انتقاله إلى دولة ذات سيادة نفسها . وحالها كدولة تحكم نفسها رغم صغرها فإن دولة ترينداد و تباغو قد وهب و أهدى إلى العالم أفرادا كثيرة من المتفوقين في مجالات مختلفة و من هؤلاء الأفراد: برايان لارا (لاعب الكريكيت), و داي أيلان (أم الرقص الصيني), و إدموندو روس (قائد قرقة الفنانين), و بيتر منشال (مصمم ألبسة متنوعة), و رودراناث كابيلديو (فيزيائي), و سام مينديز (المخرج السبمائي/ مدير الإفلام), و هيثار هيدلي (مغنية), وفي. إس نايباول (كاتب) و هذه الدولة هي المهد الأول و المنشأ الأصيل للآلة الموسيقية الوحدة التي أخترعت في القرن العشرين – آلة مصنوعة من برميل حديدي .

هذه الجمهورية محتوية من جزيرتين هي بوابة لفرص و تجارب للمستثمر و الزائر كليهما.

المقدمة

إن أول رئيس الوزراء لبلد ترينداد وتباغو – الدكتور إيريك ويليامز – في خطبته يوم الإستقلال الوطني أوصى فقال :

" مهما كان نوع التحديات التي تواجهكم من أي مصدر كانت فاجعل المصلحة الوطنية و مناصرة فضايا الوطن في المرتبة الأولى فقوة الوطن تتوقف على قوة المواطنين ."

خمسون سنة قد مضت و الرئيسة الحالية و أول امرأة تتولى رئاسة الوزراء في دولة ترينداد و تباغو سيدة – كملا برساد بيسيسار – تعهدت رئاستها للوزراء لبناء مجتمع.

" الذي يعتز الحياة,و يحترم التنوع, و يولد الازدهار , و يشجع الإبتكار و يقابل الضعفاء من المواطنين بالرأفة و الشققة . "

كلا الرئيسين في أقصى طرفي من هذه الرحلة الزمنية امتدادها 50 عاما. التي كانت بلد ترينداد و تباغو عاش مستقلا كبلد ذي جزيرتين. مع كل واحد من الجزيرتين يلعب دورا أساسيا في توجيه تطورات البلد , بلد تنوعاته تعارف عليها الناس في إطار واسع – تنوعات في تأريخه و أهله و نباتاته و حيواناته و فنونه وثقافاته و في موسيقه و في نمط الحياة و أديانه و أطعمته و فرصه الإستثمارية المتوفرة و في مبانيه و بيئاته.

دولة في الوقت الحاضر تخضع لقيادة سيدة كملا برساد بيسيسار أول امرأة من الأصول الهندية تتولى رئاسة الوزراء في المناطق الغربية من العالم. وإن بلد ترينداد و تباغو يتسعد لإبتداء تحول إجتماعي و اقتصادي لضمان بقاء البلد و التأكد من استمراره و نموه و قدرته التنافسية و استدامته. إن هذا الوطن ذو جزيرتين هو حقا ازدواج ديناميكي يوفر لنا سوقين يتميز كل واحد منه عن الآخر – ترينداد محل لإجراء الأعمال الإستثمارية و تباغو جنة تقضي فيها الفراغ تربته نظيفة خضراء هادئة.

وإن هذا البلد قد أصدر إطاره السياسي الذي تحدف اليه في الفصل المتوسط ليحدث الإزدهار و النجاح للجميع. و حكومة البلد تقوم بوضع برنامج مكون من أعمال متنوعة لسيره من خلال تحديات المشهد العالمي الجديد من الناحية الإقتصادية و السياسية و إنه تقدم فرص مغرية لإثارة تجارة داخلية و خارجية و إستثمارات ليكون ترينداد تباغو محورا و مركزا إقليميا للمنطقة الكاريبية و أمريكى اللاتينية و لتكون الدولة كذلك لاعبا عالميا في ملاذ تجاري و إستثماري.

EMBASSIES, INTERNATIONAL ORGANISATIONS, GOVERNMENT MINISTRIES AND DIPLOMATIC MISSIONS OVERSEAS

EMBASSIES

Apostolic Nunciature
1 Mary Street, St Clair
Tel: (868) 622-5009/6359
Fax: (868) 628-5457
Email:
apnunppp@googlemail.com

Embassy of the Argentine Republic
4th Floor, Tatil Building, 11
Maraval Road, Port of Spain
Tel: (868) 628-7557/7587
Fax: (868) 628-7544
Email: etrin@mrecic.gov.ar

Australian High Commission
18 Herbert Street, St Clair
Tel: (868) 628-0695/4732
Fax: (868) 622-0659
www.trinidadandtobago.
embassy.gov.au

Embassy of the Federative Republic of Brazil
18 Sweet Briar Road, St Clair
Tel: (868) 622-5779/5771
Fax: (868) 622-4323
www.brazilembtt.org

British High Commission
19 St Clair Avenue, St Clair
Tel: (868) 622-2748
Fax: (868) 622-4555
www.fco.gov.uk

High Commission for Canada
Maple House, 3-3A Sweet Briar
Road, St Clair
Tel: (868) 622-6232/3581
Fax: (868) 628-2619
www.trinidadandtobago.gc.ca

Embassy of the Republic of Chile
4 Alexandra Street, St Clair
Tel: (868) 628-0540/4763
Fax: (868) 622-9894
Email: echile@tstt.net.tt

Embassy of the People's Republic of China
39 Alexandra Street, St Clair
Tel: (868) 622-6976
Fax: (868) 622-7613

Embassy of the Republic of Costa Rica
The Mutual Centre, 3rd Floor,
Queen's Park West, Port of Spain
Tel: (868) 628-0652/0653
Fax: (868) 622-4862
Email: embrctt1@tstt.net.tt

Embassy of the Republic of Cuba
2nd Floor, 92 Tragarete Road, Port of Spain
Tel: (868) 622-6075/9142
Fax: (868) 628-4186
Email:
embacubatrinidad@tstt.net.tt

Embassy of the Dominican Republic
Suite 101, Savannah Court,
10B Queen's Park West, Port of Spain
Tel: (868) 624-7930, 623-3642
Fax: (868) 623-7779

Embassy of the Republic of El Salvador
29 Long Circular Road, St James
Tel/Fax: (868) 622-8314
Tel: (868) 628-4454

Delegation of the European Commission to Trinidad and Tobago
Sagicor Financial Centre, 16
Queen's Park West, Port of Spain
Tel: (868) 622-6628/0591
Fax: (868) 622-6355
www.deltto.ec.europa.eu

Embassy of the French Republic
6th Floor, Tatil Building, 11
Maraval Road, Port of Spain
Tel: (868) 622-7447/2388/7446
/ (868) 628-8633
French Trade Delegate:
(868) 622-7494
www.ambafrance-tt.org

Embassy of the Federal Republic of Germany
7-9 Marli Street, Newtown, Port of Spain
Tel: (868) 628-1630/1631
Fax: (868) 628-5278
www.portofspain.diplo.de

Embassy of the Republic of Guatemala
Apt 7A, Regents Tower,
Westmoorings-by-the-Sea
Tel/Fax: (868) 632-7629
Email: embagua@tstt.net.tt

High Commission for the Republic of India
6 Victoria Avenue, Port of Spain
Tel: (868) 627-7480/81
Fax: (868) 627-6985
www.hcipos.org

High Commission for Jamaica
2 Newbold Street, St Clair
Tel: (868) 622-4995
Fax: (868) 622-9043
Email: jhct@tstt.net.tt

Embassy of Japan
5 Hayes Street, St Clair
Tel: (868) 628-5991/3
Fax: (868) 622-0858
www.tt.emb-japan.go.jp

Embassy of the Republic of Korea
60 Eagle Crescent, Fairways, Maraval
Tel: (868) 622-9081
Fax: (868) 627-6317
Email: koremb.tt@gmail.com

Embassy of the Kingdom of the Netherlands
Trinre Building, 69-71 Edward Street, Port of Spain
Tel: (868) 625-1210 / 1722 / 2532
Fax: (868) 625-1704
www.holland.tt

High Commission for the Federal Republic of Nigeria
3 Maxwell-Phillip Street, St Clair
Tel: (868) 622-4002
Fax: (868) 622-7162
Email:
nigpos@nigeriahighcommission-tt.org

Embassy of the Republic of Panama
Suite 2, 1A Dere Street, Port of Spain
Tel: (868) 623-3435/6
Fax: (868) 623-3440

Embassy of the Kingdom of Spain
7th Floor, Tatil Building, 11
Maraval Road, Port of Spain
Tel: (868) 625-7938
Fax: (868) 624-4983
Email: emb.trinidad@maec.es

High Commission for the Republic of South Africa
4 Scott Street, St Clair
Tel: (868) 622-9869
Fax: (868) 622-7089
www.dfa.gov.za

Embassy of the Republic of Suriname
5th Floor, Tatil Building
11 Maraval Road
Port of Spain
Tel: (868) 628-0704
Fax: (868) 628-0086
Email:
surinameembassy@tstt.net.tt

Embassy of the United Mexican States
12 Hayes Street
St Clair
Tel: (868) 622-1422/7527/3930
Fax: (868) 628-8488

Embassy of the United States of America
15 Queen's Park West
Port of Spain
Tel: (868) 622-6371/6
Fax: (868) 822-5905
www.trinidad.usembassy.gov

Embassy of the Republic of Venezuela
16 Victoria Avenue
Port of Spain
Tel: (868) 627-9821/9823/4
Fax: (868) 624-2508
Email: embaveneztt@tstt.net

INTERNATIONAL ORGANISATIONS

The Caribbean Court of Justice
134 Henry Street
Port of Spain
Tel: (868) 623-2225, 624-2256
www.caribbeancourtofjustice.org

Association of Caribbean States
5-7 Sweet Briar Road
St Clair
Tel: (868) 622-9575, 628-0930
www.acs-aec.org

United Nations Development Programme (UNDP)
UN House, 3A Chancery Lane
Port of Spain
Tel: (868) 623-7056
Fax: (868) 623-1658
Email: registry@undp.org.tt
www.undp.org.tt

GOVERNMENT MINISTRIES

His Excellency the President
President of Trinidad and
Tobago
St Ann's
Port of Spain
Tel: (868) 624-1261/2
www.thepresident.tt/

The Honourable Prime Minister
Office of the Prime Minister
13-15 St Clair Avenue
St Clair
Port of Spain
Tel: (868) 622-1625
Fax: (868) 622-0055
www.15stclairave.gov.tt/

**Ministry of Community
Development**
Corner Jerningham Avenue and
Queen's Park East
Port of Spain
Tel: (868) 625-0639
Fax: (868) 624-2896
www.community.gov.tt/

Ministry of Education
18 Alexandra Street
St Clair
Port of Spain
Tel: (868) 622-2181-5
Fax: (868) 622-4892
www.moe.gov.tt/

**Ministry of Energy and Energy
Affairs**
Head Office
Levels 22-26, Energy Tower,
International Waterfront Centre,
1 Wrightson Road
Port of Spain
Tel: (868) 62-MOEEI (66334)/
623-6708
Fax: (868) 625-0306
Email: info@energy.gov.tt
www.energy.gov.tt/

Ministry of Finance
Eric Williams Finance Building,
Independence Square
Port of Spain
Tel: (868) 627-9700, Exts.
2805-9
Fax: (868) 627-9700 ext 2810
Email: comm.finance@gov.tt
www.finance.gov.tt/

**Ministry of Food Production
Land and Marine Affairs**
St Clair Circle, St Clair
Port of Spain
Tel: (868) 622-1221-5, 622-
6481-7
Fax: (868) 622-8202
www.agriculture.gov.tt/

**Ministry of Foreign Affairs and
Communications**
Levels 10-14, Tower C,
International Waterfront
Complex, Wrightson Road,
Port of Spain
Tel: (868) 628-6894
Fax: (868) 627-6859, 623-5853
Email: website@foreign.gov.tt
www.foreign.gov.tt

Ministry of Health
63 Park Street, Port of Spain
Tel: (868) 627-0010-2
Fax: (868) 623-9528
Email:
corpcomm@health.gov.tt
Email:
suggestions@health.gov.tt
www.health.gov.tt/

**Ministry of Housing and the
Environment**
NHA Building, 44-46 South
Quay, Port of Spain
Tel: (868) 623-4663
Fax: (868) 625-2793
www.mphe.gov.tt/

**Ministry of Labour and Small
and Micro-Enterprises
Development**
Head Office, Level 5 & 6, Tower
C, International Waterfront
Centre, 1 Wrightson Road, Port
of Spain
Tel: (868) 625-8478
Fax: (868) 624-4091
Email: rplann@tstt.net.tt
www.labour.gov.tt/

Ministry of Legal Affairs
Registration House, Huggins
Building, 72-74 South Quay,
Port of Spain
Tel: (868) 624-1660, 625-9971,
623-7163
Fax: (868) 625-9803
Email: info@legalaffairs.gov.tt
www.legalaffairs.gov.tt/

Ministry of Local Government
Kent House, Long Circular
Road, Maraval, Port of Spain
Tel: (868) 622-1669/1979, 628-
1323-5
Fax: (868) 628-7283
www.localgov.gov.tt

Ministry of National Security
Temple Court, 31-33
Abercromby St
Port of Spain
Tel: (868) 623-2441-5
Fax: (868) 627-8044
Email: info@mns.gov.tt
www.nationalsecurity.gov.tt

**Ministry of Planning, Economic
and Social Restructuring**
Eric Williams Finance Building,
Independence Square, Port of
Spain
Tel: (868) 623-3716
Fax: (868) 627-4195
www.mphe.gov.tt/

**Ministry of Gender, Youth and
Child Development**
Algico Building, Jerningham
Avenue, Belmont
Tel: (868) 625-3012/ 3112
Fax: (868) 625-3278

Ministry of Public Utilities
2 Elizabeth Street, St Clair, Port
of Spain
Tel: (868) 628-9500, 628-6129
Fax: (868) 628-6067
www.mpu.gov.tt/

Ministry of Public Administration
Levels 5-7 National Library
Building, Corner Hart and
Abercromby Streets, Port of
Spain
Tel: (868) 625-6724 (MPA4)
Fax: (868) 623-8636/624-9482/
623-6027
www.mpa.gov.tt/

**Ministry of Science, Technology
and Tertiary Education**
Levels 16-18, International
Waterfront Centre, 1 Wrightson
Road, Port of Spain
Tel: (868) 623-9922
Fax: (868) 625-5423
www.stte.gov.tt/

Ministry of Sport
12 Abercromby Street, Port of
Spain
Tel: (868) 625-5622-4
Fax: (868) 623-0174
www.msya.gov.tt/

**Ministry of the Arts and
Multiculturalism**
JOBCO Building, 51-55
Frederick Street, Port of Spain
Tel: (868) 625-8519, 625-6962,
627-1061
Fax: (868) 625-8519, 627-4991
Email: culturedivision.tt@gmail.com
www.culture.gov.tt/

Ministry of Justice
Tower C, Levels 19-21, Port of
Spain International Waterfront
Complex, #1 Wrightson Road,
Port of Spain
Tel: (868) 625-JUST (5878)
Fax: (868) 623-5596
www.moj.gov.tt

Attorney General
Cabildo Chambers, 23-27 St
Vincent Street, Port of Spain
Tel: (868) 623-7010, 625-8901
Fax: (868) 624-1986
Email: ag@ag.gov.tt
Email: communication@ag.gov.tt
www.ag.gov.tt/

**Ministry of the People and
Social Development**
ANSA Building, Cnr Independence
Sq and Abercromby St, PoS
Tel: (868) 625-9221
Fax: (868) 627-4853
www.socialservices.gov.tt/

Ministry of Tobago Development
Office of the Prime Minister
CAST Building, Jerningham
Street, Scarborough
Tel: (868) 635-1828
Fax: (868) 635-2011
www.15stclairave.gov.tt/

Ministry of Tourism
Level 9, Tower C, International
Waterfront Centre, 1
Wrightston Road, Port of Spain
Tel: (868) 624-1403/4792
Fax: (868) 625-1825, 625-3894
Email: mintourism@tourism.gov.tt
Email: touresearch@tourism.gov.tt
www.tourism.gov.tt/

Ministry of Trade and Industry
Levels 11-17, Nicholas Tower,
63-65 Independence Sq, PoS
Tel: (868) 623-2931-4
Fax: (868) 627-8488 / 0002
Email: info@tradeind.gov.tt
www.tradeind.gov.tt/

Ministry of Works
Level 6, Head Office Building,
Corner Richmond and London
Streets, Port of Spain
Tel: (868) 625-1225
Fax: (868) 625-8070
www.mowt.gov.tt/

Ministry of Transport
Level 6, Head Office Building, Cnr
Richmond and London Sts, PoS
Tel: (868) 625-1225
Fax: (868) 625-8070
www.mowt.gov.tt/

**Speaker of the House of
Representatives**
Office of the Parliament
Red House, Abercromby St,
P.O. Box 878, Port of Spain
Tel: (868) 624-7275
Fax: (868) 625-4672
E: administration@ttparliament.org
www.ttparliament.org/

DIPLOMATIC MISSIONS OVERSEAS

BELGIUM
Embassy of the Republic of
Trinidad and Tobago
Avenue de La Faisanderie 14,
150
Brussels
Tel: 011-322-762-9400
Fax: 011-322-772-2783
Email: info@embtrinbago.be

BRAZIL
Embassy of the Republic of
Trinidad and Tobago
SHIS QL 02
Conjunto 02
Casa 01
71665-028
Brasilia D.F.
Tel: (011)-5561-3365-3466 /
011)-5561-3365-3572 / (011)-
5561-3365-1132
Fax: 011-5561-3365-1733
Email:
rinbagoemb@gmail.com
Telex: 611844 EBTT BR

CANADA – Toronto
Consulate General of the
Republic of Trinidad and
Tobago
85 Sheppard Avenue West,
Toronto M2N 1M9
Tel: 1-416-495-9442-3 / 1-416-
495-7342 / 1-416-495-7847
Fax: Fax:1-416-495-6934
Email:
congen@ttcgtoronto.gov.tt
www.ttcgtoronto.gov.tt/

CANADA – Ottawa
High Commission of the
Republic of Trinidad and
Tobago
Third Level
200 First Avenue
Ottawa
Ontario K1S 2G6
Tel: 1-613-232-2418-9
Fax: 1-613-232-4349
Email: Ottawa@ttmissions.com
www.ttmissions.com/

COSTA RICA
Embassy of the Republic of
Trinidad and Tobago
Edificio Torre La Sabana,
Segundo Piso, Del ICE 300
metros Oeste y 25 Norte,
Sabana Norte
San José
Tel: (011) 506-2231-0809
Fax: (011) 506-2231-1244
Email:
embttsanjose@racsa.co.cr

CUBA
Embassy of the Republic of
Trinidad and Tobago
5ta Ave. 6603, E/66 & 68,
Miramar, Playa, Cuidad
Havana
Tel: 011 537-207-9603 / 011-
537-207-9604
Email: ttmissionscuba@enet.cu
or
admin.attache@ttmissions.co.cu

INDIA
High Commission of the
Republic of Trinidad and
Tobago
B-3/26, Vasant Vihar
New Delhi
110057
Tel: 011-9111-4600-7500
Fax: 011-9111-4600-7505
Email: info@hctt.in
Telex: TrintagoffNewDelhi

JAMAICA
High Commission of the
Republic of Trinidad and
Tobago
7th Floor, Pan Caribbean
Building, 60 Knutsford
Boulevard, Kingston 5
Tel: 1-876-926-5730 / 1-876-
926-5739 / 1-876-968-0588
Fax: 1-876-926-5801
Email:
kgnhctt@cwjamaica.com
www.kgnhctt.org/

NIGERIA
High Commission of the
Republic of Trinidad and
Tobago
No. 7 Casablanca Street
Off Nairobi Street
off Aminu Kano Crescent,
WUSE II
Abuja
Tel: 011-(234) 9461 1118 / 011-
(234) 9870-2438
Fax: 011-234-9461-1117
Email:
trinitobagoabj@yahoo.co.uk or
info@ttmissionsnigeria.com
www.ttmissionsnigeria.com/

SOUTH AFRICA
High Commission of the
Republic of Trinidad and
Tobago
258 Lawley Street
Waterkloof
Pretoria, 0181
Tel: 011-27-12-460-9688
Fax: 011-27-12-346-7302
Email: Pretoria@hctt.co.za or
hcttpretoria@telkomsa.net
www.hcpretoria.foreign.gov.tt/

VENEZUELA
Embassy of the Republic of
Trinidad and Tobago
No. 22-12, Quinta Poshika,
Tercera Avenida, Entre 6a y 7a
Transversales, Altamira,
Municipio Autónomo Chacao
de Estado Miranda, Caracas
Tel: 011-58-212-261-3748 /
011-58-212-261-5796 / 011-58-
212-261-4772
Fax: 011-58-212-261-9801
Email: embassytt@gmail.com
or embassytt@cantv.net

UGANDA
High Commission of the
Republic of Trinidad and
Tobago
Plot No. 44 Chwa II Place,
Mbuya, P.O. Box 40150,
Nakawa
Kampala
Tel: 011-256-414-562-400-5
Fax: 011-256-414-223-318/319
Email:
tthckampala@gmail.com

UNITED NATIONS – Geneva
Permanent Mission of the
Republic of Trinidad and
Tobago
37-39 rue de Vermont, 1202
Geneva
Switzerland
Tel: (011) 4122-918-0380 /
(011) 4122-918-0390
Fax: 011-4122-734-9138 / 011-
4122-734-8826
Email: Mission.Trinidad-
Tobago@ties.itu.int or
admin@ttperm-mission.ch
www.missions.itu.int/~trintago/

UNITED NATIONS – New York
Permanent Mission of the
Republic of Trinidad and
Tobago
Chanin Building, 122 E 42nd
Street, 39th Floor, New York,
N.Y. 10168
Tel: 1-212-697-7620-3
Fax: 1-212-949-4639
Email:
adminprun@trinbago.org

UNITED KINGDOM
High Commission of the
Republic of Trinidad and
Tobago
42 Belgrave Square
London, SW1X 8NT
Tel: 01-144-207-245-9351
Fax: 01-144-207-823-1065
Email: tthc@btconnect.com or
tthc.account@btconnect.com
www.tthighcommission.co.uk/

UNITED STATES –
Washington DC
Embassy of the Republic of
Trinidad and Tobago
1708 Massachusetts Avenue
N.W., Washington D.C.
20036-1975
Tel: 1-202-467-6490-3
Fax: 1-202-785-3130
Email: Info@ttembwash.com
www.ttembassy.com/

UNITED STATES – Miami
Consulate General of the
Republic of Trinidad and
Tobago
1000 Brickell Avenue
Suite 800
Miami Fl 33131 -3047
Tel: 1-305-374-2199
Fax: 1-305-374-3199
Email:
Consulate@ttcgmiami.com
www.ttcgmiami.com/

UNITED STATES – New York
Consulate General of the
Republic of Trinidad and
Tobago
125 Maiden Lane
4th Floor
New York, N.Y. 10038
Tel: 1-212-682-7272
Fax: 1-212-232-0368
Email: consulate@ttcgny.com
www.ttcgnewyork.com/

GOVERNMENT MINISTRIES

His Excellency the President
President of Trinidad and
Tobago
St Ann's
Port of Spain
Tel: (868) 624-1261/2
www.thepresident.tt/

The Honourable Prime Minister
Office of the Prime Minister
13-15 St Clair Avenue
St Clair
Port of Spain
Tel: (868) 622-1625
Fax: (868) 622-0055
www.15stclairave.gov.tt/

Ministry of Community Development
Corner Jerningham Avenue and
Queen's Park East
Port of Spain
Tel: (868) 625-0639
Fax: (868) 624-2896
www.community.gov.tt/

Ministry of Education
18 Alexandra Street
St Clair
Port of Spain
Tel: (868) 622-2181-5
Fax: (868) 622-4892
www.moe.gov.tt/

Ministry of Energy and Energy Affairs
Head Office
Levels 22-26, Energy Tower,
International Waterfront Centre,
1 Wrightson Road
Port of Spain
Tel: (868) 62-MOEEI (66334)/
623-6708
Fax: (868) 625-0306
Email: info@energy.gov.tt
www.energy.gov.tt/

Ministry of Finance
Eric Williams Finance Building,
Independence Square
Port of Spain
Tel: (868) 627-9700, Exts.
2805-9
Fax: (868) 627-9700 ext 2810
Email: comm.finance@gov.tt
www.finance.gov.tt/

Ministry of Food Production
Land and Marine Affairs
St Clair Circle, St Clair
Port of Spain
Tel: (868) 622-1221-5, 622-
5481-7
Fax: (868) 622-8202
www.agriculture.gov.tt/

Ministry of Foreign Affairs and Communications
Levels 10-14, Tower C,
International Waterfront
Complex, Wrightson Road,
Port of Spain
Tel: (868) 628-6894
Fax: (868) 627-6859, 623-5853
Email: website@foreign.gov.tt
www.foreign.gov.tt

Ministry of Health
63 Park Street, Port of Spain
Tel: (868) 627-0010-2
Fax: (868) 623-9528
Email:
corpcomm@health.gov.tt
Email:
suggestions@health.gov.tt
www.health.gov.tt/

Ministry of Housing and the Environment
NHA Building, 44-46 South
Quay, Port of Spain
Tel: (868) 623-4663
Fax: (868) 625-2793
www.mphe.gov.tt/

Ministry of Labour and Small and Micro-Enterprises Development
Head Office, Level 5 & 6, Tower
C, International Waterfront
Centre, 1 Wrightson Road, Port
of Spain
Tel: (868) 625-8478
Fax: (868) 624-4091
Email: rplann@tstt.net.tt
www.labour.gov.tt/

Ministry of Legal Affairs
Registration House, Huggins
Building, 72-74 South Quay,
Port of Spain
Tel: (868) 624-1660, 625-9971,
623-7163
Fax: (868) 625-9803
Email: info@legalaffairs.gov.tt
www.legalaffairs.gov.tt/

Ministry of Local Government
Kent House, Long Circular
Road, Maraval, Port of Spain
Tel: (868) 622-1669/1979, 628-
1323-5
Fax: (868) 628-7283
www.localgov.gov.tt

Ministry of National Security
Temple Court, 31-33
Abercromby St
Port of Spain
Tel: (868) 623-2441-5
Fax: (868) 627-8044
Email: info@mns.gov.tt
www.nationalsecurity.gov.tt

Ministry of Planning, Economic and Social Restructuring
Eric Williams Finance Building,
Independence Square, Port of
Spain
Tel: (868) 623-3716
Fax: (868) 627-4195
www.mphe.gov.tt/

Ministry of Gender, Youth and Child Development
Algico Building, Jerningham
Avenue, Belmont
Tel: (868) 625-3012/ 3112
Fax: (868) 625-3278

Ministry of Public Utilities
2 Elizabeth Street, St Clair, Port
of Spain
Tel: (868) 628-9500, 628-6129
Fax: (868) 628-6067
www.mpu.gov.tt/

Ministry of Public Administration
Levels 5-7 National Library
Building, Corner Hart and
Abercromby Streets, Port of
Spain
Tel: (868) 625-6724 (MPA4)
Fax: (868) 623-8636/624-9482/
623-6027
www.mpa.gov.tt/

Ministry of Science, Technology and Tertiary Education
Levels 16-18, International
Waterfront Centre, 1 Wrightson
Road, Port of Spain
Tel: (868) 623-9922
Fax: (868) 625-5423
www.stte.gov.tt/

Ministry of Sport
12 Abercromby Street, Port of
Spain
Tel: (868) 625-5622-4
Fax: (868) 623-0174
www.msya.gov.tt/

Ministry of the Arts and Multiculturalism
JOBCO Building, 51-55
Frederick Street, Port of Spain
Tel: (868) 625-8519, 625-6962,
627-1061
Fax: (868) 625-8519, 627-4991
Email: culturedivision.tt@gmail.com
www.culture.gov.tt/

Ministry of Justice
Tower C, Levels 19-21, Port of
Spain International Waterfront
Complex, #1 Wrightson Road,
Port of Spain
Tel: (868) 625-JUST (5878)
Fax: (868) 623-5596
www.moj.gov.tt

Attorney General
Cabildo Chambers, 23-27 St
Vincent Street, Port of Spain
Tel: (868) 623-7010, 625-8901
Fax: (868) 624-1986
Email: ag@ag.gov.tt
Email: communication@ag.gov.tt
www.ag.gov.tt/

Ministry of the People and Social Development
ANSA Building, Cnr Independence
Sq and Abercromby St, PoS
Tel: (868) 625-9221
Fax: (868) 627-4853
www.socialservices.gov.tt/

Ministry of Tobago Development
Office of the Prime Minister
CAST Building, Jerningham
Street, Scarborough
Tel: (868) 635-1828
Fax: (868) 635-2011
www.15stclairave.gov.tt/

Ministry of Tourism
Level 9, Tower C, International
Waterfront Centre, 1
Wrightston Road, Port of Spain
Tel: (868) 624-1403/4792
Fax: (868) 625-1825, 625-3894
Email: mintourism@tourism.gov.tt
Email: touresearch@tourism.gov.tt
www.tourism.gov.tt/

Ministry of Trade and Industry
Levels 11-17, Nicholas Tower,
63-65 Independence Sq, PoS
Tel: (868) 623-2931-4
Fax: (868) 627-8488 / 0002
Email: info@tradeind.gov.tt
www.tradeind.gov.tt/

Ministry of Works
Level 6, Head Office Building,
Corner Richmond and London
Streets, Port of Spain
Tel: (868) 625-1225
Fax: (868) 625-8070
www.mowt.gov.tt/

Ministry of Transport
Level 6, Head Office Building, Cnr
Richmond and London Sts, PoS
Tel: (868) 625-1225
Fax: (868) 625-8070
www.mowt.gov.tt/

Speaker of the House of Representatives
Office of the Parliament
Red House, Abercromby St,
P.O. Box 878, Port of Spain
Tel: (868) 624-7275
Fax: (868) 625-4672
E: administration@ttparliament.org
www.ttparliament.org/

DIPLOMATIC MISSIONS OVERSEAS

BELGIUM
Embassy of the Republic of Trinidad and Tobago
Avenue de La Faisanderie 14, 1150
Brussels
Tel: 011-322-762-9400
Fax: 011-322-772-2783
Email: info@embtrinbago.be

BRAZIL
Embassy of the Republic of Trinidad and Tobago
SHIS QL 02
Conjunto 02
Casa 01
71665-028
Brasilia D.F.
Tel: (011)-5561-3365-3466 / (011)-5561-3365-3572 / (011)-5561-3365-1132
Fax: 011-5561-3365-1733
Email:
trinbagoemb@gmail.com
Telex: 611844 EBTT BR

CANADA – Toronto
Consulate General of the Republic of Trinidad and Tobago
185 Sheppard Avenue West, Toronto M2N 1M9
Tel: 1-416-495-9442-3 / 1-416-495-7342 / 1-416-495-7847
Fax: Fax:1-416-495-6934
Email:
congen@ttcgtoronto.gov.tt
www.ttcgtoronto.gov.tt/

CANADA – Ottawa
High Commission of the Republic of Trinidad and Tobago
Third Level
200 First Avenue
Ottawa
Ontario K1S 2G6
Tel: 1-613-232-2418-9
Fax: 1-613-232-4349
Email: Ottawa@ttmissions.com
www.ttmissions.com/

COSTA RICA
Embassy of the Republic of Trinidad and Tobago
Edificio Torre La Sabana, Segundo Piso, Del ICE 300 metros Oeste y 25 Norte, Sabana Norte
San José
Tel: (011) 506-2231-0809
Fax: (011) 506-2231-1244
Email:
embttsanjose@racsa.co.cr

CUBA
Embassy of the Republic of Trinidad and Tobago
5ta Ave. 6603, E/66 & 68, Miramar, Playa, Cuidad Havana
Tel: 011 537-207-9603 / 011-537-207-9604
Email: ttmissionscuba@enet.cu or
admin.attache@ttmissions.co.cu

INDIA
High Commission of the Republic of Trinidad and Tobago
B-3/26, Vasant Vihar
New Delhi
110057
Tel: 011-9111-4600-7500
Fax: 011-9111-4600-7505
Email: info@hctt.in
Telex: TrintagoffNewDelhi

JAMAICA
High Commission of the Republic of Trinidad and Tobago
7th Floor, Pan Caribbean Building, 60 Knutsford Boulevard, Kingston 5
Tel: 1-876-926-5730 / 1-876-926-5739 / 1-876-968-0588
Fax: 1-876-926-5801
Email:
kgnhctt@cwjamaica.com
www.kgnhctt.org/

NIGERIA
High Commission of the Republic of Trinidad and Tobago
No. 7 Casablanca Street
Off Nairobi Street
off Aminu Kano Crescent, WUSE II
Abuja
Tel: 011-(234) 9461 1118 / 011-(234) 9870-2438
Fax: 011-234-9461-1117
Email:
trinitobagoabj@yahoo.co.uk or info@ttmissionsnigeria.com
www.ttmissionsnigeria.com/

SOUTH AFRICA
High Commission of the Republic of Trinidad and Tobago
258 Lawley Street
Waterkloof
Pretoria, 0181
Tel: 011-27-12-460-9688
Fax: 011-27-12-346-7302
Email: Pretoria@hctt.co.za or hcttpretoria@telkomsa.net
www.hcpretoria.foreign.gov.tt/

VENEZUELA
Embassy of the Republic of Trinidad and Tobago
No. 22-12, Quinta Poshika, Tercera Avenida, Entre 6a y 7a Transversales, Altamira, Municipio Autónomo Chacao de Estado Miranda, Caracas
Tel: 011-58-212-261-3748 / 011-58-212-261-5796 / 011-58-212-261-4772
Fax: 011-58-212-261-9801
Email: embassytt@gmail.com or embassytt@cantv.net

UGANDA
High Commission of the Republic of Trinidad and Tobago
Plot No. 44 Chwa II Place, Mbuya, P.O. Box 40150, Nakawa
Kampala
Tel: 011-256-414-562-400-5
Fax: 011-256-414-223-318/319
Email:
tthckampala@gmail.com

UNITED NATIONS – Geneva
Permanent Mission of the Republic of Trinidad and Tobago
37-39 rue de Vermont, 1202 Geneva
Switzerland
Tel: (011) 4122-918-0380 / (011) 4122-918-0390
Fax: 011-4122-734-9138 / 011-4122-734-8826
Email: Mission.Trinidad-Tobago@ties.itu.int or admin@ttperm-mission.ch
www.missions.itu.int/~trintago/

UNITED NATIONS – New York
Permanent Mission of the Republic of Trinidad and Tobago
Chanin Building, 122 E 42nd Street, 39th Floor, New York, N.Y. 10168
Tel: 1-212-697-7620-3
Fax: 1-212-949-4639
Email:
adminprun@trinbago.org

UNITED KINGDOM
High Commission of the Republic of Trinidad and Tobago
42 Belgrave Square
London, SW1X 8NT
Tel: 01-144-207-245-9351
Fax: 01-144-207-823-1065
Email: tthc@btconnect.com or tthc.account@btconnect.com
www.tthighcommission.co.uk/

UNITED STATES – Washington DC
Embassy of the Republic of Trinidad and Tobago
1708 Massachusetts Avenue N.W., Washington D.C. 20036-1975
Tel: 1-202-467-6490-3
Fax: 1-202-785-3130
Email: Info@ttembwash.com
www.ttembassy.com/

UNITED STATES – Miami
Consulate General of the Republic of Trinidad and Tobago
1000 Brickell Avenue
Suite 800
Miami Fl 33131 -3047
Tel: 1-305-374-2199
Fax: 1-305-374-3199
Email:
Consulate@ttcgmiami.com
www.ttcgmiami.com/

UNITED STATES – New York
Consulate General of the Republic of Trinidad and Tobago
125 Maiden Lane
4th Floor
New York, N.Y. 10038
Tel: 1-212-682-7272
Fax: 1-212-232-0368
Email: consulate@ttcgny.com
www.ttcgnewyork.com/